Read Two Books and Let's Talk Next Week

Read Two Books and Let's Talk Next Week

Using Bibliotherapy in Clinical Practice

**Janice Maidman Joshua
and Donna DiMenna**

John Wiley & Sons, Inc.

New York • Chichester • Weinheim • Brisbane •
Singapore • Toronto

ISBN 0-471-37565-9

Printed in the United States of America.

10 9 8 7 6 5 4 3 2 1

Contents

ADOPTION, 36

AGING, 49

Contents

Contents

Contents

Contents

Contents

Contents

PARENTING/FAMILIES, 248

General, 248

ADD/ADHD and Other Behavior Problems, 259

Developmental Disabilities, 264

Parenting Teens

Raising Children of Color/Multiracial Families, 270

Stepparenting and Single-Parent Families, 272

RELATIONSHIPS, 284

Adult Children and Parent Relationships, 284

Dating, 288

Difficult Relationships, 290

Contents

Contents

Contents

Preface

*R*ead Two Books and Let's Talk Next Week was conceived as the result of our awareness of the enormous and ever-growing number of self-help books on the
market. This fact gave us confidence that there was a need for counseling clinicians
to have some way to navigate this ever-growing sea of self-help literature for use in
their therapeutic practices. Our intent was to fill a void for counseling practitioners,
including psychologists, physicians, social workers, clergy, counseling chaplains,
employee assistance therapists, and educators working in the counseling arena. Our
hope is that *Read Two Books . . .* will be a powerful resource for many of these practitioners. In addition, for those clients who on their own are searching for solutions
to their problems, *Read Two Books . . .* provides an easy guide to the self-help section of their bookstore or library.

Read Two Books . . . will by no means be exhaustive or all-inclusive of the current self-help books on the market. It is meant to provide a limited but important
sampling of books easily available at libraries and bookstores, which we, our clients,
and our colleagues have found meaningful. The books we have chosen are germane,
useful, and inclusive of many mental health issues. We highlighted the insights of
each book so the practitioner could easily and quickly gage its clinical efficacy. We
intended this reference book to be a unique resource to the counseling practitioner
and are well aware that we may have missed many additional books that our colleagues or clients would have included. *Read Two Books . . .* is a compilation of
books that have come out of our combined 30 years of experience in mental health.

Our intention is to bring to the counseling community a reference book that is well organized and user friendly. To do this, in addition to a general table of contents, we have included title and topic indexes.

The book's table of contents includes 19 topics and subtopics, along with titles of books and their authors. The topics and subtopics were chosen on the basis of issues that we see daily in our clinical practices. In addition, in the back of the book, there is an alphabetized title index and a topic index for cross-referencing books. Our hope is to give the practitioner easy ways to reference the content of *Read Two Books.* . . .

The main text includes summaries of 317 books, which we have found meaningful to our clients in clinical practice. Each book includes four sections: a title summary, a "Book Byte," a "Suggested Readers" section, and a "Therapeutic Insights" section.

The title section includes the title of the book, the author(s), the publisher and the copyright date, along with the number of pages in the book. This gives the practitioner an easy way to access the book either in a bookstore or a library. The number of pages gives the practitioner a guide to the length of the book, which may be a consideration with certain clients.

The "Book Byte" section is a quick summary of the book, giving the main thrust of the subject of the book. This section is not meant to be a comprehensive summary by any means. It is simply to give the reader a "byte" of what the book is about.

The "Suggested Readers" section lists the three major groups of people that the book will pertain to. We have tried to be as specific as possible with this section, giving the practitioner a quick way to tell if it is a book that is applicable to the particular client.

In the "Therapeutic Insights" section, we have tried to encapsulate five main insights that readers may gain from the book. This gives the practitioner a bird's-eye view of what the author was intending to impart to the reader. We are well aware that in many cases, books may have more than five distinct therapeutic insights. The "Therapeutic Insights" are a snapshot of what the reader may learn from the author, not necessarily an all-inclusive picture.

Read Two Books . . . is meant to serve as a quick reference, which is well organized, user friendly, and a daily asset to the practicing clinician.

Acknowledgments

We are extremely grateful to a countless number of people who have made this project possible, including first and foremost our clients and colleagues. It was with their input and feedback that we first became aware of the importance of bibliotherapy in the therapeutic setting.

We thank our extraordinary clients who were willing to share with us the self-help books, which made a difference in their lives as they searched for solutions to their problems. We also thank our colleagues who have shared with us their favorite books, and insights regarding bibliotherapy, which they have found useful in their practices. These include the following: Ruth Markowitz, L.P.; Dr. Maxine West; Dr. Sally Moore; Dr. Jan Colwell; Dr. Nancy Ankeny; Dr. Jane Klein; Dr. Mary Frey; Dr. Kristin Benson; Dave Mathews, L.I.C.S.W.; Signe Nestingen, L.P.; Susan Reynolds, L.I.C.S.W.; and Sally Sibbit, L.I.C.S.W. We also greatly appreciate the work of Rachel Beckman, who word processed half of this book.

To our families, this project would not have come about without their support and love. I (DD) would especially like to thank my partner, Rosann Cahill, who not only bolstered, encouraged, and supported me throughout this project, but also put in innumerable hours formatting and helping to organize this book. I am also grateful and thankful to my mother, Cas DiMenna, who spent numerous hours throughout the last six months, word processing over half of the manuscript. So much for retirement. I have great appreciation for my family, the DiMennas, the Vogts, the

Schneiders, and friends who have been extremely supportive in this endeavor. Thank you.

I (JMJ) need to first and foremost thank God for giving me the gifts I have as a person. He or she has always been there to provide guidance and inspiration in my life. I also extend deep appreciation to my family, Vincent and Blake. It was their understanding and support that kept me on track and focused as I balanced family life and motherhood with my career. And I thank my original family, the Warren Carlsons, for their constant affirmations and support.

To our local libraries in the Minneapolis–St. Paul area and our local bookstores, including The Hungry Mind, Barnes & Noble, and Borders Bookstores. We appreciate their patience in providing us with the materials we needed for writing *Read Two Books. . . .*

Last, but not least, this project would not have come about without Tracey Belmont or Dorothy Lin at John Wiley & Sons. Their belief in our project provided us with continuous reassurance, support, and advice in bringing our project to fruition. We appreciate their constant guidance and expertise.

The Value and Goals of Bibliotherapy

We often get calls from colleagues, or are asked by friends, "What's a good book for ————?" Or a client comes into our office stating that a self-help book has changed their life, and that we should recommend it to everyone. Books, like many things, are personal and people respond to them quite differently. Recommending books, films, literature, or theater is as useful as suggesting exercise, support groups, relaxation, or any other of the many resources available to people. The road to recovery and healing is not only based on what happens in an hour-long session in our office; it is also based on what happens between sessions.

Self-help books have been in abundance over the last 15 years for good reason. They guide, comfort, encourage, and teach men and women who are reluctant at times to confide in their friends or families. Self-help books reduce people's isolation, particularly for those who think they are the only ones who are disheartened or confused. Bibliotherapy can be an essential part of providing services to clients. To be more specific, bibliotherapy is the clinical technique of recommending books to clients for guidance in solving their problems. It is often used as an adjunct to standard therapy techniques. Counseling is a collaborative process with therapists acting not only in the therapeutic role, but also as coaches and teachers. Recommending reading materials, specific to a client's recovery and healing, has become a primary treatment technique for mental health practitioners, physicians, school psychologists, teachers, and clergy. The goals of bibliotherapy are not to replace counseling, but to assist the helping professional to enhance and increase the resources available to the client. With the advent of restrictive Health Maintenance Organizations and cost-containment treatment, self-help books enhance and extend the therapeutic process. Individuals both in and out of therapy can make use of self-help books in constructing, repairing, and understanding their own lives.

Research in the 1990s continues to support the effectiveness of self-help books in clinical practice. Four studies found self-help books useful in treating health-related problems. Starker (1992*a,b*, 1994) found in three studies that self-help books improved clients' attitudes toward health problems and treatment, provided therapeutic comfort, and lowered stress levels in clients receiving health-related services. Matthews and Lonsdale (1992) found that children who were hospitalized benefited from self-help books. Ellis (1993) and Halliday (1991) concluded in their respective studies that self-help books enabled clients to make profound personality changes. Fiction, poetry, or inspirational readings have limited empirical support as bibliotherapeutic treatment mediums. This may be because behavioral- and cognitive-oriented self-help books are more amenable to empirical scrutiny (Pardeck, 1993). According to Baruth and Burggraf (1984) and Orton (1997), the goals of bibliotherapy include the following:

1. To provide information
2. To provide insight
3. To stimulate discussion about problems
4. To communicate new values and attitudes
5. To create awareness that other people have similar problems
6. To provide solutions to the problems
7. To provide realistic solutions to problems

Various kinds of information can be conveyed through assigned and shared reading. Insight or self-awareness, is another important goal of bibliotherapy. To select a book for a client, the practitioner should use books with which they are familiar. Therapists should be aware of the length and complexity of the book. The book should be applicable to the problem facing the client. The client's reading ability should be considered, along with the client's emotional and chronological age.

Of course, there are limitations that one should be aware of when using bibliotherapy. One of the most important limitations to this type of intervention is that it should never be used as a single approach to treatment, but rather as an adjunct (Pardeck, 1986, 1993; Orton, 1997). Second, the client may intellectualize about a problem when reading about it (Giblin, 1989). Third, individuals who are not good readers may have difficulty benefiting from bibliotherapy. However, bibliotherapy can be conducted successfully through books on tape as well as other innovative strategies. If the above points are considered, practitioners will find bibliotherapy to be a creative tool that can support the therapeutic process.

 **ABUSE**

GENERAL

Better Boundaries: Owning and Treasuring Your Life
Jan Black and Greg Enns
New Harbinger Publications, 1998
256 pages

Book Byte

The authors explain the differences between boundaries and walls and explore relationship problems associated with poor boundaries. They teach the reader to view him- or herself as a treasure to be protected. This is a good book for the client who can't say no to others. The authors help the reader to assess his or her own boundary issues and to make adjustments.

Suggested Readers

- Clients who are involved in abusive relationships
- Clients with a history of sexual abuse
- Clients with codependent issues

Therapeutic Insights

- Boundaries are the "stop signs," or borders, that we install to protect ourselves. Having good boundaries enables us to own our lives and to make authentic choices as to the way we live, love, give, and relate to others.
- Having successful boundaries involves sorting and choosing who and what to let into our lives and who and what to keep out.
- Learning the appropriate use of the words *yes* and *no* leads to stable boundaries. Boundaries define our identities and attract respectful relationships.
- A life without boundaries produces endless problems. It can open the door to victimization and confusing and unhappy relationships.
- Boundaries are not an excuse to be selfish, arrogant, or rude. They mean we, as the owners, exert choices over our lives.

DOMESTIC VIOLENCE

He Promised He'd Stop
Michael Groetsch
CPI Publishing, 1997
228 pages

Book Byte

Michael Groetsch dispels the myth that all batterers are alike. He shows readers how to identify which category of batterer they are involved with using a "batterer's continuum" from least dangerous to most dangerous. This book is a great resource for women who feel trapped in abusive relationships. He gives specific strategies for women to protect themselves and get out of violent relationships.

Suggested Readers

- Women who are in abusive relationships
- Friends and family of women who are in abusive relationships
- Females who are questioning the severity of abuse in their relationship

Therapeutic Insights

- Batterers are not all alike. Some are less dangerous than others. Some are more treatable than others.
- Batterers have many emotions and behaviors in common. Learning to recognize the warning signs can keep a woman from entering into an abusive relationship.
- Battered women should consider three strategies:
  1. Treating the batterer
  2. Leaving the batterer
  3. Prosecuting the batterer
- Battered women are often very isolated. It is imperative to build a strong support system.
- Children can be emotionally damaged if they grow up in a violent home. There is a great likelihood that boys will grow up to be adult batterers.

When Men Batter Women: New Insights into Ending Abusive Relationships

Neil S. Jacobsen, Ph.D., and John Gottman, Ph.D.
Simon & Schuster, 1998
320 pages

Book Byte

Drawing from their research of more than 200 couples over a 10-year period, Jacobsen and Gottman take a new look at the issue of battering. They dispel certain myths, including "All batterers are alike." Jacobsen and Gottman have found through research that there are two distinct categories of batterers; knowing which type determines if the relationship is salvageable. They offer advice and support with fresh new insights to women in abusive relationships. They also dispel many of the myths and the misinformation regarding domestic violence.

Suggested Readers

- Women who are in violent relationships
- Friends, relatives, and caregivers of women who are in violent relationships
- Male abusers

Therapeutic Insights

- There are many myths and much misinformation about domestic violence. Not all batterers are alike.
- Battered women experience a variety of emotions all at once. They are often frightened, angry, sad, and outraged, all at the same time.
- Often, women feel crazy while in a battering relationship. They begin to doubt their own views or reality.
- There are two categories of abusers:
    1. The "pitbulls," who are extremely dependent and have emotions that boil over quickly
    2. The "cobras," who have a history of childhood abuse and see violence as a part of life
- Battered women do get out of abusive relationships. They are more likely to leave than other women who are simply in unhappy relationships.

FAMILY ABUSE

The Drama of the Gifted Child: The Search for the True Self
Alice Miller
Basic Books, HarperCollins Publishers, 1997
136 pages

Book Byte

Alice Miller has written an unpretentious book that has great impact on child abuse survivors. She describes these children as gifted, not because they have high grades or they are talented in some way, but because they have survived, and somehow they have adapted to an unspeakable cruelty during childhood. The numbness that they experience is actually a gift that helps them survive the trauma. *The Drama of the Gifted Child* helps these survivors reclaim their lives by discovering their needs and their own truth.

Suggested Readers

- Adults who are experiencing depression as a result of childhood trauma
- Survivors of sexual abuse
- All parents

Therapeutic Insights

- Clients cannot undo the damage that was done to them as children, but they can repair and change themselves. By transforming themselves from unaware victims of the past into responsible individuals in the present, they are able to move beyond the childhood trauma and live more fully.
- When a child's needs are not met, he or she will often develop numbness, or not experiencing feelings. A child experiences feelings only when there is someone there to accept, to understand, and to support him or her.
- Depression can result from a child not experiencing his or her feelings. It is a denial of his or her own emotional reactions.
- One of the greatest wounds that a child can experience is not to be loved just as he or she truly is. A client cannot heal without the work of mourning the loss.
- Access to a client's "true self" comes when he or she no longer needs to be afraid of the intense emotions from early childhood.

FEMALE SEXUAL ABUSE

The Courage to Heal: A Guide for Women Survivors of Child Sexual Abuse
Ellen Bass and Laura Davis
Harper Perennial, 1994
608 pages

Book Byte

Ellen Bass and Laura Davis have written a comprehensive guide for women who were sexually abused as children. They provide explanations and practical suggestions for healing by sharing their personal and professional experiences. The authors explore the healing process for the reader and how she can come to terms with her past. Both Ellen Bass and Laura Davis are nationally recognized experts on healing from child sexual abuse. Their book is easy to read and covers many different issues facing a sexual abuse survivor.

Suggested Readers

- Female clients who have been sexually abused as children
- Family and friends of sexual abuse survivors
- Health care professionals who work with sexual abuse survivors

Therapeutic Insights

- Women often go to great lengths to deny their memories of abuse. Denial is a method of self-protection for abuse survivors.
- An essential part of the healing process is for these women to tell their stories.
- The backbone of healing is for a woman to be able to express her anger about the situation in a positive way. Anger is often held in, resulting in depression, anxiety, and/or addictive behavior.
- Negative self-images are the result of internalized messages from the abuser or simply from the event of being abused. For a client to learn to love herself, these internal messages must change.
- Abuse survivors can learn to be intimate. Communication and trust, along with giving and caring, are the main elements of intimacy. Relationships are places to practice intimacy.

Secret Survivors: Uncovering Incest and Its Aftereffects in Women
E. Sue Blume
Ballentine Books, John Wiley & Sons, Inc., 1990
321 pages

Book Byte

Secret Survivors expands the definition of *incest* to include all adult abusers. E. Sue Blume discusses the many different problems that may result from childhood abuse, including depression, drug and alcohol use, phobias, panic disorders, and eating and sexual disorders. The author explains how these different problems are actually coping mechanisms for dealing with childhood abuse. E. Sue Blume teaches the reader alternative nondestructive survival techniques.

Suggested Readers

- Incest survivors
- Adults with a history of any childhood sexual abuse
- Clients who exhibit symptoms of depression, alcohol or drug abuse, eating or sexual disorders, along with a memory of childhood sexual abuse

Therapeutic Insights

- The aftereffects of incest are actually survival tactics rather than problems to be overcome.
- What constitutes incest is actually an imbalance of power. This imbalance may exist between two children of the same age.
- The term *survivor* serves as a reminder that he or she was not the wrongdoer.
- The aftereffects of incest are coping mechanisms with negative side effects. Learning alternative positive coping mechanisms is paramount to healing.
- Once "remembering" begins, it is important for the victim to set limits on memory and surging emotion. The therapist can help pace the remembering. Denial serves a purpose.

The Sexual Healing Journey: A Guide for Survivors of Sexual Abuse

Wendy Maltz

HarperCollins Publishers, 1992 (reprint edition)

368 pages

Book Byte

Wendy Maltz has written a book specifically about sexual healing for the sexual abuse survivor. She takes the survivor step-by-step through the recovery of his or her sexual life to a loving and safe place, and teaches the reader to identify the effects of sexual abuse and to gain control over disturbing automatic reactions to touch and sex. She then guides the reader to creating a positive meaning for sex and improving his or her intimate relationship. This book is primarily for sexual abuse survivors, but it is also helpful for intimate partners and therapists.

Suggested Readers

- Female survivors of sexual abuse
- Male survivors of sexual abuse
- Clients with sexual intimacy issues

Therapeutic Insights

- Sexual abuse directly affects how clients feel about their bodies and how they experience physical pleasure and intimacy with others.
- The client's decision to reclaim his or her sexuality is a very affirming step in the recovery process. Identifying his or her fears, creating realistic goals, and then beginning the process of reclaiming his or her sexuality are the first three steps.
- A sexual abuse survivor's attitude toward sex is contaminated. Often, his or her mind-set includes such beliefs as sex is uncontrollable, sex is hurtful, or sex has no boundaries. These are just a few of the false ideas that a survivor may believe.
- To create a new concept of sex, clients need to change their negative attitudes to positive ones. Several healthy ideas about sex are that it is a natural biological drive, it is an expression of love, and that it is a powerful healing energy.

- Learning to recognize, to understand, and to cope with automatic reactions is a necessary part of the healing process. Automatic reactions can come in three forms:
  1. Emotional responses
  2. Physical sensations
  3. Intrusive thoughts

MALE SEXUAL ABUSE

Victims No Longer: Men Recovering from Incest and Other Sexual Child Abuse
Mike Lew
Perennial Library, 1990 (reprint edition)
352 pages

Book Byte

Victims No Longer addresses men recovering from incest and other sexual abuse. The author, Mike Lew, a psychotherapist and expert in the field of male sexual trauma, explores strategies of healing and working through issues of trust, intimacy, and sexuality. He helps male survivors identify and validate childhood traumas, and he explores strategies for survival and healing. Michael Lew takes male victims forward into recovery.

Suggested Readers

- Adult male survivors of childhood sexual abuse
- Adult homosexual males with histories of childhood sexual trauma
- Male clients with trust and intimacy issues due to childhood sexual abuse

Therapeutic Insights

- Incest is a violation by someone in authority. It is a violation of trust, power, and protection.
- In our culture, men are not supposed to be victims. Many people believe that a "real man" should be able to protect himself and solve his problems without any help.

- Sexual abuse leads the survivor to have confused feelings about his sexuality. A connection between sex and shame happens when children are sexually abused.
- Part of the recovery process includes returning to your childhood to understand what really happened and what your actual role was in the abuse.
- Recovery is possible, but the abuse and pain need to be confronted directly.

SELF ABUSE

A Bright Red Scream: Self-Mutilation and the Language of Pain
Marilee Strong
Penguin Putnam, 1999
256 pages

Book Byte

Marilee Strong explores the secret world of self-mutilation in this book. She confronts the myths and stereotypes of self-mutilation and explains how self-mutilation, such as cutting or burning is actually an effective coping mechanism for victims of child abuse. She presents her information with stories and testimonies from self-mutilators themselves and dispells the many myths surrounding self-mutilation.

Suggested Readers

- Adults who self-abuse
- Family, friends, and therapists of self-abusers
- Adolescents who self-abuse

Therapeutic Insights

- Clients deliberately harm themselves to provide relief from emotional pain caused by such symptoms as anxiety, depersonalization, and desperation.
- During childhood, people learn to regulate their emotions, which gives them a sense of self-control. Feeling helpless and out of control can stem from traumatic childhood experiences.

- Disassociation is a useful coping mechanism when experiencing a traumatic event. When it becomes an automatic response to even minor stresses, clients feel out of control and unconnected to their bodies. Cutting or self-abusing is a way of reconnecting with their bodies and knowing they are alive, human, and whole.
- Severe trauma may alter the structure and chemistry in a person's brain. The body becomes hardwired to a state of fear and anxiety. Research has shown that this can change with talk therapy, medication therapy, or having new experiences.
- There is no single approach to healing self-abusers. The underlying trauma must be resolved or other self-destructive behaviors may emerge when the self-injury stops, such as alcohol abuse, drug abuse, or eating disorders. A combination of medication, psychotherapy, and cognitive-behavioral techniques contributes to successful treatment.

The Scarred Soul: Understanding and Ending Self-Inflicted Violence

Tracy Alderman
New Harbinger Publications, 1997
216 pages

Book Byte

Tracy Alderman has written a book specifically for victims of self-inflicted violence. She teaches the reader what he or she can do to stop hurting him- or herself by using insight and logical solutions. In addition, Alderman educates therapists, family, and friends on how to be helpful and supportive to self-abuse victims and how to end the secrecy of their abuse and begin to experience and express their feelings.

Suggested Readers

- Adults who inflict violence on themselves
- Friends, family, and therapists of self-abusers
- Adolescents who are self-abusers

Therapeutic Insights

- Clients learn that self-inflicted violence serves as a relief for overwhelming feelings. Often, these victims are unable to express or control their emotions, possibly because it was physically unsafe to express emotions in their family.
- Some negative coping methods to deal with overwhelming feelings include self-inflicted violence, alcohol abuse, overeating, or sex. Positive and healthy coping forms may include talking, exercising, writing, crying, breathing, doing artwork, or resolving the underlying problem.
- When clients experience detachment from their bodies, dissociation serves as a defense mechanism and protects them from overwhelming emotional pain. Self-inflicted violence can help reduce or end this detachment. Often, it produces feelings of euphoria. The human brain, during physical trauma, releases endorphins that are similar to morphine. This is why abusers do not feel pain while hurting themselves.
- Shame stemming from events that happened earlier in a client's life is often the overwhelming emotion that precedes self-inflicted violence. One way for clients to reduce this shame is to change the way they view the events that have happened in their lives.
- Clients need to thoroughly explore the reasons why they use self-inflicted violence and then why they might want to stop before making a decision to stop. A solid support system is paramount in making this decision.

VERBAL ABUSE

Tongue Fu!
Sam Horn
St. Martin's Press, Inc., 1996
236 pages

Book Byte

Sam Horn's book, *Tongue Fu!*, is written on how to deflect, disarm, and defuse verbal conflict. It is easy to read and gives specific tactics for verbal self-protection. Sam Horn teaches us how to handle bullies, complainers, and angry individuals and how to do it in such a way as to disarm the attacker and preserve the relationship. It is a book far beyond assertiveness training. It is about disarming and connecting with individuals who verbally and psychologically attack. Horn writes about communication and how to conduct ourselves with confidence to avoid being verbally abused.

Suggested Readers

- Clients with communication issues
- Women or men who are in verbally abusive relationships
- Adults who want to diffuse conflict in relationships

Therapeutic Insights

- Responding to unpleasant and irritable people with compassion and understanding can often transform their hostility into harmony. Learn to respond to others rather than simply to react to them.
- There are certain words that set up adversarial relationships. Use the word *and* instead of *but. But* negates what has been said and turns discussions into debates. Lose the words *no* and *can't because.*
- Giving someone our undivided attention is the single most important thing we can do to make them feel significant. Active listening includes looking at the person, lifting eyebrows and establishing eye contact, and leaning forward in an attentive posture. Active listening is learning what the other person is saying.
- We can learn to get more of what we want, need, and deserve by knowing what battles to pick, by learning how to say *no,* by learning to end conversations tactfully, and by acting and projecting confidence.
- We can learn to take control of our emotions. It is only with our consent that someone can make us angry.

The Verbally Abusive Relationship: How to Recognize It and How to Respond, Second Edition

Patricia Evans
Adams Media Corp., 1996
221 pages

Book Byte

In this book, Patricia Evans explores the damaging effects of verbal abuse. The book is oriented toward women, although it is excellent for all clients. The author's main purpose is to teach the reader how to recognize verbal abuse and to change how he or she reacts to it. The author uses a self-evaluative questionnaire in Part I and defines "Power Over" someone versus "Personal Power." In Part II, she defines the categories of abuse (e.g., withholding, countering, discounting, and trivializing), and she gives appropriate methods of communicating and making changes.

Suggested Readers

- Women who feel disrespected in relationships or are in a verbally abusive relationship
- Couples with issues of anger
- Parents who are constantly angry with their children

Therapeutic Insights

- This book teaches the reader how to recognize verbal abuse and helps the reader understand that verbal abuse is an issue of control in which a person holds power over another.
- Clients learn how verbal abuse is generally denied by the abuser and often takes place behind closed doors.
- Clients learn the progression of how verbal abuse can proceed to physical abuse.
- In verbally abusive relationships, clients are often told their perception of reality is wrong.
- Readers learn to recognize a verbally abusive relationship, and to respond to it in a way to create change. By doing so, the victim often encounters the fear of *loss of love;* by not doing so, the victim may encounter a *loss of self.*

You Can't Say That to Me!: Stopping the Pain of Verbal Abuse: An 8-Step Program

Suzette Haden Elgin, Ph.D.
John Wiley & Sons, Inc., 1995
206 pages

Book Byte

Suzette Elgin, the creator of the *Gentle Art of Verbal Self-Defense,* teaches us, in an eight-step program, how to counter verbal abuse by spouses, friends, employers, and relatives. She does this by teaching us specific language techniques to neutralize verbal attacks. She teaches us how to establish an environment in which verbal abuse almost never happens, and how to handle it directly and efficiently if it does.

Suggested Readers

- Adults who are victims of verbal abuse
- Adults who use verbal abuse to control their spouses, friends, relatives, or employees
- Parents who wish to teach their children how to diffuse verbally abusive situations

Therapeutic Insights

- Verbal abuse is exhausting. It consists of unanswerable questions, scalding accusations, sarcasm, and insinuations.
- Verbal violence is the root of all other violence.
- To put an end to verbal abuse, two resources are needed:
  1. Knowledge of our native language
  2. Basic common sense
- We can expect dramatic improvements in our relationships with others by learning to neutralize verbal attacks.
- Our productivity and creativity increase automatically when we are no longer drained by verbal conflict.

ADDICTIONS AND RECOVERY

ADDICTIVE ORGANIZATIONS

The Addictive Organization: Why We Overwork, Cover Up, Pick Up the Pieces, Please the Boss, and Perpetuate Sick Organizations

Ann Wilson Schaef and Diane Fassel

Harper San Francisco, 1990

240 pages

Book Byte

Everyone in society lives and works in some kind of organization, group, or system. Beginning with the family, and incorporating environments such as schools, the workplace, clubs, and civic organizations, most of us spend the majority of our lives within organizations or relating to organizations. Often, persons who come from dysfunctional families find their organizations repeating the same patterns they learned in their families. This book explains how people can become tied to an organization to the point at which they will do anything to please it. Schaef and Fassel reflect on the signs that show that a person is an addict. They explain how an organization becomes addictive, and they also tell of the four major forms of addiction in an organization.

Suggested Readers

- Employees in organizations in which they see addictive processes occurring
- Adults who report to addicts
- Those who feel few options in their workplace due to its closed systems

Therapeutic Insights

- An addictive system is a closed system.
- An addictive system calls for addictive behaviors.
- Self-centeredness is a prominent characteristic of addicts and an addictive system.

- Confusion plays a vital role in an addictive system and prevents workers from taking responsibility.
- Addictive organizations can be identified by perfectionism, workaholism, rigidity in thinking, crisis handling, and lack of teamwork.

ADDICTIVE PERSONALITY

The Addictive Personality: Understanding the Addictive Process and Compulsive Behavior, Second Edition
Craig Nakken
Hazelden Publishing Group, 1996
120 pages

Book Byte

Since its first publication in 1988, Nakken's powerful and poignant description of the addiction process—the causes, stages of development, and consequences—has helped thousands of people understand better the depth and dimension of this costly illness. The author sees addiction as an attempt to control life's cycles, a process that is progressive, and as an illness that undergoes continuous development from a beginning to an end point. Addiction and the mood change created by acting out are very seductive processes in which the addict is emotionally seduced into believing that he or she can be nurtured by objects or events. Addicts keep delaying life issues as a way of nurturing themselves.

Suggested Readers

- Those who are caught up in the cycle of addiction
- Adults who are seeking to understand the progressive nature of addiction
- Individuals who are attempting to find recovery from their addictions

Therapeutic Insights

- Addicts achieve an illusion of being in control through acting out.
- Everyone has the potential to form addictive relationships with objects or events during stressful times.
- The addict builds a defense system to protect the addictive belief system against attacks from others.

- The longer an addictive illness progresses, the less a person feels the ability to have meaningful relationships with others.
- Practicing addicts want to be first and demand to come first.

The Angry Heart: Overcoming Borderline and Addictive Disorders: An Interactive Self-Help Guide
Joseph Santoro, Ph.D., and Ronald Cohen, Ph.D.
New Harbinger Publications, 1997
224 pages

Book Byte

The transition from a newborn infant to an out-of-control adult progresses over the course of many years. The failure to develop basic trust as an infant leads to an inability to enter into close and meaningful relationships with others. When someone is unable to trust others, he or she secretly uses relationships to fulfill desperate unmet needs for belonging, love, and survival. Such a person cannot give to relationships in the same measure that he or she takes; therefore, the relationships frequently become unstable battlegrounds where misperceptions, self-defeating manipulations, broken promises, and resentment are briefly interrupted by seductive truces. Thus, the borderline personality is described. Santoro and Cohen have written a guide and a valuable resource for this disorder and its relationship to addictive behaviors. Significant exercises are included throughout the book.

Suggested Readers

- Those individuals who are looking for skills and support to change their destructive behaviors
- Adults with a history of childhood trauma
- Individuals with poor impulse control, with poor anger control, and with a propensity toward self-harm

Therapeutic Insights

- To be successful, one must recondition the way he or she thinks.
- Chronic exposure to traumatic stress overloads the brain systems responsible for self-protection.

- Poor decision-making skills and an attitude of neediness cause impulsive gratification.
- People with borderline personalities lack the skills needed to make thoughtful decisions, and they are driven by intense feelings, which they cannot soothe.
- Taking more than one gives is a red flag in any relationship.

Facing Love Addiction: Giving Yourself the Power to Change the Way You Love—The Love Connection to Codependence
Pia Mellody, Andrea Wells Miller, and J. Keith Miller
Harper San Francisco, 1992
256 pages

Book Byte

Mellody has written three books that unravel the intricate and debilitating dynamics of coaddictive relationships. She outlines the toxic patterns played out by "love addicts" and the unresponsive "avoidance addicts" to whom they are painfully and repeatedly drawn. She shares personal experiences and real case histories that clarify the distinctions between codependence and coaddiction; she describes how love at first sight can be the first step in the addictive cycle of attraction, and how childhood experiences of abandonment or engulfment influence the choice of partners or friends. She includes journaling exercises for recovery.

Suggested Readers

- Those who are learning to accept another's value system
- Adults who are attempting to correct distorted thinking
- Adults who have grown up in families in which there was either engulfment, abandonment, or both

Therapeutic Insights

- Relationships between love addicts and avoidance addicts usually involve intensity, obsession, and compulsion.
- When avoidance addicts notice that their partners have given up pursuit and are gone, their fear of abandonment is triggered.

- When both people alternate between both roles, it creates the most intense, crazy, and sometimes violent relationship of all.
- Love addicts perceive avoidance addicts to be more powerful.
- An addiction functions in a person's life to remove intolerable reality through a series of obsessive compulsive experiences.

ADULT CHILDREN OF ALCOHOLICS

Children of Alcoholism: A Survivor's Manual
Judith S. Seixas and Geraldine Youcha
Harper & Row, 1986 (reprint edition)
224 pages

Book Byte

At lease 22 million American adults were raised by an alcoholic parent; as a consequence, nearly all of them live with scars, both psychological and physical. Coming from homes filled with loneliness and terror, children of alcoholics grow up unable to lead lives that are free from guilt, deep insecurity, lack of self-esteem, and intense sadness. This book exposes the family secret of alcoholism and draws on interviews with over 200 survivors to share the realities of family alcoholism, the occurrence of child abuse, the ruined family holidays, and the crazy atmosphere of an alcoholic home. The authors suggest invaluable techniques for reversing destructive patterns learned in the alcoholic family.

Suggested Readers

- Adult children of alcoholics
- Spouses of adult children of alcoholics
- Children of adult children of alcoholics

Therapeutic Insights

- Adult children of alcoholics, who are depressed, experience a lingering sadness that underlies their depression.
- Coming from an alcoholic family means that a person can't be sure of others even when they are reliable.

- When a person cannot allow him- or herself to believe in others, there is a reflexive pulling back in order to feel safe.
- Most adult children of alcoholics live with anger that began as a result of the contradictions built into life with an unstable parent.
- Children of alcoholics may accept the critical feelings that their parents expressed toward them, or they may assume that there is something unlovable in them.

My Mama's Waltz: A Book for Daughters of Alcoholic Mothers
Eleanor Agnew and Sharon Robideaux
Simon & Schuster, 1998
299 pages

Book Byte

With stunning honesty, this book brings to light the painful legacy of daughters of alcoholic mothers—the first book to focus solely on this fractured relationship. The authors share their own personal accounts, along with the memories and experiences of hundreds of women from all ages and backgrounds. This book gives a voice to the millions who, as children, lost their mothers to alcoholism. Being the daughter of an alcoholic mother always means having *more*—more secrecy, more social stigma, more family responsibilities while growing up, more worrying about her mother, more self-doubt about her own behaviors, more confusion in her home, and more unanswered questions about being a teenager and a young woman. These authors offer tremendous insight so that adult daughters of alcoholic mothers can better understand themselves.

Suggested Readers

- Adult daughters who are seeking to unlock the secret of having an alcoholic mother
- Adult daughters of alcoholic mothers who want to face their shame and self-doubt
- Those who want to understand the dynamics and consequences for adult women of alcoholics

Therapeutic Insights

- All family members must "waltz" carefully with an alcoholic, but this sinister dance is particularly terrifying for children.
- The alcoholic mother is inconsistent in her behavior, personality, and emotional availability.
- Hiding becomes a way of life for children of alcoholics.
- Adding to the pain of a mother's alcoholism is society's presumption that the mother-daughter relationship is always close and mutually fulfilling.
- Traditionally, or at least mythologically, a mother is the glue that holds the family together—until she becomes an alcoholic. Then, she tears it apart.

Perfect Daughters: Adult Daughters of Alcoholics

Robert J. Ackerman, Ph.D.
Health Communications, Inc., 1989
197 pages

Book Byte

Robert Ackerman is a leading expert on alcoholism and the family, especially on children of alcoholics of all ages. He has brought together the thoughts, ideas, and feelings of more than 1,200 women who are daughters of alcoholics. This book is about recovery. All adult daughters are not affected the same nor do they have the same issues. It is very difficult to get an accurate and consistent perception of something when it is chaotic, when it changes constantly, when it contains mixed messages, or when it is impossible to understand what is happening. Many adult daughters were not only confused as children, but also about how they should behave now in their own families. Ackerman assists the readers in understanding the issues of parenting, identity, control, trust, attempts to please, and shame and fear for the adult daughter of an alcoholic.

Suggested Readers

- Adult daughters of alcoholics
- Family members who are seeking more understanding regarding their parent's alcoholism
- Women who find it difficult to trust

Therapeutic Insights

- In adult daughters, there are at least eight different patterns of behavior that have been carried over from their childhood.
- Not all characteristics can be traced to being a daughter of an alcoholic.
- Types of adult daughters include the achiever, the triangulator, the passive one, the other directed one, the conflict avoider, the hypermature, the detacher, and the invulnerable one.
- Adult daughters are at high risk for codependency.
- There is a difference between being a warm loving person and a codependent.

ALCOHOLISM

The Alcoholic Man: What You Can Learn from the Heroic Journeys of Recovering Alcoholics, Second Edition

Sylvia Cary, M.A., MFT
Lowell House, 1999
288 pages

Book Byte

Getting sober can be easy compared with staying sober. Now, read of courage and inspiration from 21 heroic men who've learned the benefit of staying sober. In this edition, the reader also finds strategies for staying sober, steps that can trigger a remission, how sexual energy and creativity soar with sobriety, how to upgrade his or her character, and what he or she should know about the phases of recovery.

Suggested Readers

- Men who are interested in long-term recovery
- Men who are making their first steps into sobriety
- Helping professionals who need assistance in recognizing addiction

Therapeutic Insights

- Fifty percent of those who try sobriety relapse within the first few months.
- Health maintenance organizations can be the biggest threat to the treatment of alcoholics and addicts.

- Alcoholism is a disease, and effective treatment requires total abstinence.
- All recovery does not look alike.
- Addiction is progressive.

Cool Water: Alcoholism, Mindfulness and Ordinary Recovery
William Alexander
Shambhala Publications, 1997
160 pages

Book Bytes

According to Alexander, the key to ongoing freedom from alcoholism or from any kind of addiction is right before us, here and now, in the present moment. The foremost problem is that addictions are often the result of people's efforts to escape living in the present. Alexander uses mindfulness, stories, meditation, Buddhist teachings, and the 12 steps to help alcoholics and others learn how to come back to the moment and to find healing there. He writes that ordinary recovery is not complicated, not special: It is about waking up to what is real.

Suggested Readers

- Those who are learning that the way to the healing moment is through paying attention
- Adults who are in recovery from addiction
- Addicts who are seeking other roads to recovery

Therapeutic Insights

- The practice of mindfulness is the path of wholeness in the midst of chaos.
- An active alcoholic or addict lives in a state of chronic apartness, separated from the gods and people who love him or her.
- Alcoholism is the disease of living "elsewhere."
- There will be times when the world will not feel familiar and, seemingly, when there are only the rawest wounds to hang on to.
- Drinking causes suffering, suffering causes drinking.

A Ghost in the Closet: Is There an Alcoholic Hiding?: An Honest Look at Alcoholism

Dale Mitchel
Hazelden Publishing Group, 1999
250 pages

Book Byte

In an alternately objective and personal voice, Mitchel presents a comprehensive and compelling view of alcoholism and the recovery process. He reveals blindness and grandiosity as common aspects of the disease, and he shines the light of self-understanding and self-forgiveness on the recovery path. At the root of all alcoholism is a shame-based personality and low self-worth. Shame-based people do not believe they have *done* something wrong, they believe they *are* something wrong. Mitchel has exhausted the literature on alcoholism, passing it through the filters of his own experience as an active, and now recovering, alcoholic. This book includes extensive tools for recovery, humor, prayers, and meditations.

Suggested Readers

- Adults who are in recovery for alcoholism
- Individuals who are active alcoholics
- Families and friends of alcoholics

Therapeutic Insights

- If a person is having trouble in any particular area of his or her life due to alcohol use, the odds are great that he or she is an alcoholic.
- With a mastered ability to deceive, an alcoholic holds his or her pain deep below the levels of public perception.
- One way that an alcoholic tends to rationalize behavior is through performing occasional good deeds.
- In an alcoholic, there is a complete feeling of total inadequacy.
- Although alcoholics are generally self-centered individuals, they also possess a heightened sensitivity to their emotions and, at times, their feelings.

I'll Quit Tomorrow: A Practical Guide to Alcoholism Treatment

Vernon E. Johnson

Harper San Francisco, 1990 (Revised edition)

192 pages

Book Byte

This best-selling recovery classic has helped many alcoholics on the way to recovery. Johnson presents the concepts and methods that have brought hope to alcoholics and their families, friends, and employers. His therapy aims at restoring the alcoholic's ego strength to assure permanent recovery. This book outlines a dynamic intervention and treatment plan, leading the alcoholic to a more productive life.

Suggested Readers

- Those who suspect themselves to be an alcoholic
- Family and friends of alcoholics
- Alcoholics who are seeking sobriety

Therapeutic Insights

- No one can survive alcoholism if it remains unchecked.
- Alcoholism involves the whole person—physically, mentally, psychologically, and spiritually.
- Ultimately, alcoholism causes people to behave in destructive and antisocial ways.
- The buildup of crises forces people to recognize their alcoholism.
- Different sorts of people become alcoholics, but ultimately, all alcoholics are alike in their powerlessness.

The Thinking Person's Guide to Sobriety

Bert Pluymen

St. Martin's Press, Inc., 1999

288 pages

Book Byte

Bert Pluymen, a highly successful attorney, was the last person anyone would have considered an alcoholic. He never missed work, never drank in the morning, never woke up with the shakes, and never lost a job due to drinking. Nevertheless, Pluymen was an alcoholic, and this is his insightful, witty, and uplifting story of his triumph over alcohol addiction. This book sheds new light on how alcohol can ruin people's lives.

Suggested Readers

- Those who are wondering if they are, in fact, alcoholic
- Adults who want to change their drinking habits
- Those alcoholics who never thought it could happen to them

Therapeutic Insights

- Drinking offers the allure of temporary pain relief, but the death risk is great.
- The cumulative effect of drinking includes an undercurrent of low-level exhaustion.
- *Insanity* is doing the same thing repetitively, expecting a different result.
- As time goes on, the alcoholic imperceptibly loses most friends who are not heavy drinkers and becomes more isolated.
- Women suffer heart, liver, and brain damage after drinking less and for a shorter time than men.

BOOKS FOR CHILDREN ABOUT ALCOHOLISM

I Wish Daddy Didn't Drink So Much

Judith Vigna
Albert Whitman & Co., 1993
32 pages

Book Byte

For children, having an alcoholic parent can be a double blow: Not only must they cope with the drinking parent; often, they also feel ignored by the sober parent who may be overwhelmed by the drinker's problems. This is a very sensitive book about a little girl named Lisa who is constantly confused and disappointed by her alcoholic father. After a great disappointment at Christmas when her father doesn't show up, Lisa and her mother work through all the feelings that she has about her father. Lisa talks about her sadness, anger, and betrayal; she learns to think positively about herself.

Suggested Readers

- Children between ages 5 and 10 who are dealing with an alcoholic parent
- Parents who need help in processing alcoholism with their young children

Therapeutic Insights

- Children will create fantasies to buffer their real feelings about an alcoholic parent.
- Children will think that they are responsible for a parent's drinking.
- A parent's alcoholism can make a child feel worthless and unlovable.

COCAINE AND OTHER DRUGS

Cocaine Addiction: Treatment, Recovery, and Relapse Prevention
Arnold M. Washton
Norton, 1991
236 pages

Book Byte

Cocaine use has become recognized as a nationwide epidemic, and the drug is now universally considered highly dangerous and addictive. Use has spread increasingly to women, minority groups, lower-income groups, and adolescents. The cocaine outbreak has also forced the existing treatment system to better adapt itself to the clinical needs of the employed middle class. Mr. Washton is an internationally known clinician, researcher, and public speaker. He writes effectively about cocaine addiction, effective treatment ingredients, cocaine and the family, and treating special populations.

Suggested Readers

- Adults who are attempting to end their cocaine addiction
- Families who are looking for information regarding cocaine addiction
- Individuals who are involved in cocaine prevention programs

Therapeutic Lesson

- Requiring total abstinence ensures the widest safety margin against potential relapse to cocaine and prevents the development of a substitute addiction.
- Chemical dependency is almost always a family disease in terms of its etiology, maintenance, and negative impact.
- Relapse rates among cocaine addicts remain unnecessarily high, especially for those without a highly structured relapse prevention program.
- Identifying external cues and internal feeling states that trigger drug cravings is essential to achieving abstinence.
- Cocaine use significantly alters virtually every aspect of the neural transmission process in the brain.

How to Quit Drugs for Good: A Complete Self-Help Guide

Jerry Dorsman
Prima Publishing, 1998
384 pages

Book Bytes

Although quitting drugs may be the best thing that one can do, it can also be the hardest challenge an individual can face. In this book, Dorsman helps the addict to find the best approach to beating any drug habit—from barbiturates and prescription drugs to marijuana, cocaine, and heroin. Through a series of self-discovery exercises, worksheets, and checklists, the reader will learn how to determine if he or she has a drug problem, examine his or her individual reasons for using drugs, develop a personal treatment plan, and choose the techniques that will work.

Suggested Readers

- Those who are addicted to prescription drugs
- Addicts who are attempting to recover from cocaine addiction
- Adults who want to be in charge of their own treatment plan

Therapeutic Insights

- Acupuncture is a new method for treating drug addiction and alcoholism.
- Acupressure attempts to achieve the same results as acupuncture without the needles by applying finger pressure and massage.
- Solitude gives the addict an opportunity for self-examination and plans for self-renewal.
- The addict must stop denying the problems caused by drugs.
- People who have quit using drugs often feel overwhelmed with too much to do.

Prescription Drug Abuse: The Hidden Epidemic: A Guide to Coping and Understanding

Rod Colvin
Addicus Books, 1995
142 pages

Book Byte

Twelve of the top 20 most abused controlled substances in the nation are prescription drugs. Legions of Americans are abusing, misusing, and becoming addicted to prescribed drugs. As public awareness goes, this is a hidden epidemic, often misunderstood and underreported. This is a resource book to spotlight this serious national problem. Colvin balances compelling anecdotes of personal recovery with insightful reports from addiction medicine specialists, pharmacists, pain management researchers, and consumer educators. Treatment referral agencies are listed for all 50 states.

Suggested Readers

- Adults who are addicted to prescription drugs
- Family members and friends who need information regarding a loved one's addiction to pills
- Interested helping professionals who work with prescription addiction

Therapeutic Insights

- Prescription drug abuse is difficult to recognize.
- Prescription drug overdoses outnumbered heroin overdoses by a ratio of 6 to 1.
- In the top-20 list of the most abused controlled substances are marijuana, Xanax, Valium, Atrivan, Klonopin, Darrocet, Vicodin, Restoril, Percodan, Librium, and Methadone.
- More than 50 percent of prescriptions are used incorrectly.
- Doctors misprescribe because they are either duped by the patient, dishonest or disabled themselves.

RECOVERY

Codependent No More: How to Stop Controlling Others and Start Caring for Yourself, Second Edition
Melody Beattie
Hazelden Publishing Group, 1987, 1996
250 pages

Book Byte

This book has been a healing touchstone for millions, and spent over three years on *The New York Times* best-seller list. The book is essentially about self-care in the faces of relationships with the alcoholic, workaholic, foodaholic, rebellious teenager, gambler, and so forth. Codependency is a self-defeating, learned behavior that results in a diminished capacity to initiate or participate in loving relationships. Beattie believes that we don't have to take other people's behaviors as reflections of our self-worth. We don't have to react, we have options. Beattie's book teaches how to regain faith and confidence in our ability to think and reason.

Suggested Readers

- Spouses or significant others who are involved with addicts
- Addicts who don't trust their ability to problem solve and make decisions
- Those who are in dysfunctional painful relationships

Therapeutic Insights

- Sometimes, no human being can be there the way one may need them to be.
- People may even convince themselves that they would die if a certain person weren't in their life.
- A beneficial act is facing and coming to terms with what is.
- At times, people prefer to stay angry, using anger as a protective shield.
- Forgiveness comes in its own time.

The Serenity Principle

Joseph Bailey
Harper San Francisco, 1990
128 pages

Book Byte

Bailey's new approach to recovery from addiction shows people how to tap their own source of positive energy in the search for serenity, a quest long recognized as the key to recovery. By identifying four principles of psychological function—thought, separate realities, levels of consciousness, and emotions as "delusion detectors"—Bailey shows how our thoughts actually control our reality. If we understand this, we have the power to create sane and serene lives.

Suggested Readers

- Those who seek serenity, and those who want to regain it
- Adults who are looking for mature harmonious relationships
- Individuals who want to give up the need to control

Therapeutic Insights

- Listening can occur only when the mind is quiet.
- Open-mindedness is the key to personal evolution and growth.
- Becoming addicted represents a desperate search outside ourselves for a positive feeling.
- Individuals tend to blame "outside reality" for negative experiences that create a feeling of powerlessness and unhappiness.

- It is in the lower levels of understanding that people click into the thought system that triggers learned habits and addictions.

Vastly More than That: Stories of Lesbians and Gay Men in Recovery
Guy Kettlehack
Hazelden Publishing Group, 1999
224 pages

Book Byte

For gay men and lesbians who are overcoming addiction—whether to alcohol, drugs, food, sex, or unhealthy relationships—the answer may be as complex and as difficult to grasp as the problem itself. This book highlights issues unique to gay men and lesbians in recovery, many of whom must confront crippling self-hatred. A loose and varied tribe, gays and lesbians have consistently been at the vanguard of creative recovery. This community has often mixed New Age approaches with any number of therapies in addition—sometimes, *but not always*—to the traditional 12-step route. They have forged many paths through the jungle. Lesbians and gay men as a group have taught others that sobriety and recovery are enormously open-ended and encompassing terms.

Suggested Readers

- Gays and lesbians who are fighting addiction
- Gays and lesbians who are looking for new opportunities for growth
- Family members and friends of gays and lesbians

Therapeutic Insights

- Drinking and drug taking may have once been a profoundly necessary defense.
- *Sobriety* is another word for being conscious.
- Everyone, gay or not, has inner and outer levels, contradictions, and internal conflicts.
- Sobriety is exasperating, sometimes unnerving in its clarity, but never boring.

- The damage caused by internalized homophobia is insidiously crippling and pervasive.

SEXUAL ADDICTION

Out of the Shadows: Understanding Sexual Addiction, Second Edition
Patrick Carnes, Ph.D.
Hazelden Publishing Group, 1992
182 pages

Book Byte

This book is the first ever published on sexual addiction and remains the premier text in the field. A moment comes for every addict when the consequences are so great or the pain is so bad that the addict admits life is out of control because of her or his sexual behavior. One of the greatest myths that allows the addict to repeat sexual behaviors is that sexual addiction does not adversely affect other relationships, especially a marriage. The corollary myth is that the family does not know about the addict's secret sexual life. Carnes' book is about treatment and hope, and breaking the isolation of the addict's life.

Suggested Readers

- Those who lead a secret life as a sex addict
- Family members who are attempting to understand their loved one's compulsive sexual behavior
- Men and women who are attempting to recover from sexual addiction

Therapeutic Insights

- Sincere delusion is believing one's own lies.
- Sexual addicts are hostages of their preoccupation.
- The first two phases of the addictive cycle (preoccupation and ritualization) are not always visible. The addict struggles to present an image of normalcy to the outside world.
- The addictive system starts with a belief system containing faulty assumptions, myths, and values, which support impaired thinking.

- All three levels of addiction transcend personality, gender, and socio-economic status.

Women, Sex and Addiction: A Search for Love and Power

Charlotte Davis Kasl, Ph.D.
Harper & Row, 1990 (reprint edition)
416 pages

Book Bytes

In our society, sex can easily become the price that many women pay for love and the illusion of security. A woman who seeks a sense of personal power and an escape from pain may use sex and romance as a way to feel in control. But sex never satisfies her longing for love and self-worth. In this very wise book, Kasl shows women how they can learn to experience their sexuality as a source of love and positive power, and how to experience sex as an expression that honors the soul as well as the body.

Suggested Readers

- Women who want to heal from sex addiction
- Women who want to develop a clearer sense of boundaries
- Men who are attempting to find ways to connect intimacy with sexuality

Therapeutic Insights

- When someone tries to control another person, intimacy is impossible.
- Women are taught to turn their anger inward.
- Women, who hide from the truth in their lives, immerse themselves in a web of addiction.
- Successful couples maintain separate identities.
- Addictive people are attracted to those who reinforce their negative core beliefs.

SPIRITUALITY AND ADDICTION

Addiction and Grace: Love and Spirituality
in the Healing of Addictions
Gerald G. May, M.D.
Harper San Francisco, 1998
200 pages

Book Byte

This book is about May's classic exploration of the psychology and physiology of addiction. It offers inspiration for those who desire to explore the mystery of who they really are. May examines the processes of attachment that lead to addiction, and he describes the relationship between addiction and spiritual awareness. He also details the various addictions from which we suffer—addictions not only to substances like alcohol and drugs, but to work, sex, performance, responsibility, and intimacy. May draws on his experience as a psychiatrist working with the chemically dependent. He emphasizes that addiction represents an attempt to assert complete control over our lives.

Suggested Readers

- Those who are looking for a scientific, psychological, and theological understanding of addiction
- Adults who seek clear and simple insights regarding addiction
- Those who seek to understand the paradoxes of addiction

Therapeutic Insights

- Addiction is a self-defeating force that abuses our freedom.
- Addiction attaches desire, it bonds, and it enslaves the energy of desire to certain specific behaviors, things, or people.
- Grace can transcend repression, addiction, and any other power that seeks to oppress the freedom of the human heart.
- Addiction is a state of compulsion, obsession, or preoccupation that enslaves a person's will and desire.
- Willpower and resolutions come and go, but the addiction process never sleeps.

 **ADOPTION**

GENERAL

Being Adopted: The Lifelong Search for Self
David M. Brodzinsky, Ph.D., Marshall D. Schechter, M.D.,
and Robin Marantz Henig
Doubleday, 1993 (reprint edition)
213 pages

Book Byte

Being adopted means different things to different people. There is no right or wrong way to experience it. For some, it is a sense of always feeling unsettled; for many, there is the gratitude of having been raised by loving parents; for others, there is a continuous pain of feeling out of place. This book is a way to share the author's model of normal adjustment to being adopted as it occurs through the lifespan. This model is based on years of clinical and research work with adoptees and their families. There are six themes that are illustrated throughout the book:

1. Adoption through the eyes of the adoptees
2. Developmental perspective
3. Normality
4. Individuality
5. Search for self
6. Sense of loss

Suggested Readers

- Adoptees who are addressing identity issues
- Parents and family members of adopted children
- Adoptees who want to understand the common developmental pathways on the way to adoption adjustment

Therapeutic Insights

- For children who are adopted late, the loss can be traumatic and overt, placing greater stress on the child.

- Children adopted at birth may grieve the loss of origins, of a completed sense of self, and of genealogical continuity.
- Most young adoptees love their adoption stories.
- The developmental task of separation for an adolescent is further complicated if the adolescent is adopted.
- Becoming a parent is often one of the landmarks of adulthood that pushes an adult adoptee to search for his or her birth parent.

The Essential Adoption Handbook
Colleen Alexander-Roberts
Taylor Publishing, 1993
242 pages

Book Byte

Understanding all the steps, paperwork, and legal requirements can make the difference between adopting now and adopting years from now. This book walks the reader through the entire process, step-by-step, covering all types of adoption and the situations that he or she may encounter. This definitive resource offers both answers and advice, including the pros and cons of each type of adoption; samples of necessary letters, forms, and documents; preparing for a home study; adopting independently or through an agency; differences between a U.S. adoption and from another country; and the expenses to expect.

Suggested Readers

- Families who are considering adoption
- Adults who want specific information regarding costs
- Families who are preparing for a home study

Therapeutic Insights

- Open adoptions sidestep some problems that are inherent in confidential adoptions.
- Some families who are trying to adopt explore the possibility of foster parent adoption.
- A home study is an evaluation regarding the suitability of single people or couples to become parents.

- An independent adoption is one in which the birth mother places her child instead of an agency.
- Newspaper advertising is a very controversial issue.

How to Raise an Adopted Child: A Guide to Help Your Child Flourish from Infancy Through Adolescence

Judith Schaffer and Christina Lindstrom
Plume Books, 1991 (reprint edition)
310 pages

Book Byte

Adoption is an act of love; however, it is only successful when parents are prepared to deal with the special needs and circumstances of the adopted child. These two authors/psychotherapists use their experience to create a guide that anticipates most any situation adoptive parents can encounter. They give special advice for single adoptive parents, multiracial families, and children who have special needs. They give assistance in handling the racism often expressed against children of interracial adoption, as well as ways to handle a child's request to find his or her parents.

Suggested Readers

- Adoptive parents who want information regarding developmental stages
- Single adoptive parents
- Multiracial families

Therapeutic Insights

- Children usually start to speculate about who their birth parents are when they are between ages 6 and 9.
- Other children in the family will need their own time to prepare for an adopted sibling to join the family.
- There still remains too much secrecy and pretending in adoption.
- All children are born with their own psychological tendencies.
- Adoptive parents' support groups are an excellent source of help.

Making Sense of Adoption: A Parent's Guide

Lois Ruskai Melina

Harper Perennial, 1989

288 pages

Book Byte

Children who are adopted have predictable and often unspoken concerns about themselves and how they joined their families. In this guide, Melina helps parents anticipate and respond to those concerns in ways that build self-esteem. Through sample conversations, reassuring advice, and age-specific activities, parents can find answers to many difficult questions. Whether parents adopted traditionally, as step-parents, through donor insemination, through surrogacy, or through in vitro fertilization, this book will open the door to understanding for adoptive families.

Suggested Readers

- Parents of adopted children
- Families and friends who are involved in relationships with adopted children
- Parents who have been asked by their children to help them find their birth parents

Therapeutic Insights

- Children have the right to know who they are and how they joined their families.
- Children should be able to ask freely about their origins.
- Adoptive parents should encourage their children to have a positive attitude about their birth parents.
- The ages of 7 to 11 are critical years for children who have been adopted.
- Children's grief and anger at their birth parents may be directed at their adoptive parents.

The Primal Wound: Understanding the Adopted Child

Nancy Newton Verrier
Verrier Publications, 1997
252 pages

Book Byte

This book clarifies the effects on adopted children of separation from the birth mother. It presents information about pre- and perinatal psychology, attachment, bonding, and loss. In addition, to those children whose pain has long been unacknowledged or misunderstood, this book gives validation for their feelings, as well as explanations for their behavior. The author believes the primal wound is caused by the separation of the child from the biological mother, the connection to whom seems mystical, mysterious, spiritual, and everlasting.

Suggested Readers

- Adult adoptees
- Parents of adopted children
- Adoptees who are attempting to reconcile their feelings of loss

Therapeutic Insights

- Mother-and-child bonding doesn't begin at birth: It is a continuum of events, which begin in utero.
- The lack of personal history is difficult for the adoptee because of the importance of knowing one's past.
- The child experiences the separation as abandonment, no matter how altruistic the reason for giving a child up for adoption.
- It is very difficult for the adoptive mother of a newborn to comprehend the concept of the primal wound.
- Sometimes children may feel guilty for having been born.

ADOPTION AND REUNION

Shadow Mothers: Stories of Adoption and Reunion
Linda Back McKay
North Star Press, 1998
155 pages

Book Byte

Behind the sensationalism, talk shows, and tabloids, lie the truths of real women who each placed their child for adoption and were reunited years later. There is great complexity woven into the quilt of their lives—more than simply the pain and loss of the reunion. This book is about 10 women who tell their stories. They do not show the same histories, but they do have a common bond.

Suggested Readers

- Mothers who wish to be reunited with a child they placed for adoption
- Adoptees who are looking for their birth parents
- Support systems of people who want to reunite with their birth families

Therapeutic Insights

- A striking aftereffect of a reunion is the enhancement of the relationship between adoptees and their adoptive parents.
- Reunions make it possible for the adoptee to complete a new circle that encompasses both birth and adoptive parents.
- Most adoptees (90 percent) are satisfied with the outcome of the reunion.
- Reunions resolve genealogical concerns and diminish identity conflicts.
- The number of female adoptees searching and effecting reunions far outstrips the number of male adoptees doing the same.

BOOKS FOR CHILDREN ABOUT ADOPTION

Adoption Is for Always

Linda Walvoord Girard and Judith Friedman
Albert Whitman & Co., 1987
32 pages

Book Byte

This is a book about Celia, who becomes frustrated and upset when she realizes for the first time that she is adopted. As she gradually discovers the bits and pieces of her life, she begins to understand not only why her birth mother gave her up, but also that her adoptive parents will be her mommy and daddy forever.

Suggested Readers

- Children, between ages 5 and 9, who are adopted
- Families with adopted children

Therapeutic Insights

- Children may have a painful reaction to the fact that they were adopted.
- Children will question why they were given up for adoption.
- Children often have fantasies about their birth parents.

Happy Adoption Day

John McCutcheon and Julie Paschkis
Little, Brown & Co., 1996
32 pages

Book Byte

This children's book is a celebration of adoption. It honors the day the child was adopted through song and pictures. It includes beautiful illustrations and a story about families who chose to adopt a baby. The babies are represented well across all races and ethnicity.

Suggested Readers

- Children, between ages 2 and 6, who have been adopted

Therapeutic Insights

- Some parents look different, some look the same.
- No matter what color the skin, family is family.
- Adoptions are to be celebrated.

Let's Talk About It: Adoption
Fred Rogers (*Mr. Rogers's Neighborhood*)
Family Communications, 1998 (reissue edition)
32 pages

Book Byte

Different children find different ways to handle their feelings about adoption. How they want to talk about it, or even *if* they want to talk about it, will be an individual decision. This book by Fred Rogers is a way for children to share their uncertainties about difficult things with people who care about them. The issues of adoption are represented by beautiful photographs of children and families of all races and ethnicity.

Suggested Readers

- Children, between ages 4 and 8, who are adopted
- Families with adopted children

Therapeutic Insights

- It helps for children to talk about their confusion regarding adoption with their parents.
- Everyone has different feelings about their families.
- Every family is special.

We Adopted You, Benjamin Koo

Linda Walvoord
Albert Whitman & Co., 1989
32 pages

Book Byte

This is a book about Benjamin Koo, who was adopted from Korea as an infant, and he describes what it is like to grow up adopted from another country. Benjamin talks about his thoughts of his past, the details that he now knows about his orphanage experience, and the process of being adopted by his family in America. The story also includes Ben's experience when his parents adopted a little girl from Brazil.

Suggested Readers

- Children, between ages 7 and 11, who have been adopted
- Families with adopted children

Therapeutic Insights

- America is full of all different sorts of families.
- Sometimes, adopted children can help others learn about the meaning of family.
- Adopted children may be angry at times for feeling different.

PLACING A CHILD FOR ADOPTION

The Third Choice: A Woman's Guide to Placing a Child for Adoption

Leslie Foge and Gail Mosconi
Creative Arts Book Co., 1999
150 pages

Book Byte

This is a comprehensive guide for adults who are facing the difficult and complex decision of placing a child for adoption. This book takes potential birth mothers through their pregnancies, the birth, the relinquishing of the child, and the grief and recovery periods afterward. Choosing adoption instead of abortion or opting to parent is a very personal choice. This book is clear, sensitive, and compassionate. The book also includes a resource section on other reading materials and helpful organizations.

Suggested Readers

- Adults who are considering placing their child for adoption
- Families and friends supporting those who are considering adoption
- Helping professionals who assist birth mothers through this process

Therapeutic Insights

- It is important to identify any preconceived notion that one may have about adoption.
- The reasons for choosing adoption are varied, personal, and complicated.
- There is no way to avoid grief after placing a child for adoption.
- There is a wide range of normal feelings during the first year following an adoption placement.
- After the birth and placement of a baby, a parent may need to redefine his or her identity.

SPECIAL-NEEDS ADOPTION

Adopting the Hurt Child: Hope for Families with Special-Needs Kids: A Guide for Parents and Professionals

Gregory C. Keck, Ph.D., and Regina M. Kupecky, L.S.W.
Pinon Press, 1998 (revised edition)
256 pages

Book Byte

Many adoptions these days involve emotionally wounded older children who have suffered the effects of abuse or neglect in their families and who carry complex baggage with them into their adoptive families. In this book, Keck and Kupecky address the frustrations, heartaches, and hopes that surround the adoptions of these special-needs kids. The authors also explain how trauma and interruption affect these children's normal development and often severely undermine their capacity to function in a loving family and society.

Suggested Readers

- Parents of adopted children
- Therapists and teachers who are in the lives of adopted children
- Families who are welcoming an adopted child into their family

Therapeutic Insights

- As of 1995, there were 100,000 children in the United States waiting for adoption.
- Children bring into new families the remnants of the problems that began with the birth families and have never been resolved.
- Many children and adolescents have experienced multiple traumas prior to adoption.
- Repeated failed reunification trials complicate future attachments.
- Every child must learn that they have choices, and with choices come consequences.

TEENS AND ADOPTION

How It Feels to Be Adopted
Jill Krementz
Knopf, 1988 (reprint edition)
107 pages

Book Byte

This is a moving and sensitive book that allows adopted children to speak for themselves about their hopes, dreams, and fears—especially about their sense of belonging. Nineteen kids from every social background confide their feelings about being adopted, and they reveal questions, frustrations, difficulties, and joys.

Suggested Readers

- Children, between ages 8 and 16, who have been adopted
- Parents of adopted children
- Family members and other support people who are in the lives of adopted children

Therapeutic Insights

- Being adopted needs to be discussed openly and freely in the family.
- Adolescents often have great fantasies about who their birth parents are.
- Children often feel that bringing up the topic of their birth parents will hurt their adopted parents' feelings.
- It is natural for small children to be curious about their birth parents.
- Many adopted children give little thought to their birth parents.

TODDLER ADOPTION

Toddler Adoption: The Weaver's Craft
Mary Hopkins-Best
Perspective Press, 1998
272 pages

Book Byte

This is a book about the journey of building a family through the adoption of a child between the ages of one and three. This book is about exploring the decision to adopt, the preparation for adoption, and the adjustment to the adoption of a toddler. The book is rich in examples of challenges and strategies from families whose children were adopted as toddlers. Also included is information on toddler development, parenting the grieving toddler, behavior management, and becoming attached.

Suggested Readers

- Adults who are considering the adoption of a toddler
- Family and friends who want to assist and support toddler adoption
- Helping professionals who are involved with families where there is a toddler adoption

Therapeutic Insights

- Parents need to deal with adoption-related issues over and over again as children reach new levels of cognitive and language development.
- Toddlers need to be prepared carefully for their pending adoption.
- Toddlers deserve to get to know their parents prior to placement.
- Toddlers are creatures of habit, and most are upset by changes in their routines.
- Parental expectations significantly influence parental adjustment.

 **AGING**

GENERAL

Aging

Henri J. M. Nouwen and Walter J. Gaffney
Doubleday, 1976
160 pages

Book Byte

We are all aging. No one can stop the ongoing cycle of growth. In this book, the authors share some moving and inspirational thoughts on what aging means, and on what it *can* mean, regardless of one's chronological age. Enhanced by 85 photographs, this is about making the later years a source of hope, rather than of loneliness. The authors offer a somewhat Christian perspective.

Suggested Readers

- Men and women who want to celebrate aging
- Men and women who want to repair the connections between generations
- Men and women who are embracing their aging process

Therapeutic Insights

- Aging is not a reason for despair; rather, it is a basis of hope.
- Many people start to consider themselves old when certain institutional arrangements (mandatory retirement) say they are.
- In many older people, one finds more uniqueness and special talents than in the young.
- Preoccupation with the past imprisons older people.
- Segregation and desolation create a severe alienation for the elderly.

Another Country: Navigating the Emotional Terrain of Our Elders

Mary Pipher, Ph.D.

Riverhead Books, 1999

328 pages

Book Byte

Another Country is about navigating the emotional terrain of our elders. As parents and grandparents grow older, it is often difficult to find words to talk about medicine, loneliness, forgetfulness, love, or selling the house and car. Elders find it difficult to ask for what they need, and their children and grandchildren find it difficult to understand or anticipate what they need. Pipher offers the reader scenarios to bridge the communication gap. She gets inside the minds and hearts of men and women in their 70s, 80s, and 90s.

Suggested Readers

- Children and grandchildren who want to decrease the isolation felt by parents and grandparents
- Those who want to understand aging
- Those who want to improve their relationships with aging parents or grandparents

Therapeutic Insights

- Never before have so many people lived so far away from the older people they love.
- Many older people are living in a world designed for younger people.
- Old age is not interesting until one gets there.
- A great deal of the social sickness in America comes from age segregation.
- Situations that work for people in the young-old stage are not feasible for the old-old.

Awakening at Midlife: A Guide to Reviving Your Spirits, Recreating Your Life, and Returning to Your Truest Self

Kathleen A. Brehony, Ph.D.
Riverhead Books, 1997 (reprint edition)
384 pages

Book Byte

The transition to midlife can be a difficult one, fraught with relational, professional, physical, and emotional changes. Questions of personal identity will often arise at this time, forcing people to reexamine all of the beliefs that seemed to be true the first half of their lives. Brehony suggests that the "transformation at midlife offers unparalleled opportunities for a rich, meaningful second half of life." This book is a wake-up call for those who want to make the most of this transitional journey.

Suggested Readers

- Adults who want to recover childhood dreams
- Adults who recognize the importance of prayer and meditation
- Adults who are attempting to recover their sense of self and purpose

Therapeutic Insights

- The cultural belief that there are few changes expected in adulthood is a dangerous one.
- Many experience midlife as a full-blown crisis.
- At midlife, some people notice the subtle and not so subtle effects of aging on their bodies, whereas others are in the best form of their lives.
- The frightening and painful symptoms of midlife are necessary for the individual's growth.
- At the most basic level, one must let go of who they are in order to become what they are suppose to be. The key to becoming a late bloomer is the secret of attitude.

The 50 Year Dash: The Feelings, Foibles and Fears of Being Half a Century Old

Bob Greene
Doubleday, 1998
304 pages

Book Byte

Nationally syndicated columnist Bob Greene offers his clever musings on a midlife milestone in this poignant, funny book. It is about all the things that being 50 is about: family, career, body, money, sex, mortality, friendships, regrets, dreams, heartaches, and hopes. Greene states that being 50 feels like being a teenager who's been in a fight: battered, weary, sometimes confused, a little worse for the wear, but surprisingly eager for the next round.

Suggested Readers

- Men and women who want a guidebook about midlife
- Fifty-somethings who want to explore dreams and regrets
- Midlifers who want to feel good about the journey ahead

Therapeutic Insights

- Prime-time television has nothing to do with the 50-year-old.
- Aches and pains that used to be a meaningless phrase turn out to be literal.
- At 51, we finally understand that there are certain irrefutable truths, not open to debate.
- Even on days when rewards seem elusive, it is good to keep in mind that they do show up at their own pace.
- If at this juncture one can't have a candy bar and beer for dinner, then when can he or she?

It's Only Too Late If You Don't Start Now:
How to Create Your Second Life at Any Age

Barbara Sher
Dell Publishing, 1999
288 pages

Book Byte

Sher believes it is never too late to reclaim your creativity, to recapture long lost dreams, or to embark on a new life. In this provocative book, she offers a bold new strategy for creating a second life, no matter what your age is. Combining motivational techniques with step-by-step exercises, Sher reminds the reader of the dreams that he or she abandoned along the path to adulthood.

Suggested Readers

- Those who are trying to overcome illusions that act as obstacles to achieving one's dreams
- Adults who want to resolve regrets that have gotten in the way
- Individuals who are trying to rediscover the inspired self they use to be

Therapeutic Insights

- The knowledge that one will never be young again can be a wake-up call.
- Aging is about transition, not decline.
- The goals of one's second life come from his or her deepest gifts and desires.
- Aging is the luxury of not being impeded by the obstacles of youth.
- Being calm completely changes one's experience of time.

Secrets of Becoming a Late Bloomer: Extraordinary Ordinary People on the Art of Staying Creative, Alive, and Aware in Mid-life and Beyond
Connie Goldman and Richard Mahler
Stillpoint Publishing, 1995
297 pages

Book Byte

Some late bloomers are legendary. Grandma Moses didn't start painting until she was nearly 80. Winston Churchill was in his 70s when he led Britain through World War II. Everyone has the potential to keep blooming or to become a late bloomer. During the retirement years, people go through dramatic changes in a shorter span of time. The latter years bring the loss of loved ones, physical limitations, and other activities that were once taken for granted. However, it also brings a richness, intimacy, humor, creativity, spirituality, and for some an ability to forgive.

Suggested Readers

- Men and women who want to respond creatively to their changing lives
- Men and women who are anxious about getting older
- Men and women who want to dispel many of the fears and myths about aging

Therapeutic Insights

- Everyone has the power to set in motion a chain of events that can enrich his or her life.
- Visualization and affirmations are proven empowerment tools.
- The secret of remaining youthful means tapping into the best energies and qualities with which one associates being young.
- An attitude that accepts change and encourages growth can be a guiding force in remaining healthy and upbeat.
- The key to becoming a late bloomer is the secret of attitude.

Successful Aging
John W. Rowe, M.D., and Robert L. Kahn, Ph.D.
Dell Publishing, 1999
272 pages

Book Byte

How much aging is genetic and how much does one control? What are the factors that put one 80-year-old in a wheelchair and another on a bike? This book investigates and reveals the importance of lifestyle choices, which determine how well people age. The authors discuss preventable declining physical functioning, mental ability, staying independent, Alzheimer's, fragility, sexuality, and other aging issues.

Suggested Readers

- Men and women who want to understand the aging process
- Men and women who want to age healthily
- Men and women who want to focus on the many positive aspects of aging

Therapeutic Insights

- Aging is not to be understood through a disease framework.
- The topic of aging is durably encapsulated in a layer of myths in society.
- The less people are challenged, the less they can perform.
- Successful aging is about the active engagement with life.
- The linking of social relationships to longevity has been unequivocally demonstrated.

MEN AND AGING

Understanding Men's Passages: Discovering the New Map of Men's Lives

Gail Sheehy
Ballentine, 1999
352 pages

Book Byte

Gail Sheehy has been documenting and mapping the changes that men and women experience from youth to maturity. This book continues that journey as she guides men through the turbulent changes and surprising pleasures that begin at 40. Work anxieties, marital stress, family responsibilities, power, and concerns over sexual potency—all take on new urgency as men contemplate the years ahead. Sheehy believes that it is in midlife when men are most likely to reinvent themselves and to become the masters of their fates.

Suggested Readers

- Men who are looking to find more passion in their lives
- Men who are attempting to defeat depression and *mano*pause
- Men who crave intimacy and renewal

Therapeutic Insights

- The values with which many men grew up have been subverted and changed.
- Men have not been taught to ask questions about their sexual life cycle or their psychological well-being.
- More often than not, men are not aware that they are depressed.
- If there is anything certain about passage, it is uncertainty.
- Underneath the whole male *mano*pause syndrome may be a man who feels he is losing control.

WOMEN AND AGING

The Estrogen Alternative: What Every Woman Needs to Know About Hormone Replacement Therapy and SERMS, the New Estrogen Substitutes
Steven R. Goldstein, M.D., and Laurie Ashner
Perigee Books, 1999
208 pages

Book Byte

For years, postmenopausal women have been faced with the estrogen dilemma. Replacing estrogen has been proven to lower the incidence of heart disease, osteoporosis, and Alzheimer's disease. It has also been shown to increase the risk of breast and uterine cancer. New synthetic hormones [e.g., selective estrogen receptor modulators (SERMs)] provide many of estrogen's benefits without the risk. This book answers questions regarding traditional estrogen therapy, herbal estrogen therapy, and SERMs, as well as which form of hormone replacement is best for the reader.

Suggested Readers

- Women who are debating the appropriate hormone replacement for themselves
- Women who are questioning traditional estrogen replacement
- Women who are confused and afraid of their options

Therapeutic Insights

- There are 37 million women in the United States who are in or past menopause.
- Estrogen levels in the body affect a broad range of tissues and organs.
- After menopause, the body may experience bone loss faster that it can be replaced, due to the estrogen loss.
- There is a new category of drugs known as SERMs, including Raloxifene (Evista).
- Raloxifene acts like estrogen, prevents bone loss, reduces the incidence of new onset breast cancer, lowers cholesterol, and does not cause proliferation of the uterine lining.

Good Daughters: Loving Our Mothers As They Are

Patricia Beard

Warner Books, Inc., 1999

289 pages

Book Byte

Millions of daughters ask one another, "What shall we do about our mothers?" Often, this question is precipitated by their mother's age, illness, loneliness, and financial issues. Caught between caring for their mothers and other responsibilities, women in midlife are affected by guilt, anger, and anxiety as they struggle to be good daughters. In this sensible book, Beard explores the tension of the mother-daughter relationship, the reality of aging, and the new roles that daughters take on.

Suggested Readers

- Daughters who are caring for elderly parents
- Daughters who feel a sense of responsibility to care for their mothers
- Daughters who feel both ancient bonds and conflicts with their aging mothers

Therapeutic Insights

- It is difficult for daughters to overcome resentment and to learn to accept a mother's accomplishments and failures.
- For many daughters and mothers, the principle issue is fear of loss.
- The mother-daughter relationship is like no other.
- By not asking them, daughters miss the chance to find out what their mothers feel they need.
- Many daughters hide their bitterness and disappointments until their mothers die.

The Hormone of Desire: The Truth About Sexuality, Menopause, and Testosterone
Susan Rako, M.D.
Harmony Books, 1996
121 pages

Book Byte

Susan Rako is at the forefront of the research into testosterone replacement therapy, educating women and their doctors about the essential role that testosterone plays in a woman's sexual and physical well-being. Millions of women experience a traumatic loss of sexual desire during menopause. Doctor Rako's research links decreased testosterone levels with the onset of diminished sex drive, as well as with the heart and bones.

Suggested Readers

- Women who want to make informed decisions
- Doctors who are assisting women in issues related to sexual desire and menopause
- Women who want to appreciate their potential for a fulfilling sex life during and after menopause

Therapeutic Insights

- Research and treatment of female sexual dysfunction, particularly in older women, has received little attention or funding.
- A critical amount of testosterone decreases after menopause, resulting in a vital loss of energy and sexual libido.
- Testosterone is the hormone responsible for the expression of sexual desire not only for men, but also for women.
- There is a heterosexual bias in the medical establishment regarding these issues.
- Testosterone deficiency is a quality-of-life-threatening condition.

Menopause and the Mind: The Complete Guide to Coping with Memory Loss, Foggy Thinking, Verbal Confusion, and Other Cognitive Effects of Perimenopause and Menopause
Claire L. Warga, Ph.D.
Simon & Schuster, 1999
304 pages

Book Byte

This book gives women the survival kit that they may need to manage the thinking and memory symptoms that accompany the onset of perimenopause and menopause. These symptoms occur with greater frequency as women enter their 40s, 50s, and beyond. Neuropsychologist Claire L. Warga provides the scientific explanation for this common hormonal misconnection syndrome. Forgetfulness, malapropisms, and lost concentration result from an estrogen depletion in the brain cells of women as they enter perimenopause and menopause. Treatment options are suggested.

Suggested Readers

- Women who are in the midst of perimenopause
- Menopausal women who want to understand their memory loss and foggy thinking in the context of hormonal changes
- Women who don't respond to hormone replacement therapy

Therapeutic Insights

- There is evidence that estrogen loss impacts verbal learning and memory.
- Menopausal women are very often misdiagnosed.
- Changes produced by estrogen loss can often be reversed considerably or partially with replacement estrogen.
- When estrogen replacement therapy is not an option, there are some safe nonhormonal agents and behaviors that are known to mimic some of the estrogen's functions.
- Glucose is a potent memory agent, apart from being the brain's only nonstorable source of fuel.

 **ANGER**

ADULTS

Anger: How to Live With It and Without It
Albert Ellis
Citadel Press, 1997
282 pages

Book Byte

Albert Ellis offers a solution to the problem of anger: a step-by-step technique based on Rational-Emotive Therapy to help the reader explore and understand the nature of his or her anger. Doctor Ellis explains his theory of Rational-Emotive Therapy and demonstrates how a person can be assertive without being angry. By challenging and eliminating anger, one can be more successful in his or her daily life.

Suggested Readers

- Clients with issues of anger
- Clients with issues of depression and anxiety
- Adults with stress management issues

Therapeutic Insights

- Anger, as a consequence, is not the direct result of an activating event. There is a belief system attached to that event that triggers the feeling.
- Everyone has rational and irrational beliefs.
- People need to first acknowledge and accept responsibility for their anger. After acceptance of their thoughts, they can then look for the belief system attached to the event. People need to look for the "shoulds," "musts," or "oughts" of the situation.
- By disputing and debating one's absolutistic musts, shoulds, or oughts with regard to themselves, they can then begin to eradicate these irrational beliefs.
- Rational-Emotive Therapy gears the client toward acting assertively. It teaches a person how to distinguish assertion from aggression.

The Anger Workbook

Les Carter, Ph.D., and Frank Minirth, M.D.
Thomas Nelson Publications, 1993
237 pages

Book Byte

This is a 13-step interactive workbook that will help the reader identify anger and the best ways to handle it. The authors look at the myths surrounding anger and identify the learned patterns of relating, thinking, and behaving, which influence a person's anger. Carter and Minirth look at anger as more than just violent outbursts such as shouting, slamming fists, or throwing things: They explain how it can also be exhibited in many other emotional ways such as frustration, discouragement, annoyance, and irritability.

Suggested Readers

- Adults with issues of anger
- Clients with depression
- Clients motivated by a workbook style of learning

Therapeutic Insights

- Anger has many different faces. Learning to manage one's anger starts with identifying it in his or her life.
- Five ways to handle anger include:
  1. Suppression
  2. Open aggression
  3. Passive aggression
  4. Assertiveness
  5. Simply dropping it
- Anger thrives on unmet needs. Learning to let go of dependencies can help a person manage his or her anger rather than having it triggered by external situations.
- Feeling controlled or wanting to control can lead to anger. Pride, fear, loneliness, and inferiority can also lead to anger.
- By learning to manage one's anger, a person can directly influence his or her children and how they handle their anger.

The Anger Workbook
Lorrainne Bilodeau, M.S.
Hazelden Publishing Group, 1992
128 pages

Book Byte

This workbook helps us explore our attitudes about anger and discover the roots of our anger. Lorrainne Bilodeau teaches us, through exercises and techniques, how to use our anger beneficially. She stresses the need to make our anger work for us.

Suggested Readers

- Clients with issues of anger
- Adults with depression or anxiety
- Clients motivated by a workbook style of learning

Therapeutic Insights

- Anger is neither good nor bad; it is a natural emotion that is functional for us. When used as intended, it is productive and useful.
- Anger can be expressed destructively through depression or aggression. This is distorted anger.
- Acknowledge the completeness of anger. The circular character of an emotion includes the event; the thought; the physical, the chemical, and the physiological sensations; and the behavior we then choose.
- Problems with our thoughts or beliefs that affect anger include misinterpretation of the event, inaccurate judgments of ourselves and others, and excessive negative self-statements.
- When encountering another person's anger, we tend to return to a child's perspective of powerlessness and vulnerability. We do not have to deal with another person's anger. It belongs to him or her; therefore, he or she is responsible for it.

Angry All the Time: An Emergency Guide to Anger Control

Ron Potter-Efron, M.S.W.
New Harbinger Publications, 1994
136 pages

Book Byte

This is an emergency guide, which offers real help and answers to a person wishing to control his or her anger. It gives practical advice and definitive steps to anger management. This book can offer genuine relief to those who frequently lose their tempers.

Suggested Readers

- Clients with anger issues
- Adults with issues of abusive behavior
- Adults with chemical dependency issues

Therapeutic Insights

- Normal anger tells a person that he or she has a problem, and he or she needs to think and do something about it. After doing this, a person can let go of his or her anger.
- With problem anger, everything is a problem. The person constantly thinks about the problem and comes onto others too strong in what he or she says and does. Ignoring the bad results and thus failing to change his or her actions, the person then fails to let go of anger because nothing has changed.
- The six reasons for staying angry include the following:
  1. Power and control
  2. Giving away responsibility
  3. Poor communication skills
  4. Avoiding other feelings or people
  5. Habit
  6. Anger rush
- Very angry people are trapped by their emotions. They often lose control and say and do damaging things.
- Anger comes in many stages, from sneaky anger to blind rage, but it can intensify into violence if it isn't addressed.

- Real change can only begin with the angry person, but it takes honesty and courage.

The Angry Book
Theodore I. Rubin, M.D.
Simon & Schuster, 1998
198 pages

Book Byte

An excellent book on anger, this best-seller looks at anger as a natural human emotion, which we all experience. Theodore I. Rubin speaks extensively on how denying our anger can lead to depression, anxiety, insomnia, alcoholism, and other health-related problems. He calls this the "anger suppression syndrome," and he shows the reader how to understand and how to release his or her anger.

Suggested Readers

- Adults who have difficulty expressing anger
- Clients who are experiencing depression or anxiety
- Clients with chemical dependency or eating disorders issues

Therapeutic Insights

- Clients need to normalize the emotion of anger and learn how repressed anger leads to overindulgent behavior with food, alcohol, or drugs, along with psychosomatic illness.
- By understanding the connection between repressed anger, depression, and anxiety, a client can be guided into a healthier view of anger.
- A person can learn how to see anger as a basic human emotion that needs expression.
- Understanding and verbalizing anger can reduce a person's depression and anxiety and can lead to greater happiness and emotional wholeness.
- Anger is constructive if it is expressed appropriately. Suppressed anger can lead to many health problems (e.g., high blood pressure, heart disease, headaches, and anxiety).

The Angry Teenager: Why Teens Get So Angry and How Parents Can Help Them Grow Through It
Dr. William Lee Carter
Thomas Nelson Publishers, 1995
251 pages

Book Byte

William Lee Carter, a licensed psychologist who specializes in children and adolescents, has written this book for parents to better understand their teenagers' emotions. In this book, Carter tries to bring parents into the world of their teenagers' emotions. His goal is to help parents overcome their own anxieties and fears in dealing with teenagers' anger and to be a positive influence during their teen years. Doctor Carter explores adolescence and anger from the teenagers' perspective.

Suggested Readers

- Parents of teenagers
- Parents or caretakers of teens
- Parents of angry teens

Therapeutic Insights

- Doctor Carter teaches parents how to recognize their teens' anger and how to determine how prevalent it is. He does this in his first chapter with a rating scale. He helps parents understand whether this anger is a natural teenage stage or more.
- He discusses how anger impacts teenagers' self-esteem and how it is useful as a communication device.
- The book discusses the many faces of teenage anger, from passive aggressive, to stubbornness, to depression, and to aggression.
- Anger can get pushed out of control.
- Parents need to learn specific ways to respond to their angry teenagers.
- Anger, if properly understood, can be a useful emotional tool between parents and teens.

The Dance of Anger: A Woman's Guide to Changing the Patterns of Intimate Relationships
Harriet Lerner, Ph.D.
HarperCollins Publishers, 1997
239 pages

Book Byte

In Harriet Lerner's best-selling book, she writes about how anger influences our relationships. She teaches women to identify the source of their anger and then to use that information to create change in their relationships. This is a classic book on the patterns of intimate relationships, and it will be useful to men and women alike.

Suggested Readers

- Women with anger issues
- Couples with relationship issues
- Women with depression or anxiety issues

Therapeutic Insights

- Anger is a message that women should listen to. It tells them that something is wrong. It is a warning signal.
- Making a committed relationship work means striking a balance between being an individual (the "I") and togetherness (the "we").
- Deselfing, or compromising oneself, is often at the heart of a person's anger problems. Only by changing oneself can a relationship change.
- Emotional overfunctioning can create anger. Only by understanding who is responsible for what, can a person learn to change this pattern.
- A person often lowers his or her anxiety in a relationship by involving or focusing on a third party. Getting out of the middle can be difficult.

Letting Go of Anger: The 10 Most Common Anger Styles and What to Do About Them

Ron Potter-Efron, M.S.W., and Pat Potter-Efron, M.S.
New Harbinger Publications, 1995
158 pages

Book Byte

This book examines the 10 most common styles of anger. Ron and Pat Potter-Efron begin their book with a quiz to determine the reader's style of anger. With this information, the reader can see which style of anger he or she expresses and what to do about it. The authors also define healthy anger and how to express it.

Suggested Readers

- Clients with issues of anger
- Clients with a diagnosis of depression or anxiety
- Clients with chemical dependency issues

Therapeutic Insights

- Anger is a natural part of the human condition.
- Anger is an accurate signal of real problems.
- Anger is temporary. When handling anger, one can let go of it after the issue is resolved.
- Anger is often masked and comes in many different styles. Many styles of anger actually prevent healthy anger from happening.
- Each style of anger poses a challenge to its owner. The more a person knows about his or her own style of thinking and acting, the more control that person has over his or her life.

BOOKS FOR CHILDREN ABOUT ANGER

Andrew's Angry Words

Dorthea Lachner

NorthSouth Books, 1995

32 pages

Book Byte

This book, illustrated with cartoonlike watercolors, is geared toward children. Through a fantasy story, the author teaches children the importance of expressing anger appropriately. She does this by showing the power of good and kind words versus angry and ugly words. It is a story about a boy named Andrew, who has an argument with his big sister and says very angry words to her. His angry words then fly across the world from person to person causing harm. The story then reverses itself as Andrew learns to use kind and good words, which, in turn, causes goodwill.

Suggested Readers

- Children between ages 4 and 9
- Children who are learning to express anger with words appropriately

Therapeutic Insights

- Young children can learn an appropriate way to use words when angry.
- By verbalizing anger, children do not have to use violent behavior to express themselves.
- Angry words can hurt people. Nice words can have positive effects on other people.

Don't Pop Your Cork on Mondays: The Children's Anti-Stress Book

Adolph Moser, Ed.D.

Landmark Editions, 1988

48 pages

Book Byte

This book for children explores the causes and effects of stress. Adolph Moser teaches kids practical tools for controlling and coping with stress. The book, written for children, has lots of colorful illustrations. It is a great tool for counselors, teachers, and parents. The book provides exercises for reducing and managing stress.

Suggested Readers

- Parents of children who are between ages 5 and 10
- Children who are struggling with anger or depression issues
- Children who are easily frustrated

Therapeutic Insights

- Adults often underestimate the stresses with which young children deal.
- Children need to understand that they are not alone in feeling the pressures in our society. Stress affects everyone, adults and children.
- Stress affects children in different ways: Some children get angry, some become sad and cry, and others become very quiet.
- Exercises can help lower stress and burn off energy: Tightening and relaxing your muscles can lower stress; breathing slowly and deeply can lower stress; imagining a relaxing place can lower stress.
- Kids can change their lives by how they react to it. They can control their own stress.

Don't Rant and Rave on Wednesdays: The Children's Anger Control Book
Adolph Moser, Ed.D.
Landmark Editions, 1994
61 pages

Book Byte

Adolph Moser examines children's feelings of anger. This book, written for children between ages 5 and 10, offers practical tools to help them control their behavior when they are angry. Doctor Moser does this in a humorous but sensitive way. He explores the causes of anger and the various ways in which anger can be expressed.

Suggested Readers

- Children between ages 5 and 10
- Children who are learning to express anger appropriately
- Children with issues of depression

Therapeutic Insights

- Anger can be a very frightening emotion for children to see in themselves and in others, but everyone becomes angry at some time.
- Anger can be expressed in many ways, but it affects our thinking and makes our muscles become tight.
- We can become angry about many different things. When we become angry, we do not think clearly. Anger can be like a car speeding down the hill at 100 miles per hour with no steering wheel.
- Anger is neither good nor bad. It is a feeling, and feelings are neither bad nor good. How we express our anger can be either good or bad.
- Ways to control anger include calming down with counting, listening to our thoughts, reading something funny, exercising, or talking to someone. Learning to control anger takes practice.

 **CHRONIC ILLNESS**

ALZHEIMER'S DISEASE

Alzheimer's Disease: Prevention, Intervention and Treatment
Elwood Cohen, M.D.
NTC/Contemporary Publishing Group, 1999
253 pages

Book Byte

Elwood Cohen has written a book in which he gives hope to Alzheimer's patients and their families. In his book, he shows how new research and technological advances have demystified the disease. Doctor Cohen presents practical strategies for detecting and managing the disease along with the newest medical treatments and genetic markers of the disease. He combines medical knowledge with homeopathic approaches. This is an excellent and current resource on the disease of Alzheimer's.

Suggested Readers

- Adults with a diagnosis of Alzheimer's
- Adults who suspect they might be having an onset of Alzheimer's disease
- Friends, family, or caregivers of Alzheimer's patients

Therapeutic Insights

- There are a number of prescription and nonprescription drugs that are surprisingly effective against Alzheimer's disease.
- There are certain herbs (such as gingko biloba and gotu kola, among others) that can delay the progression of Alzheimer's or alleviate some of the disease's symptoms.
- Abnormalities occur in patients long before the onset of the disease. Some of these include changes in fingerprint patterns, loss of the sensation of smell, vision disturbances, and hearing loss.
- There are four cornerstones in the treatment of Alzheimer's:
  1. Avoidance of causative entities
  2. Intensive caregiving

3. Medication
4. Diet and nutrition

- The key to effective treatment of Alzheimer's is early diagnosis.

The Alzheimer Sourcebook for Caregivers: A Practical Guide for Getting Through the Day, Third Edition
Frena Gray-Davidson
Lowell House, 1999
252 pages

Book Byte

In Frena Gray-Davidson's newly revised edition of *The Alzheimer Sourcebook for Caregivers,* she gives the reader the latest information on Alzheimer's research, along with information on possible signs and symptoms of a person experiencing Alzheimer's disease. This unique resource teaches the caregiver how to manage the stress and how to work through the difficult personal issues surrounding caregiving. Frena Gray-Davidson writes this book from her own experiences as a caregiver and from the experiences of hundreds of other home caregivers. It's a great reference book.

Suggested Readers

- Adults with a diagnosis of Alzheimer's
- Family and friends of patients with Alzheimer's
- Caregivers of patients with Alzheimer's

Therapeutic Insights

- To make the task of caregiving more meaningful, a person must explore the meaning of the journey and face the task of caregiving on a daily basis. A person must not get locked into despair or hopelessness, which can only consume his or her energy.
- Unless caregivers tend to their own needs, they cannot tend to another's.
- Caregivers need to ask others for help. One person cannot handle the total care of an Alzheimer's patient.

- If we can face the fear of the disease and take the risk of feeling our pain and loss, we can then be free to love the Alzheimer's patient. Human beings need love all the way until death. Love matters.
- Caregivers need to be aware of how they are handling their own stress. Are they an overachieving caregiver? Do they know when to get help or when to let go?

Coping with Alzheimer's: The Complete Care Manual for Patients and Their Families

R. E. Markin, Ph.D.
Citadel Press, 1998 (revised edition)
128 pages

Book Byte

This is a how-to book for coping with Alzheimer's. Doctor Markin discusses practical subjects from legal aspects to living wills to self-preservation. He also includes a list of resources for finding help and support. Doctor Markin is the former director of the Alzheimer's Research Foundation. This book is designed for recently diagnosed patients along with their friends and families.

Suggested Readers

- Adults with a recent diagnosis of Alzheimer's disease
- Family members of an Alzheimer's patient
- Caregivers of Alzheimer's patients

Therapeutic Insights

- Acceptance can be very difficult when a family member is first diagnosed. This is a good time to take advantage of the calm and take practical steps toward getting organized.
- Being prepared legally is important, as there will come a time when the Alzheimer's patient can no longer think clearly.
- The average life span for an Alzheimer's patient after diagnosis is approxi-

mately four to eight years. Understanding a person's financial state and the particulars of their health insurance is paramount.

- Physical and emotional depletion of the caregiver is inevitable unless the caregiver takes certain precautions for self-preservation.
- A client's local chapter of the Alzheimer's Association can be an important asset for any caregiver. They can provide direct help, referrals, support, and simple suggestions for coping.

The 36 Hour Day: A Family Guide to Caring for Persons with Alzheimer's Disease, Related Dementing Illness, and Memory Loss in Later Life, Third Edition

Nancy L. Mace, M.A., and Peter V. Rabins, M.D., M.P.H.
Johns Hopkins University Press, 1999
339 pages

Book Byte

This book is written for family, friends, and caregivers who are caring for loved ones with any disease causing the loss of memory and reasoning skills. It is written for those who face the daily challenges and adjustments that result from caring for someone with dementia. It is an excellent and practical book full of specific advice and recommendations for making care easier on a daily basis and improving the quality of life for all involved.

Suggested Readers

- Friends and family of persons who are suffering from Alzheimer's or dementia
- Caregivers of persons with chronic illness
- Friends, family, or caregivers of persons who suffer from any illness that affects memory and reasoning skills

Therapeutic Insights

- Sick people must adjust to their changing role in the family. Caregivers can help maintain their position as important members of the family by listening to and consulting with them to let them know they are still respected.

- Caregivers may lose their tempers with a person who seems unable to do simple tasks. Although losing one's temper occasionally is not terrible remember that the person is not doing this intentionally. Take a deep breath and try to approach the situation calmly. If caregivers are angry and frustrated frequently, this is a warning that they are overtired. Time away from the person is essential at this point.

- A chronic dementing illness places a heavy burden on the family system in many ways. Family members' expectations change as the sick person's role changes. Change can lead to conflict and misunderstanding. Adjusting to these changes and facing problems can also bring families closer.

- There are six *R*s of behavior management: restrict, reassess, reconsider, rechannel, reassure, and review.

- Persons with memory problems should be carefully diagnosed for major depression. Alcohol, tranquilizers, or other drugs may blot out the sadness temporarily, but these will also compound the problem.

CANCER

Cancer as a Turning Point: A Handbook for People with Cancer, Their Families, and Health Professionals
Lawrence LeShan, Ph.D.
Plume/Penguin Books, 1994
244 pages

Book Byte

With over 35 years' experience working with cancer patients, Lawrence LeShan has written a book about new and effective ways of patients fighting for their lives. Doctor LeShan contends that when a cancer patient's whole environment is mobilized toward living through psychological change and medical treatment, a compromised immune system often begins a unique healing process. For many patients, life can be prolonged; for others, genuine miracles can happen. In his book, Doctor LeShan includes a workbook of hands-on exercises for the reader to improve his or her inner self and to get the most from his or her immune system.

Suggested Readers

- Clients with a recent diagnosis of cancer
- Family and friends of clients with cancer
- Health professionals working with cancer patients

Therapeutic Insights

- Who people are depends on two factors: (1) their genetic inheritance and (2) their inner and outer life experiences. Considering that genetic inheritance cannot be changed, inner and outer life experiences need to change to minimize the return of the illness.
- To mobilize patients' healing resources, their therapies must be focused on what would be zestful and enthusiastic for them as a whole versus a search for pathology.
- Patients need to learn not to worry about what the world wants from them, but to worry about what makes them come alive as individuals.
- Respect and communication are the most important elements on which families must focus.
- Cancer patients die when they are in a negative state of stress and are overcome with hopelessness. It is a death or a loss of zest and enthusiasm for life.

Cancer Talk: Voices of Hope and Endurance from "The Group Room," The World's Largest Cancer Support Group

Selma R. Schimmel with Barry Fox, Ph.D.
Broadway Books, 1999
324 pages

Book Byte

Cancer Talk provides a support group in a book. Based on *The Group Room,* a talk-radio cancer support show, the book is an invaluable and informative guide for coping with cancer. Selma R. Schimmel has brought together the voices of cancer patients, cancer survivors, family, friends, and health care clinicians to give the reader hope and inspiration.

Suggested Readers

- Cancer patients and survivors
- Family and friends of cancer patients and survivors
- Anyone whose life has been touched by cancer

Therapeutic Insights

- Fear is a perfectly normal emotion. Recognizing it and acknowledging it helps a person to learn to live with it.
- Couples need to keep talking. Spouses of cancer victims feel as if they have cancer, too. Recognize the difficulties that each other is experiencing. When feeling good, try to spend quality time together.
- Never underestimate the role of the caregiver. It takes its toll. The caregiver needs time out, along with support, to replenish his or her own needs. It is natural to feel angry and resentful. Cancer is an unwelcome intruder.
- Often, cancer can be a catalyst for positive personal changes—emotionally, psychologically, and spiritually.
- A person's spirituality often expands when faced with a life-threatening illness. Many people find comfort in their faith in God or in a greater power. It can help them surrender to the unknown.

What to Do When They Say "It's Cancer!": A Survivor's Guide
Joel Nathan
Allen & Unwin Pty., Limited, 1999
320 pages

Book Byte

Joel Nathan, a survivor of cancer, writes of his experiences with the aim of helping others with their life-threatening illnesses. He brings light to the many issues facing cancer patients. He goes beyond diagnosis and treatment options (conventional and alternative) to feelings, legal matters, relationships, children, and actually facing death. His book brings inspiration, compassion, and practical guidance to the seriously ill.

Suggested Readers

- Clients with a diagnosis of cancer
- Family and friends of cancer patients
- Terminally ill clients

Therapeutic Lessons

- A person needs to first understand and confirm his or her diagnosis. Always get a second opinion.
- Survivors are people who believe that they are worth saving. Cancer patients who feel worthless or who rely on others to do things for them unnecessarily, may not have the courage to survive the struggle.
- Patients have the choice when it comes to treatment. They need to know the right questions to ask, and they need to take the time to understand the treatment.
- It is important to honor and to give expression to one's moods and feelings. Bottled-up or unexpressed feelings will, in turn, bring feelings of being overwhelmed, which can adversely affect the healing process.
- Communication is vital with family, friends, and the treatment team.

CHRONIC PAIN

Conquering Pain
Randall S. Prust and Susan Luzader
Berkley Publishing Group, 1997
255 pages

Book Byte

Conquering Pain is a practical guide for people feeling hopeless about their chronic pain. Randall S. Prust and Susan Luzader give the reader hope for relief. They focus on traditional and alternative treatments, prescription and nonprescription drugs, along with the new developments in pain management. They give the reader not only medical information but also information on how to cope with the psychological aspects. Their book focuses on giving the chronic pain sufferer new hope for relief.

Suggested Readers

- Clients with chronic headaches
- Clients with chronic back and neck pain
- Clients with any chronic pain issues

Therapeutic Insights

- Knowledge and understanding of pain and its treatments gives a person power and, thus, a better chance of conquering the pain.
- Pain can come from four different sources:
  1. Nerve pain
  2. Bone pain
  3. Muscle pain
  4. Central pain

  Pain can be useful or nonuseful for the pain sufferer. Treatments vary according to the variety of pain.
- There are many new medicines and technologies to help patients. Having a physician who is abreast of these new treatments is important. No particular treatment works for everyone.
- Chronic pain patients should know their insurance coverage. Patients should ask their physicians if they are bound by the gag rule, which restricts physicians from telling patients about medical procedures that the insurance company does not cover.
- When selecting a pain center for treatment, select one that has credentials and that is multidisciplined in its approach.

Facing and Fighting Fatigue: A Practical Approach
Benjamin H. Natelson, M.D.
Yale University Press, 1998
208 pages

Book Byte

Facing and Fighting Fatigue, written by Benjamin H. Natelson, a specialist in fatigue disorders, is a practical approach to coping with severe chronic fatigue and pain. He gives the reader information on improving their sleep, on managing the stress associated with chronic fatigue and pain, and on finding understanding and sympathetic physicians. Doctor Natelson discusses what fatigue is, what causes it, and how to cope with it. It is a book filled with information on fatigue disorders.

Suggested Readers

- Clients with chronic fatigue or a diagnosis of chronic fatigue
- Clients with chronic pain
- Family and friends of clients who are suffering from chronic fatigue and pain

Therapeutic Insights

- There are no specific treatments or remedies for chronic fatigue syndrome. At this time, the treatment needs to be focused on relief of the symptoms.
- Clients must develop a specific and individual strategy for the management of excessive fatigue.
- The most common cause of fatigue is often stress, and although fatigue and exercise or effort seem incompatible, exercise actually relieves stress, thus relieving fatigue.
- Sleep disturbance can be caused by poor sleep hygiene (e.g., eating late, drinking too much caffeine or alcohol, or being overweight). Sedatives are no longer the first treatment for insomnia; instead, low doses of antidepressants that have a side effect of sedation seem to be a better alternative.
- Having a positive attitude, as difficult as this may be, will actually make the client feel better. Laughter can help keep someone more positive and reduce the symptoms.

The Fibromyalgia Handbook, Second Edition
Harris H. McIlwain, M.D., and Debra Fulghum Bruce
Henry Holt & Co., Inc., 1999
231 pages

Book Byte

Harris H. McIlwain, a leading arthritis specialist, and Debra Fulghum Brice have written a handbook that addresses one of the most commonly misdiagnosed and misunderstood illnesses, fibromyalgia. Their book is set up as a seven-step treatment program, and it includes the latest in medications and medical treatments, including alternative medical treatments. The authors teach the reader how to recognize symptoms and how to manage the symptoms so as to lead an active life.

Suggested Readers

- Adults with a diagnosis of fibromyalgia
- Adults with chronic pain and chronic fatigue
- Family and friends of clients with fibromyalgia or chronic pain and chronic fatigue

Therapeutic Insights

- The goal of living with this disease is to change it from something disabling to an illness that is manageable.
- The most common symptom of fibromyalgia is pain. This pain is usually not specific to a part of the body; rather, it can be felt all over the body. The pain is usually deep, sharp or dull, and throbbing. Next to pain, fatigue is the major complaint.
- Handling everyday issues and major life stressors while experiencing pain and fatigue may become impossible without getting the help of a trained professional.
- An effective treatment program includes medication, exercise, reducing stress, learning ways to enhance restful sleep, improving nutrition, increasing a client's support system, and using alternative treatments as necessary.
- A client should seek out a comprehensive and accredited pain clinic for supportive care if he or she is unable to get relief from McIlwain and Bruce's seven-step treatment program.

The Fibromyalgia Help Book: Practical Guide to Living Better with Fibromyalgia

Jenny Fransen, R.N., and I. Jon Russell, M.D., Ph.D.
Smith House Press, 1997
239 pages

Book Byte

This is a how-to book written by a physician and a nurse clinician. The authors aim to give the reader practical tools for managing fibromyalgia syndrome (FMS). The book addresses the many different questions that patients and their families have. Fransen and Russell also look at the recent research that is shedding some light on the cause of this mysterious condition and on new developments in treatment.

Suggested Readers

- Clients with a diagnosis of fibromyalgia
- Families and friends who seek to understand FMS
- Medical professionals who treat patients with fibromyalgia

Therapeutic Insights

- A client is not alone with this illness. Fibromyalgia syndrome is one of the most common types of chronic pain conditions. A frustrating aspect of this illness is that others cannot see it. A person may look fine but be trapped in a body that feels terrible.
- Positive overall management of fibromyalgia requires a trusting and open relationship with one's physician. Building such a relationship often takes time.
- A patient's understanding of the illness is critical in order to manage it. The patient knows his or her body the best; thus, he or she can also determine the most effective treatment.
- Restorative sleep is essential in the self-management of fibromyalgia. Understanding the nature of restorative sleep is a first step toward achieving quality sleep.
- The purpose of making lifestyle changes is to minimize the negative impact that fibromyalgia has on the patient's life. He or she needs to learn to organize his or her daily tasks to conserve energy.

Living with Chronic Pain: One Day at a Time
Mark Allen Zabawa
Freedom Enterprises in Chronic Pain, 1994
404 pages

Book Byte

This is a daily meditation book, written for chronic pain sufferers, to help them cope with life's daily stresses. Mark Zabawa wrote the meditations based on his own and on others' experiences with chronic pain. It is a great little book with an emphasis on hope, faith, courage, peace, acceptance, and recovery.

Suggested Readers

- Clients with chronic pain
- Clients with chronic and life-threatening illness
- Clients who acknowledge a higher power in their lives

Therapeutic Insights

- There are many personal changes that a person must make when coping with pain on a daily basis.
- A person with chronic pain may not necessarily have the power to erase pain, but he or she does have the power to reduce the pain and its effects.
- To survive with chronic pain, a person's attitudes and outlook on life must change. Being open to change keeps a person from being a prisoner of his or her pain.
- When feeling desperate, a person has a choice to react to his or her desperation or to step back and ask why he or she is feeling that way.
- Courage is when a person decides not to be trapped as a prisoner of his or her pain. It is when the person decides to take back the relationships he or she had and, once again, begins to have dreams.

Managing Pain Before It Manages You

Margaret A. Caudill, M.D., Ph.D.
The Guilford Press, 1999
207 pages

Book Byte

Margaret A. Caudill has designed and presented a program in workbook form for managing pain. It is a straightforward program designed to help the reader develop skills for coping with chronic pain. Doctor Caudill gives step-by-step techniques, activities, and homework assignments in her book to understand the pain process and to recognize what actually increases and decreases pain. She teaches the reader to set realistic goals and to learn problem-solving techniques.

Suggested Readers

- Adults with chronic pain
- Clients who are motivated by workbook-style learning
- Family and friends of clients with chronic pain

Therapeutic Insights

- For clients to begin to take control of their pain, they must first take ownership of it. They must look at how to live a life of quality while suffering from chronic pain.
- There are ways in which clients can alter their brain activity in order to change their pain experience, including increasing endorphins, relaxation techniques, and engaging in pleasurable activities. Responding to chronic pain is both emotional and physical.
- Clients can learn that during that time when they are intensely focused on an activity, their pain slips away. Time management and pacing activities let the body recuperate. Learning to label body sensations as more than just painful will help these people become more in tune with their bodies.
- The mind gives meaning to the experience of pain. A hopeless frame of mind will interpret pain signals differently than an optimistic mind. The mind is like a filter in which the pain signal passes. It can either be intensified or dampened within the mind's filter.

- Attitudes of learned helplessness and of anger and hostility are not uncommon in chronic pain clients. Adopting a positive attitude can actually decrease the level of pain.

The Mind Body Prescription: Healing the Body, Healing the Pain

John E. Sarno
Warner Books Inc., 1999
210 pages

Book Byte

In John E. Sarno's best-selling book, he specifically addresses the connection between the mind and the body. He reveals how almost all painful conditions are connected to a person's unexpressed emotions, and he demonstrates how physical disorders can be cured without medication, therapy, or surgery. Doctor Sarno writes his book in easy-to-understand language that clearly explains how emotions can influence and cause illness. This is his second best-selling book, after *Healing Back Pain*. He is a professor of clinical rehabilitation medicine at New York University School of Medicine and a physician at Howard A. Rusk Institute of Rehabilitation Medicine, New York University Medical Center.

Suggested Readers

- Adults with chronic fatigue or fibromyalgia
- Clients with chronic back pain or migraine headaches
- Clients with any chronic pain issues

Therapeutic Insights

- Life's pressures produce reactions internally in the unconscious. These reactions often elicit physical symptoms. Clients are unaware of the connection between the two.
- Rage and pressure in the unconscious can come from three possible sources:
  1. Unresolved childhood issues
  2. Self-imposed pressure (as with driven, perfectionistic people)
  3. Reaction to the everyday pressures of life

- The brain actually reduces blood flow to areas of the body, thus causing distress. The pain becomes a distraction and a diversion from the powerful unresolved feelings. Complete knowledge of this process is essential to being cured.
- Pain will cease when clients can change their unconscious minds' reactions to emotional stress.
- Feelings of rage will diminish and become less frightening as clients come to know themselves better and acknowledge it more.

We Are Not Alone: Learning to Live with Chronic Illness
Sefra Kobrin Pitzele
Workman Publishing Co., 1986
336 pages

Book Byte

Sefra Kobrin Pitzele has written an inspirational book with practical living strategies for persons suffering from chronic illnesses. She writes about how to live better, not just differently. Based on her own experiences, the author teaches readers how to maintain healthy relationships, find the right doctor, control the symptoms so they don't take control, and balance their needs for independence and getting help. It is a comprehensive manual with priceless advice for chronic pain sufferers.

Suggested Readers

- Men and women with a chronic illness
- Adults with chronic pain
- Clients with migraines, fibromyalgia, and chronic fatigue

Therapeutic Insights

- Chronic illness does not mean that a person must give up his or her life, dignity, pleasures, or relationships. Having one's illness diagnosed is not the end of his or her healthy life. It is the end of not knowing what is wrong and the beginning of a new kind of life.
- Grieving is natural. A person can move forward with new dreams and hopes by letting go of his or her loss.

- Although a person's body and physical abilities have changed, his or her thoughts, feelings, and interests, particularly with loved ones, will remain. Having two-way relationships is still important.
- Chronic pain and stress are intertwined. Managing a person's stress will be key in managing his or her pain.
- Clinical depression is not uncommon. Being alert to the symptoms and knowing when to get help is important knowledge for the chronic illness sufferer. Depression is treatable.

HIV/AIDS

The AIDS Dictionary

Sarah Barbara Watstein with Karen Chandler, M.D.
Checkmark Books, 1998
352 pages

Book Byte

The AIDS Dictionary is a comprehensive resource for nonspecialists. The book covers the basics of symptoms, diagnosis, and treatment, and it does this in a clear and easy-to-understand language for the nonspecialist. Written by Sarah Barbara Watstein, a long-time AIDS activist, and Karen Chandler, a practicing physician, the book is designed as a reference book for those seeking information about HIV, AIDS, and related topics. It is meant to be neither a medical text nor a diagnostic manual; rather, it is meant to give the reader as much information as possible, ranging from symptoms and diagnosis to emotional and psychological issues. The authors also include resources for additional information and assistance, including Internet addresses and phone numbers.

Suggested Readers

- Clients with a diagnosis of HIV or AIDS
- Clients who suspect they may be HIV positive
- Family and friends of clients with HIV or AIDS

Therapeutic Insights

- The medical vocabulary of HIV and AIDS has grown more complex in the second decade of this epidemic. It is important for a person with HIV or AIDS to become knowledgeable of the terms.

- The psychological challenges vary from individual to individual when he or she is diagnosed with HIV or AIDS. Confronting fear and denial while maintaining hope is the difficult balance that a person must come to terms with.

- Confronting and examining a person's sexual identity or drug and alcohol use with the behavioral choices that he or she has made are some of the issues that a person must face.

- Isolation is one of the biggest stressors that someone with HIV and AIDS must face. Withdrawal from friends and family is not uncommon.

- Feeling dependent on family, friends, and social services can feel demoralizing. A person with HIV or AIDS may feel a wide range of emotions as he or she begins to lose his or her independence and self-sufficiency.

Sometimes My Heart Goes Numb: Love and Caregiving in a Time of AIDS

Charles Garfield
Harvest Books, 1997 (reprint edition)
352 pages

Book Byte

Charles Garfield, founder of Shanti Project, and clinical professor in the Department of Psychiatry at the University of California School of Medicine, has written a book specifically for caregivers. He describes his book as a support group in a book for family members, professionals, clergy, and volunteers. The book is composed of 20 vignettes of exemplary caregivers, with commentaries on the skills of the individual caregivers. Garfield looks at the importance of setting healthy boundaries and how to avoid compassion exhaustion and bereavement overload. This is an inspirational book for anyone in a caregiving position.

Suggested Readers

- Caregivers of AIDS patients
- Friends of loved ones with AIDS
- Families of AIDS patients

Therapeutic Insights

- Caregivers are in a position to give the gift of dignity and self-pride to women and men with AIDS.
- Genuine compassion is often more important than knowing the right words to say. Often, there are no "right" words.
- Witnessing and listening with an open heart to a loved one's pain may be the greatest gift that a caregiver can give.
- Caregivers can put a person in touch with life and death and can provide an opportunity for that individual to discover his or her own spiritual path.
- Self-care is imperative for caregivers. This may mean time-outs or time off, getting support, or backing up and seeing the larger picture of their work and of their lives.

 **DIVORCE**

GENERAL

Can This Marriage Be Saved?: Real-Life Cases from the Most Popular, Most Enduring Woman's Magazine Feature in the World
Edited by Margery D. Rosen
Workman Publishing Co., 1994
352 pages

Book Byte

Here are selected cases, presented for the first time in book form, from the column, "Can This Marriage Be Saved?", featured in *Ladies' Home Journal*. Couples on the verge of divorce tell their stories to a marriage counselor in intimate detail, spotlighting the danger points common to every relationship. Issues include affairs, stepchildren, communication, sex, money, in-laws, impotence, gambling, alcoholism, and violence. First, the woman speaks about these issues, then the man, then the counselor. This column was introduced in the *Ladies' Home Journal* in 1954.

Suggested Readers

- Women who are struggling with unmet expectations
- Men who are attempting to improve communications
- Couples looking for other points of reference for their problems

Therapeutic Insights

- Two-thirds of the couples who seek counseling after an affair do get their marriages back on track.
- Couples must remind themselves that there are no bosses in a marriage.
- Couples who haven't made love for a long time have to rediscover how to be intimate.
- Couples will benefit if they can recognize the behavioral clues that often mask depression.

- Couples must acknowledge that they both play a part in the problems that they are having.

The Complete Idiot's Guide to Handling a Break-up

Rosanne Rosen
MacMillan Distribution, 1999
284 pages

Book Byte

This book teaches someone how to successfully initiate a breakup, as well as how to survive a breakup when it comes as a total surprise. The reader learns how to go from victim to victor and how to move on to the next relationship with confidence. In this guide, there are expert tips on determining if it is the right time to initiate a breakup, the inside story on the differences between how men and women break up, and then helpful quick fixes to get beyond the painful heartache. Rosen writes with expertise on how to cope with the uncertainty of love, how to prevent sexual mistakes, and how to handle anger and rejection.

Suggested Readers

- Adults who are learning how to separate truth and lies
- Those who want to understand the unintentional precipitators of breakups
- Men and women who are seeking to emerge whole after the loss of love

Therapeutic Insights

- One cannot change the basic character of an individual.
- The duration of attraction and infatuation is not always equal among two parties.
- Ambivalence should be expected in forming and breaking attachments.
- Rejection can be a self-fulfilling prophecy.
- Broken engagements are more common than realized.

Divorce for Dummies
John Ventura and Mary Reed
IDG Books, 1998
354 pages

Book Byte

This book is a sound and exceptionally thorough guide to practical advice for dealing with the legal, financial, and emotional ramifications of divorce. This information assists the reader in assessing whether he or she is financially and emotionally ready for a divorce, increases his or her understanding of basic legal rights and responsibilities, helps in the decision-making process in relation to dividing assets and debts, and lastly, makes recommendations regarding how to hire an attorney. Also included are excellent web sites regarding children and divorce.

Suggested Readers

- Couples who are considering divorce
- Soon-to-be-divorced individuals with concerns about the process
- Those who need legal and financial advice regarding an impending divorce

Therapeutic Insights

- Many couples who are committed to working things out use mediation as a way to structure divorce agreements and negotiations.
- From the law's perspective, divorce is about dollars and cents.
- At times, during the healing process, one may respond to the divorce by trying to strike up bargains with his or her spouse.
- Anger, depression, and shock are normal responses to the demise of a marriage.
- Some states have begun to require divorced parents to attend parenting classes in order to learn how to help their children adjust.

The Healing Journey through Divorce: Your Journal of Understanding and Renewal

Phil Rich, Ed.D., MSW, and Lita Linzer Schwartz, Ph.D., A.B.P.P.
John Wiley & Sons, Inc., 1999
264 pages

Book Byte

This is a unique journal and workbook to help clients through issues of divorce and separation. Written by experienced psychotherapists, this book guides readers through the painful emotions that are associated with the breakup of a relationship. *The Healing Journey through Divorce* contains writing exercises to guide readers through the feelings of anger, fear, confusion, remorse, grief, and hopelessness that come with the dissolution of a marriage.

Suggested Readers

- Clients in the process of separation
- Clients who have filed for divorce
- Divorced clients

Therapeutic Insights

- There are two parallel aspects involved in the dissolution of a marriage:
    1. The legal aspect
    2. The emotional aspect
- Everyone's experience of divorce is personal and unique, but there are general stages that are common to all. These stages include shock and disbelief, initial adjustment, active reorganization, and life reformation.
- Allowing the healing process to happen is allowing oneself to experience his or her feelings and then being able to sort through and express them.
- Expressing one's feelings may not change the situation, but it can change the way the person thinks and feels about the situation.
- It is often difficult for a person to inform others about a failed marriage. Social interaction and relationships can often damage or enhance self-image. Self-esteem is more connected with how one sees the world than to the actual reality of the world.

Uncoupling: Turning Points in Intimate Relationships

Diane Vaughan
Vintage Books, 1990 (reprint edition)
206 pages

Book Byte

Uncoupling begins with a secret. One of the partners starts to feel uncomfortable in the relationship. The world that the two of them have built together no longer fits. This book combines extensive research with in-depth interviews, and it offers a vision of what happens when relationships come apart. What it reveals is a process that begins with the secret that gradually becomes public, implicating not only the partners, but also their social milieu. This book is also about power. It considers how cues and signals can be manipulated to foster desired impressions.

Suggested Readers

- Couples who are in the process of uncoupling
- Those who are initiating a breakup
- Individuals who feel their partner's ambivalence toward the relationship

Therapeutic Insights

- The secret keeper can hold back information, consider it privately, and shape it in ways that influence the present and the future.
- The uncoupling begins as a quiet, unilateral process.
- The initiator who is unfamiliar with the path that he or she is contemplating begins to explore and consider information that allows him or her to anticipate the transition.
- By focusing on the negative attributes of his or her partner and the relationship, the initiator begins to create something to leave behind.
- The partner focuses on the bond, the initiator on the disintegration.

BOOKS FOR CHILDREN ABOUT DIVORCE AND SINGLE-PARENTING

At Daddy's on Saturdays

Linda Walvoord Girard and Judith Friedman
Albert Whitman & Co., 1991
31 pages

Book Byte

This is a story about Katie's father moving out of the house when he and her mom get divorced. Katie is angry, sad, and most of all afraid that her dad will never come back. However, on Saturdays, he's there, and Katie comes to understand that even though her parents don't live together anymore, they still both love her.

Suggested Readers

- Children, between ages 5 and 9, who are going through divorce

Therapeutic Insights

- It is hard to say good-byes to a parent each week, but trust does not have to be broken between the child and the parent.
- Parents divorce each other, not their children.
- Children need permission to express all of their feelings.

Dinosaurs Divorce: A Guide for Changing Families

Laurene Krasny Brown and Marc Brown
Little, Brown & Co., 1988 (reprint edition)
31 pages

Book Byte

Divorce takes place between mothers and fathers. Children are not to blame if their parents get divorced. Parents divorce when they don't love each other or can't get along together anymore, no matter how much they try. When parents divorce, it is natural for the child to feel sad, angry, afraid, ashamed, confused, relieved, guilty, and worried about who will take care of them. This book talks to children about why parents divorce, how to talk about feelings, what to do after the divorce, and how to handle visitation.

Suggested Readers

- Children, between ages 6 and 9, who are going through divorce

Therapeutic Insights

- For a child, visiting the parent that he or she used to live with can be very uncomfortable.
- Divorce can also bring about positive changes for the children.
- Children may need permission to still love both parents.

Divorced But Still My Parents
Shirley Thomas, Ph.D., and Dorothy Rankin
Springboard Publishing, 1997
90 pages

Book Byte

This book is organized according to the five stages of grief first outlined by Elizabeth Kubler Ross in her studies about human reaction to death. Though there are differences between loss of the original family and loss of a loved one through death, the stages of adjustment are the same: denial, anger, bargaining, depression, and acceptance. Children cannot achieve a lasting acceptance of their parents' divorce without working through the painful stages of grief. Children under the age of 9 usually benefit from having a parent, a counselor, or a family member read this with them.

Suggested Readers

- Children, between ages 6 and 12, who are going through divorce
- Children who are confused about their feelings
- Children who are feeling scared about the future

Therapeutic Insights

- Families live together and do lots of things as a group.
- Children never cause divorce.
- Divorce means families change, but the parents' love for the child never changes.
- Some kids have just one parent.
- Even when parents don't see their children, they have a special place for them in their hearts.

Do I Have a Daddy?: A Story for a Single-Parent Child, Second Edition

Jeanne Warren Lindsay and Cheryl Boeller
Morning Glory Press, 1992
46 pages

Book Byte

This is a book about a young boy named Erik, who gets teased by a friend for not having a father. His mother explains that he, like all other children, has a daddy, but that she and his daddy were never married. She explains that after he was born, his daddy went away because he wasn't ready for the big job of caring for a baby. This is a sensitively written book, which also includes a special section for single parents. This section contains conversations between single parents and psychologists and counselors regarding critical issues such as the never-married parent and the totally absent father.

Suggested Readers

- Single-parented children between ages 4 and 8
- Single parents who are looking for support and guidance in raising their children alone

Therapeutic Insights

- The choice to remain single can be a good choice for both the parent and child.
- It is helpful to be both honest and positive when talking to a child about the absent parent.
- Children will look to the parent for cues as to how to feel about the family with one parent.

Let's Talk About It: Divorce

Fred Rogers (*Mr. Rogers' Neighborhood*)
Penguin Putnam, 1996
32 pages

Book Byte

Mr. Rogers' talent for calmly explaining scary, emotional upheaval to young children shines in this latest book on divorce. He offers caring support and validation for children who are working through such trauma, and he supplies concrete examples of ways that kids can deal with the stress.

Suggested Readers

- Children, between ages 4 and 8, who are going through divorce

Therapeutic Insights

- When going through a divorce, children often wonder who is going to take care of them.
- Children often worry about the parent who has left the home.
- Children may need to hear over and again that the divorce is not their fault.

CHILDREN AND DIVORCE

Does Wednesday Mean Mom's House or Dad's?: Parenting Together While Living Apart
Marc J. Ackerman, Ph.D.
John Wiley & Sons, Inc., 1996
206 pages

Book Byte

Marc J. Ackerman, a psychologist and child custody expert, teaches readers what to expect during divorce and how to act so as to reduce the devastation on their children. His focus is not on how to "win" custody battles, but rather on how to work with one's spouse to effectively coparent while living apart. He also gives expert advice on all aspects of the legal process and the ins and outs of various custody arrangements and visitations plans. This is a book that gives clear practical guidelines for all parents faced with separation and divorce.

Suggested Readers

- Divorced and separated parents
- Parents who are considering a divorce or a separation
- Parents who want to understand divorce and separation from their children's vantage point

Therapeutic Insights

- Divorce affects numerous areas of children's lives. Be alert to changes in their level of play interaction with friends, physical health, and school performance.
- Children model their parents' thoughts and feelings, including sadness, depression, and inappropriate expressions of anger.
- Parents should not argue in front of their children, pull children into a custody battle, or be abusive to each other in front of their children. They should be effective and sensitive with their communication.
- It is natural for children to feed into how their parents interact with each other. Whether the family is intact or not, children try to play one parent

against another. Parents must learn to communicate and check things out with each other.

- Parental alienation happens most often with children who are between ages 9 and 12. Children often become angrier with the alienating parent than with the alienated one. They eventually become angry that they were pressured into hating one parent.

Helping Children Cope with Divorce

Edward Teyber, Ph.D.
Lexington Books, 1998 (reprint edition)
221 pages

Book Byte

The biggest concern for almost all divorcing parents is whether their children will be hurt by the breakup. Children do not understand the changes that are occurring, and they are naturally afraid of what's going to happen to them. Edward Teyber writes in the mature voice of a seasoned clinician providing parents not only with his observations, but a substantial amount of conclusive research regarding the effects of divorce on children. He advises on numerous topics, such as children wanting to reunite their parents, parental conflict and cooperation, custody, mediation, loyalty conflicts, and stepfamilies.

Suggested Readers

- Parents of children who are going through divorce
- Families who are supporting children through divorce
- Support systems that are involved in caring for children of divorce

Therapeutic Insights

- Divorcing parents can learn to recognize behavior patterns that signal children's separation anxieties.
- Parents should tell their children about the divorce when it is a firm decision.

- Children develop unrealistic infatuation fantasies to deny the reality of the breakup.
- Chronic parental conflict hurts children.
- Hostilities are often acted out irresponsibly by undermining the former spouse's relationship with the children.

Joint Custody With a Jerk: Raising a Child With an Uncooperative Ex
Julie Ross, M.A., and Judy Corcoran
St. Martin's Press, Inc., 1996
241 pages

Book Bytes

If a person is raising a child with an uncooperative ex-spouse, there are probably countless scenarios that created a great deal of pain and frustration. Whether someone is dealing with an ex-spouse who intentionally tries to manipulate him or her and the child, or with a former partner who inadvertently confuses and complicates their lives, there is help. Ross and Corcoran have written a book that offers simple yet effective tools to help communicate with an ex-spouse, whether he or she is an occasional or chronic jerk.

Suggested Readers

- Men or women who are dealing with disrespectful ex-spouses
- Men and women who are unable to communicate with their ex-spouses
- Support systems for families who are dealing with mean-spirited ex-spouses

Therapeutic Insights

- All people bring to their marriages the entire history of their relationships with their parents, siblings, and peers.
- Jealousy can cloud judgment.
- Anger can create stubbornness and an unwillingness to change.
- "I" messages are difficult to respond to in a defensive way.

- Rather than rehearsing anger and frustration, writing down some alternative thoughts prior to the discussion may lead to a more constructive conversation.

Mom's House, Dad's House: A Complete Guide for Parents Who Are Separated, Divorced or Remarried
Isolina Ricci, Ph.D.
Fireside Books, 1997 (revised edition)
381 pages

Book Byte

This comprehensive guide looks anew at the needs of families with more creative options and commonsense advice in the legal, emotional, and practical realities of creating two happy and stable homes for your children. Isolina Ricci gives age-specific advice regarding reestablishing children's sense of home and family, negotiating parenting agreements, breaking away from "negative intimacy" with a difficult ex-spouse, sidestepping destructive myths, and handling long-distance parenting.

Suggested Readers

- Adults who are attempting to maneuver through the divorce and custody process
- Adults who are separated, divorced, or remarried
- Ex-spouses who are preparing for mediation

Therapeutic Insights

- Children have a history—just as their parents have.
- Most children will display some emotional or physical reaction to the crisis of divorce.
- Differences between separated and married parenting do exist.
- The specter of a bleak financial future often haunts the end of a relationship.
- The more supportive a network is to the parents and children, the easier it is for them to survive a crisis.

The Sandcastles Way: Helping Your Kids Cope with Divorce
M. Gary Neuman
Random House, 1999
480 pages

Book Byte

No matter what their age, children of divorce have a limited capacity to understand exactly what is happening, what they are feeling, and why. This does not stop them from forcing together a "big picture" from the few puzzle pieces they have. Neuman developed the Sandcastle Program, which is a tool for learning to create an environment conducive to effective and honest communication by entering the children's world. The book covers the impact of divorce on children from birth to adulthood. Incorporated through the text are samples of children's artwork and writings. Excellent games and exercises are included in this book.

Suggested Readers

- Parents who are going through divorce who have young children
- Parents of adolescents and young adults
- Those in the legal profession who are dealing with families of divorce

Therapeutic Insights

- As hard as it is to accept, parents cannot rescue their children from disappointment and pain.
- Attitudes and emotions are contagious.
- Children of divorce need more consistency and less change.
- Divorced adults must be aware of their own internal push to find someone new.
- Parents often mistakenly assume that their adolescent children should share in the excitement of their dating.

GRANDPARENTING AND DIVORCE

The Essential Grandparent's Guide to Divorce: Making a Difference in the Family

Dr. Lillian Carson
Health Communications, Inc., 1999
200 pages

Book Byte

Lillian Carson offers this guide that teaches the reader how to handle the complicated and delicate situations resulting from divorce in the family. This book details practical down-to-earth advice and tips on how to maintain support for one's grandchildren, as well as one's grown children through such challenging and emotional times. Few families escape the heartache of divorce. Divorce does affect everyone in a family.

Suggested Readers

- Grandparents who are experiencing the divorce of the adult children
- Grandparents who want to understand how they can best care and support their grandchildren
- Parents who need to assist the entire family in coping with a divorce

Therapeutic Insights

- Parents are often tied up in their own world of heartbreak and are unavailable emotionally to their children.
- Grandparents can cushion the transition for their grandchildren.
- Grandparents can raise topics that children are too afraid to ask about.
- Divorce is like a death and requires a mourning process.
- Though grandparents have little control in children's divorce, they can help by keeping a clear perspective and just being there.

MEN AND DIVORCE

Men on Divorce: Conversations with Ex-Husbands
Ellie Wymard, Ph.D.
Hay House, Inc., 1994
208 pages

Book Byte

To explore the male side of divorce is not to betray documented evidence regarding the economic hardship and psychological stress that divorce plays on ex-wives. Women and children are still the financial losers in most divorces. This reality encourages the perception that men are callous to disappointment, hurt, and do not require nurturing even when going through one of life's worst personal crises. Ellie Wymard believes the public's critique of divorce suppresses the men's voices. This book is an effort to break the silence and to allow men to explore the power of their own words so that others may "enter the phase of empathy."

Suggested Readers

- Dispelling myths about divorced men
- Men who want to participate in a dialogue on divorce
- Divorced men who are looking for reassurance that they are not alone

Therapeutic Insights

- Men have not been encouraged to claim the truths of what divorce does to them.
- Many presume men are always in control of their own destinies.
- The first impulse of many men who are rejected by their wives is to cut themselves off from the world and to carry their grief in silence.
- Myths, which vanish in terms of real life, are plentiful about male and female behavior.
- One of the most difficult truths for men to see is that blind loyalty to patriarchal tradition ultimately thwarts their own self-definition.

TEENS AND DIVORCE

Voices of Children of Divorce
David Royko
Golden Books, 1999
224 pages

Book Byte

This book provides sage observations from the children who have been witness to divorce. In its wisdom it allows children with vastly different experiences to share their perspectives with clarity and focus, in the process of teaching adults how to better manage divorce. This collection of candid observations should move divorcing parents to reevaluate their priorities and behaviors. David Royko interviewed more than 1,000 children of divorce and shares their insights with the reader.

Suggested Readers

- Adolescents, between ages 12 and 19, who are experiencing the pain of divorce in their family
- Parents who need more understanding of how their divorce affects their children
- Parents who want to help their children grow into healthy adults

Therapeutic Insights

- Hurtful comments, made by one parent about the other parent, have a way of being taken personally by the children.
- Parents should help their children stay out of their conflicts with each other.
- No matter what age, children in the middle cannot win.
- Parents must be appropriate models for grieving.
- A parent may underestimate the reaction that children, especially older children, will have to a divorce.

When Your Parents Split Up: How to Keep Yourself Together
Alys Swan-Jackson
Price Stern Sloan, 1998
90 pages

Book Bytes

More than 7 million American children and teenagers have divorced parents. Although that's a huge number, when divorce hits a family, teens can feel very alone. In this book, teens write about their experiences of going through their parents' divorce. They talk honestly about the feelings they had during this time. They tell exactly how they coped and what they did to help themselves. In some families, the separations were friendly and carefully planned. In others, there was anger and violence. Divorce is not a single event; rather, it's an ongoing process of readjustment.

Suggested Readers

- Teenagers, between ages 13 and 17, who are going through the divorce of their parents
- Parents who are looking for assistance in helping their teens process their feelings
- Teens who want to do more than just survive the family breakup

Therapeutic Insights

- Strong pain and a deep feeling of loss often take the place of anger.
- Parents often turn to alcohol, drugs, or food to help them cope with the stress.
- Problems will not be resolved unless they are forced into the open.
- Sometimes, parents can have problems that can get in the way of a relationship with their teenagers.
- Children need help in telling others about the divorce.

WOMEN AND DIVORCE

Dumped: A Survival Guide for the Woman Who's Been Left by the Man She Loved
Sally Warren and Andrea Thompson
HarperCollins Publishers, 1999
253 pages

Book Byte

Sally Warren was dumped by her husband after 19 years. She never saw it coming. This book is about her experience. It is also a survival guide for other women. Her goals are to teach other potential dumpees the following: how to see it coming; how to survive the initial shock; how to get through the wallowing stage; how others may respond to the dumpee; what to do about new men in one's life; and finally, how to have some laughs about it.

Suggested Readers

- Women who are learning how to navigate their lives after being left
- Women who need to recognize that they are sabotaging moving forward
- Those having to make the transition from being part of a couple to being single

Therapeutic Insights

- To be dumped is not the same thing as splitting up, seeing less of each other, or deciding mutually to end the relationship.
- If a woman's husband doesn't want to be married, she ceases being married.
- There are signals that a husband is going to dump his wife.
- It will be very difficult for the dumpee to reemerge into the couple's old crowd as a solo act.
- Going public as a new dumpee takes courage and stamina.

Exorcising Your Ex: How to Get Rid of the Demons of Relationships Past
Elizabeth Kuster
Simon & Schuster, 1996
191 pages

Book Byte

This is a hilarious and even helpful collection of real-life tricks and techniques all designed to help people get rid of the demons of relationships past. With cutting-edge wit, Kuster presents tried-and-true solutions from dozens of women who have survived the trauma of breaking up, along with clever methods for getting over men who think they can live without these great women. This book includes an exclusive equation to help recalculate your postbreakup recovery time, harmless revenge tactics, and what to do with his ratty bathrobe.

Suggested Readers

- Women who are looking for a humorous way to handle their breakup
- Women who can't stop looking for ways to reinforce their sadness
- Women who are looking for alternatives to distract themselves

Therapeutic Insights

- It may be helpful to read books that make one's problems seem small in comparison, like the Helen Keller's autobiography.
- The best revenge is living well.
- Postbreakup feelings serve two functions:
  1. They can be used to control an ex-spouse's emotions.
  2. They can be clung to obsessively.
- One should expect lingering regrets after a breakup.
- Unfinished business is the kiss of death to moving forward.

How to Survive Your Boyfriend's Divorce: Loving Your Separated Man Without Losing Your Mind

Robyn Todd and Lesley Dormen
M. Evans & Co., 1999
224 pages

Book Bytes

With 65 percent of marriages ending in divorce, an average of 1 million men every year are "not quite unattached." In most cases, they are dating long before the divorce is final. Although this creates new options for single women, it also creates situations fraught with frustrations, pitfalls, and disappointments. Drawing from her own experience, Robyn Todd has created a practical guide for an emotional journey, written in a positive, down-to-earth, and sometimes humorous tone. Additionally, there are profiles of real women's experiences, important statistics, chapter checkpoints by a psychologist, and a state-by-state guide to divorce laws.

Suggested Readers

- Women who have fallen in love with men who are going through a divorce
- Women who are involved with men who have children
- Women who are feeling both impatience and resentment as their boyfriend's divorce drags on

Therapeutic Insights

- A conflict-free divorce is an oxymoron.
- The boyfriend's divorce is the central drama in his life.
- It is helpful to negotiate a strategy for the immediate future.
- When in doubt, err on the side of caution; put the interests of the children first.
- When a woman is in love with a still-married man, jealousy is especially perilous and all too common.

EATING DISORDERS

GENERAL

The Eating Disorder Source Book: A Comprehensive Guide to the Causes, Treatments, and Prevention of Eating Disorders, Second Edition

Carolyn Costin, M.A., M.Ed., M.F.C.C.
Lowell House, 1997
304 pages

Book Byte

Carolyn Costin, a recovered overeater with 16 years' experience as a specialist in eating disorders, writes this book from a personal and professional viewpoint. It is a sourcebook providing current information about the cause, identification, treatment, and prevention of an eating disorder. The book's chapters are written to provide answers to the most commonly asked questions by lay and professional people regarding eating disorders.

Suggested Readers

- Parents who want to prevent eating disorders
- Significant others who wish to support friends or family with an eating disorder diagnosis
- Adolescents who suspect that they might have an eating disorder

Therapeutic Insights

- The exact cause of eating disorders is still uncertain. Some of the variables include cultural pressure, biochemical factors, nutritional deficiencies, and psychological variables.
- There are three main perspectives in the nature and treatment of eating disorders:

1. The psychodynamic model
2. The cognitive-behavioral model
3. The addictive model

- Eating disorders are on the increase with 86 percent of victims reporting their onset of illness by age 20. The longevity of the illness, the high cost of treatment, and the high mortality rate make it imperative to have preventative programs.

- Treatment of an eating disorder should be multidimensional, involving nutritional, biochemical, and psychological interventions.

- Family and friends are often the forgotten victims of eating disorders. Their support and encouragement may be crucial to the loved one's recovery. Family and friends need to know they can support, encourage, and be there for someone with an eating disorder, but they cannot cure or fix the illness.

Making Peace with Food

Susan Kano
Harper & Row, 1989
272 pages

Book Byte

Susan Kano provides a step-by-step self-help workbook for freeing people who are caught up in diet and weight obsession. She focuses on overcoming yo-yo dieting, binge eating, food anxiety, body anxiety, and self-defeating guilt. In addition, she shows readers how to eat spontaneously, thus gaining freedom from overeating by being less preoccupied by food.

Suggested Readers

- Clients with weight and diet obsessions
- Women with body image issues
- Clients with eating issues who are motivated by workbook-style learning

Therapeutic Insights

- Women are taught to view their bodies as ornaments, rather than as instruments in which to act and live.
- Clients will learn that their set point weight is a result of genetic influence, diet, and lifestyle.
- Hunger is not governed by one's stomach. There is actually no known way to tell if hunger is imaginary or real.
- To gain freedom from overeating, clients must learn to eat spontaneously. They must learn that they never need to deprive themselves of what they want to eat, nor eat anything they don't want.
- There are three main goals for spontaneous eating:
  1. Enjoy eating.
  2. Be less preoccupied with food.
  3. Stop the battle between mind and body by maintaining a comfortable set point level.

A Parent's Guide to Eating Disorders and Obesity

Martha M. Jablow
Dell Publishing, 1992
164 pages

Book Byte

This is a guide to parents from pediatricians, neurologists, psychologists, and social workers from the Children's Hospital and Philadelphia Child Guidance Center in Pennsylvania. Martha M. Jablow discusses how to recognize and examine the symptoms of an eating disorder, whether it be anorexia, bulimia, or compulsive overeating. The author profiles three young women with eating disorders and examines the differences in signs and symptoms. She discusses how to approach these symptoms and how to tell your doctor.

Suggested Readers

- Parents who suspect an eating disorder in their adolescent
- Teachers or caretakers of adolescents who want to recognize the early warning signs of eating disorders
- Teens with body image issues

Therapeutic Insights

- Ninety percent of people with eating disorders are female; however, the percentage of males is increasing.
- Some of the early warning signs of anorexia include the following: feeling fat when actually looking thin, losing a lot of weight in a short period of time, constant dieting with lower and lower goals, denial of being hungry, spending a lot of time alone, and appearing depressed.
- Some of the early warning signs of bulimia include the following: eating large quantities of food without gaining weight, disappearing to the bathroom right after meals, eating secretly, dieting but still maintaining weight, abusing alcohol or drugs, appearing depressed, and experiencing mood swings.
- Unlike anorexia or bulimia where weight may fluctuate, a compulsive overeater is obviously overweight and does not engage in bingeing or purging.
- There are similarities between anorexia and bulimia, and there can be a crossover from anorexia to bulimia, although rarely the opposite way. Parents need to be aware of what is normal and when normal becomes abnormal.

When Food's a Foe

Nancy J. Kolodny, M.A., M.S.W., L.C.S.W.
Little, Brown & Co., 1998 (revised edition)
224 pages

Book Byte

This is a self-help guide for young adults focusing on the facts of anorexia and bulimia and how to treat and prevent these disorders. The author discusses developing self-awareness and self-esteem along with setting realistic goals. She also explores when to get outside help and how to find the best therapist. It is a useful and practical book for any young person struggling with food or body issues.

Suggested Readers

- Adolescents with possible eating disorders
- Teens with body image issues
- Female teens with self-esteem issues

Therapeutic Insights

- An eating disorder develops when habits move from the normal range to destructive obsessions. In anorexia and bulimia, obsessive thoughts and compulsive behaviors replace normal eating habits.
- Due to extreme weight loss, the chemicals in the brain actually change and a person's perceptions can become distorted. This person may see him- or herself as an obese person when, in fact, he or she is actually underweight.
- Bulimia involves thoughts and actions. A person becomes obsessive about not gaining weight, and at the same time, he or she becomes obsessive about eating. Purging becomes a way to control the urge to binge, and it is often strongest on days when a person is particularly bored, tense, angry, or depressed.
- Admitting that there is a problem and developing self-awareness are the first steps in fighting an eating disorder.
- "Coming out," or sharing honestly, about having an eating disorder can be very difficult. Maintaining secrecy can also be difficult and emotionally draining. Eventually, friends and family will notice. "Coming out" is one of the first steps in the healing process.

ANOREXIA AND BULIMIA

Anorexia Nervosa: A Guide to Recovery
Lindsey Hall and Monika Ostroff
Gurze Books, 1998
192 pages

Book Byte

This book was written specifically for anorexics, and it answers the most commonly asked questions. Lindsey Hall and Monika Ostroff provide insights from recovered and recovering anorexics, and they give specific tasks to get started on the recovery process. In this book, the authors combine facts and personal anecdotes; they also speak about how to stay committed to the process and how to know what healthy eating and ideal weight are. Hall and Ostroff include a special section for parents.

Suggested Readers

- Adults with a diagnosis of anorexia
- Parents and significant others of persons with anorexia
- Adolescents with a diagnosis of anorexia

Therapeutic Insights

- Anorexia is caused by a complex mixture of cultural, social, familial, psychological, and biochemical variables. Why people become anorexic is also a very individual mixture of these variables. Different people develop anorexia for different reasons.
- Self-starvation can have many medical complications, including heart, kidney, and organ failure, or immune system illness. Between 5 and 20 percent of anorexics die from these complications.
- Anorexia colors one's perception of the world. Preoccupation with food is only intensified as weight loss progresses. Weight gain is imperative for successful recovery because of the mental and emotional disabilities associated with weight loss. Sufferers of anorexia cannot think clearly to solve problems, make decisions, or benefit from therapy.
- Anorexia is an isolating disorder. Food becomes more important than relationships. Clients lose not only their relationships with family and friends, but also with themselves.
- Recovery is a process, unique to every individual, that demands commitment, determination, and willingness.

Bulimia: A Guide for Family and Friends

Roberta Trattner Sherman, Ph.D., and Ron Thompson, Ph.D.

Jossey-Bass, Inc., Publishers, 1997 (revised edition)

167 pages

Book Byte

Roberta Trattner Sherman and Ron A. Thompson examine the basic ingredients and causes of bulimia. They have written this book for family and friends of those who suffer from bulimia, and they attempt to answer the most common questions. It is a good basic resource for family and friends who are trying to understand the disorder.

Suggested Readers

- Clients with the diagnosis of bulimia
- Family and friends of someone with a diagnosis of bulimia
- Family and friends who suspect an eating disorder in a loved one

Therapeutic Insights

- Bulimia is a very complex disorder that requires a multidimensional treatment approach.
- Bulimia is more similar to anorexia nervosa than to compulsive overeating. Both eating disorders include a preoccupation with dieting, food, weight, and body size.
- Bulimics, as compared with normal eaters, have an emotional intensity prior to, during, and following their bingeing and purging.
- Bulimia has three components:
  1. The behavioral
  2. The cognitive
  3. The emotional
- The causes of bulimia are varied. There are certain commonalities (e.g., closed emotional systems, issues of control, and an inability to communicate needs) that exist within families and individuals.

Living with Anorexia and Bulimia
James Moorey
Manchester University Press, 1993 (reprint edition)
144 pages

Book Byte

James Moorey has written a straightforward book that addresses the questions most commonly asked about anorexia and bulimia. It contains practical information about the nature, cause, and treatment of these disorders, and it addresses practical suggestions for coping with these disorders. The author, a clinical psychologist, writes from his experience at Manchester Royal Infirmary in New York. He gives specific suggestions in a self-help section.

Suggested Readers

- Clients who are diagnosed with anorexia or bulimia
- Parents of children with anorexia or bulimia
- Siblings, relatives, partners, and friends who wish to have a better understanding of anorexia and bulimia

Therapeutic Insights

- Anorexia and bulimia involve similar preoccupations and misperceptions of a person's body image.
- A clear-cut identification of bulimia and anorexia is not easy. Concerns of dieting and body image are not sufficient to warrant a diagnosis. There are many additional features to be looked at when diagnosing these disorders.
- Self-esteem and self-worth are tied to the pursuit of weight control. This pursuit of thinness can become relentless and addictive.
- Families are not to blame for their children's anorexia or bulimia. There are many variables. Families may be just one factor among others, which predispose an individual to an eating disorder.
- Recognizing the early signs, seeking help, and assisting in recovery are the three areas where parents can be of help.

Wasted: A Memoir of Anorexia and Bulimia

Marya Horenbacher

Harper Perennial, 1999

298 pages

Book Byte

Marya Horenbacher writes a candid memoir of the trials and triumphs with anorexia and bulimia. She takes readers through her five hospitalizations, endless therapy, and loss of what it means to be normal. In her book, she recreates the complexity underlying eating disorders, explaining the triangle of family, personal, and cultural causes. She discusses the desperate need to binge.

Suggested Readers

- Parents and family of adolescents with eating disorders
- Teens who are diagnosed with anorexia
- Teens who are diagnosed with bulimia

Therapeutic Insights

- The underlying causes of eating disorders are complex, involving family, cultural, and personal variables.
- Women use their obsession with weight as a way to connect with one another. Thinness is revered in our society.
- People who suffer from eating disorders are usually perfectionistic, highly critical, and competitive individuals. An eating disorder is not an insignificant problem solved by therapy or a pill, nor is it a stage that girls go through.
- Getting well is a slow process. Therapy, along with support from family and friends, will help, but a person needs to fix it him- or herself and learn to have the desire to live.
- Family often creates an environment that is like a hothouse for the development of eating disorders.

COMPULSIVE OVEREATING

Self Esteem Comes in All Sizes: How to be Happy and Healthy at Your Natural Weight
Carol A. Johnson
Diane Publishing Co., 1999
331 pages

Book Byte

Carol Johnson speaks to women and to men about issues of self-esteem and their body weight. She explains why "thin" is not synonymous with "healthy" and that genetics may actually predetermine one's body weight. Carol Johnson's mission in this book is to help the reader understand that self-worth is not measured by one's weight. This is a great book for those who have put their happiness on hold while they lose weight.

Suggested Readers

- Women and men with body image issues
- Women and men with self-esteem issues
- Clients with obsessive dieting issues

Therapeutic Insights

- Weight is governed by many different factors just as is the color of a person's eyes or hair. Being big is not a sin.
- Our culture is obsessed with thinness. The many eating and body image disorders are a result of this obsession.
- Who a person is is a combination of his or her personality, along with his or her talents and accomplishments. Who a person is is not his or her weight.
- The body will find its natural body weight when a person concentrates on his or her health rather than on weight.
- The first step in living a healthy lifestyle is to like oneself. A person should not put his or her life on hold.

Take It Off and Keep It Off: Based on the Successful Methods of Overeaters Anonymous
Anonymous
Contemporary Books, Inc., 1989
167 pages

Book Byte

Based on the principles of Overeaters Anonymous, this book gives a foundation for taking weight off permanently. It focuses on people's relationships with food and helps them change their thinking about food. The author, who is anonymous, was a veteran of fad diets; not until she addressed her connection between food and emotional hunger did she lose and maintain a 50-pound weight loss. She believes the problem must be viewed as spiritual and emotional as well as physical. She includes inspiring stories from her experience and from others.

Suggested Readers

- Overweight clients with emotional issues
- Clients who are struggling with yo-yo dieting
- Overweight clients with assertiveness issues

Therapeutic Insights

- It's not entirely the client's fault. Our culture is obsessed with being thin. Women are fat obsessed.
- Overeating is a symptom of the person not handling the emotions in his or her life. Learning to say *no* is difficult when a person is used to saying *yes.*
- Some of the reasons clients overeat are stress, fear, and to reward themselves. It is important to understand why people overeat.
- Overeating can be a substitute for expressing emotions including fear, sadness, and loneliness.
- Recovery includes a rebalancing of physical, emotional, and spiritual needs.

The Thin Books: Daily Strategies and Meditations for Fat-Free, Guilt-Free, Binge-Free Living
Jeane Eddy Westin
Hazelden Publishing Group, 1996 (revised edition)
500 pages

Book Byte

This is a combination of two books written for overeaters. The first book contains the key principles of eating right and maintaining a positive attitude toward food. It explores the issues of people changing their attitude about food, along with changing their self-concept. Jeane Westin stresses the need for people to take charge of their own process of weight loss and shows readers how to deal with the "shame blame" game often associated with weight loss. She gives tips and insights to help overeaters gain control of their overeating. The second book contains daily motivational messages to inspire readers on a journey toward a more positive life.

Suggested Readers

- Food-obsessed yo-yo dieters
- Clients who are discouraged with dieting programs and who want to gain control of their lives
- Clients with body image issues

Therapeutic Insights

- What people think is how they feel. When they think positive thoughts about themselves, they will feel positive.
- People need to have the courage to be imperfect. A perfectionistic attitude toward weight loss sets them up for failure. People need to allow themselves mistakes and to learn from them.
- Negative thoughts or feelings pile on the pounds.
- Positive doing is the first step. Clients need to make an honest assessment of their eating patterns and then construct a personal eating plan.

- Losing weight is a one-day-at-a-time process. Overeaters need to learn to feel their emotions rather than numbing them out.

When Food Is Love: Exploring the Relationship Between Eating and Intimacy

Geneen Roth
Plume Books, 1993 (reissue edition)
265 pages

Book Byte

Geneen Roth explores the relationship between eating and intimacy. She shows how compulsive eating is often a substitute for intimacy and that overeating is an attempt to satisfy a person's emotional hunger. This book is aimed at giving the reader help in breaking destructive and self-perpetuating patterns. An additional book by Geneen Roth is *Feeding the Hungry Heart*.

Suggested Readers

- Adults with overeating issues
- Clients with a history of yo-yo dieting
- Adults with self-esteem and overweight issues

Therapeutic Insights

- Patterns of eating were formed by early patterns of loving. It is important that people take responsibility for changes in their present lives.
- Being obsessed with food or anything else does not allow people to be truly intimate with themselves or with anyone else. Compulsive eating is a way of hiding or protecting themselves.
- If overeaters continue to believe that they are in control of everyone and everything in their life, they will continue to be frustrated, disappointed, and confused. They need to learn that they are only in charge of themselves and no one else.

- Wanting what is forbidden prevents people from living in the present moment.
- Diets do not work, because food and weight are only symptoms of underlying repressed traumas that overeaters experienced as children. Food protects these clients from getting hurt again.

GAY, LESBIAN, BISEXUAL, AND TRANSGENDER

BISEXUALITY

Bi Any Other Name: Bisexual People Speak Out
Loraine Hutchins and Lani Kaahumanu
Alyson Publications, 1991
379 pages

Book Byte

These authors debunk the concept that people are either straight or gay and that bisexual women and men are fence-sitters. This book helps to secure for the bisexual community a rightful place within the larger movement of progressive social change. Bisexuals, rejected by both the gay and straight worlds, have been a community in exile. The writing is challenging and authentic.

Suggested Readers

- Women or men who identify themselves as bisexual
- Bisexuals who are seeking more information about their community
- Women or men who are questioning their sexuality

Therapeutic Insights

- Bisexuals must deal with bi-phobia from both gay and straight people.
- Development of a bisexual identity is a very individual process.
- Barriers to developing a self-affirming bisexual identity include intrapsychic, interpersonal, and societal obstacles.
- There is a virtual absence of a bisexual community.
- Validation is probably the single most important factor determining whether an achieved bisexual identity can be positive.

GAY AND LESBIAN FAMILIES

The Lesbian and Gay Parenting Handbook: Creating and Raising Our Families
April Martin, Ph.D.
HarperCollins Publishers, 1993
416 pages

Book Byte

Drawing on in-depth interviews with families and experts, along with her own personal and professional experience, April Martin walks the readers through many issues involved in forming and nurturing a lesbian or gay family. These issues include: the decision to parent; different options for creating a family, from artificial insemination to adoption or surrogacy; legal considerations, coming out, relationships and communication within the family, the special circumstances of a relationship breakup, and where to turn for additional information and support.

Suggested Readers

- Gays and lesbians who are contemplating adoption or artificial insemination
- Gays and lesbians who are coparenting children
- Families and friends who support gay and lesbian families

Therapeutic Insights

- The children of gays and lesbians are the most considered and the most planned-for children.
- The key to single parenting is support.
- Having a known donor requires careful planning, talking, thinking, and negotiating.
- Some children will express an intense longing for their biological parents, talking about it frequently and emotionally.
- Parenting can be the great equalizer between gay/lesbian parents and straight parents.

What About the Children?: Sons and Daughters of Lesbian & Gay Parents Talk About Their Lives

Lisa Saffron
Cassell Publishing, 1997
224 pages

Book Byte

A question that is often expressed about children who are raised by gays and lesbians is, what about the children? In this book, this question is addressed through the life stories of 20 sons and daughters of gay and lesbian parents. There is a combination of humor and serious reflection as they examine their own upbringing on their adult lives. Stereotypical representations of gay and lesbian parents are firmly rejected in these stories. The core of this book is that parents must equip their children to deal with discrimination and injustice that they may encounter in their lives. Saffron also includes an excellent bibliography.

Suggested Readers

- Lesbians and gays who are contemplating parenting
- Childcare professionals who want more understanding regarding the diversity of families today
- Parents who are helping their children live with prejudice

Therapeutic Insights

- Children are usually very selective as to whom they tell about a gay parent.
- For many children, family is simply who they live with.
- Most children don't see any disadvantages to having lesbian or gay parents.
- Children of gay and lesbian parents are more open and accepting of people than many other children.
- Gay and lesbian parents who are comfortable with their identity are likely to impart a liberal understanding of sexuality to their children.

GAY, LESBIAN, AND BISEXUAL TEENS

The Journey Out: A Guide For and About Lesbian, Gay and Bisexual Teens

Rachel Pollack and Cheryl Schwartz
Viking Children's Books, 1995
148 pages

Book Byte

A person's discovery of his or her sexuality doesn't happen overnight. Confusion is just the beginning of what can be a real uphill battle. Adding to the confusion are dealing with parents, friends, love, health, hormones, and homophobia. These are the personal stories and experiences of gay, lesbian, and bisexual youth. It is also a commonsense approach to coming out, dating, gay youth, politics, harassment, and religion.

Suggested Readers

- Teens who see themselves as gay, lesbian, or bisexual
- Teens who are looking for up-to-date information on gay youth issues
- Teens who need strategies to prepare for coming out

Therapeutic Insights

- Teens may or may not know if they are gay, lesbian, or bisexual.
- It is always easier to come out when an individual feels a sense of self-acceptance and his or her self esteem is high.
- Current research strongly suggests that sexual orientation is determined from birth, as part of one's genetic inheritance.
- Young gay people cannot work alone for change, but must work hand in hand with other human rights organizations.
- Eighty percent of lesbian, gay, and bisexual youth report severe feelings of isolation.

Lesbian and Gay Youth: Care and Counseling

Caitlin Ryan and Donna Futterman
Columbia University Press, 1998
256 pages

Book Byte

This is a handbook on the care, counseling, and support needs of lesbian and gay youth. It is for providers, advocates, parents, and interested readers. The authors include guidelines for assessment, treatment, prevention, and referral, along with the latest research and practical wisdom on lesbian and gay youth. Adolescents face many barriers in accessing appropriate primary care. Lesbian, gay, and bisexual youth are the most underserved population.

Suggested Readers

- Advocates and helping professionals who work with gay and lesbian youth
- Parents of gay and lesbian youth
- Teachers and other school personnel who work with gay and lesbian youth

Therapeutic Insights

- Lesbian and gay youth face the same health and mental health challenges as their heterosexual peers, with the addition of social and health challenges that are associated with having a stigmatized identity.
- AIDS is the sixth leading cause of death in youth between ages 15 and 24.
- Lesbian and gay youth who lack adequate support may develop maladaptive coping behaviors that persist into adulthood.
- Negative experiences related to coming out make it imprudent, even dangerous, to come out in many settings.
- A common theme that is identified by gay and lesbian youth is the experience of chronic stress from harassment.

The Shared Heart: Portraits and Stories Celebrating Lesbian, Gay and Bisexual Young People
Adam Mastoon
William Morrow & Co., Inc., 1997
87 pages

Book Byte

This is a compelling combination of narrative and photography, which celebrates young people who are facing the challenges of growing up gay, lesbian, or bisexual. It is through this book that the reader will see these people for who they are, not as a statistic. These stirring portraits recount experiences that are as different as their backgrounds. It also includes an excellent resource guide.

Suggested Readers

- Gay, lesbian, and bisexual adolescents
- Gay, lesbian, or bisexual teens who are looking for support and acknowledgment
- Families and friends of gay, lesbian, and bisexual teens

Therapeutic Insights

- Gay, lesbian, and bisexual adolescents are always looking for signs that they are not alone.
- It is difficult to reconcile sexual orientation with one's heritage.
- Discovering one's sexual identity does not happen quickly.
- Gay adolescents search for a place of safety in order to be who they really are in the world.
- Growing up gay, lesbian, or bisexual is an extraordinary experience that many teens have to face.

GAY MEN

Finding the Boyfriend Within

Brad Gooch

Simon & Schuster, 1999

171 pages

Book Byte

Brad Gooch offers single and coupled gay men a provocative, sophisticated, and inspirational guide that addresses the big issues of love, romance, and being alone. Part memoir and part self-help, this is a practical and helpful guide in the quest for self-discovery for gay men. Gooch believes that within each gay man are both an ideal lover and the self that must be nurtured to help prepare for sustaining a real-life relationship.

Suggested Readers

- Single gay men
- Gay men who are in relationships
- Gay men who want to increase their self-awareness and self-respect

Therapeutic Insights

- Ignoring the boyfriend within is tantamount to denying one's creativity.
- Everyone has a guiding voice within.
- There's much more work involved in meeting the good partner than wishful thinking or philosophizing.
- One is good at loving and being happy with others to the extent that he loves and is happy with himself.
- People can turn around suffering, challenges, disappointments, and rejections.

How to Survive Your Own Gay Life: An Adult Guide to Love, Sex and Relationships
Perry Brass
Belhue Press, 1998
224 pages

Book Byte

In this book, Perry Brass starts out with the basics: how to meet men, how to have a relationship that is both emotionally and sexually satisfying, how to deal with financial problems, how to survive antigay violence, and how to arrive at a core group of beliefs that will sustain one through a difficult time. He writes about keeping one's mind and soul open, realizing one's intentions, and clearing the way for what one wants.

Suggested Readers

- Gay men who are creating their own personal stories
- Gay couples who are seeking to increase their level of intimacy
- Gay men who want to change their lives

Therapeutic Insights

- Gay men do not have to apologize for who they are.
- Gay men must connect with the great source of strength inside them.
- Surviving a gay life is also about recognizing both internal and external homophobia.
- Many gay men feel that their lives are those of unrealized intentions.
- The importance of a relationship must rise above money arrangements.

Intimacy Between Men: How to Find and Keep Gay Love Relationships

John Driggs, M.S.W., and Stephen Finn, Ph.D.
Plume Books, 1991 (reprint edition)
242 pages

Book Byte

More and more gay men are seeking to find, create, and preserve intimate, long-lasting relationships. With success stories and exercises, this guide offers innovative strategies for overcoming many problems faced by gay men in society. These authors explore the coming-out process, conquering setbacks and roadblocks to intimacy, recognizing the differences between sex and intimacy, and coping with personal safety issues and AIDS.

Suggested Readers

- Gay men who are attempting to build lasting relationships
- Gay men who want to improve their communications skills
- Gay men who are exploring their personal development

Therapeutic Insights

- AIDS has complicated the task of forming intimate relationships for gay men.
- Sexuality involves considerations of health, safety, politics, ethics, and law.
- Sexuality and intimacy are different.
- Same-sex relationships benefit from a lack of stereotyped sex roles.
- The scarcity of models for gay male relationships is a part of the larger problem of the lack of support for gay couples.

Life Outside—The Signorile Report on Gay Men

Michelangelo Signorile
HarperCollins Publishers, 1998 (reprint edition)
352 pages

Book Byte

It's been nearly 30 years since the Stonewall riots ushered in the modern gay rights movement. The gay community has experienced victories, adversity, discrimination, movement, disease, despair, activism, and hope. Michelangelo Signorile offers in this book what he calls the "cult of masculinity" within contemporary gay male culture, while at the same time he finds hope and renewal among people who consider themselves to be outside the "scene." He shows the pressure that gay men are under to conform to an impossible physical ideal and how that pressure filters down. He includes conversations about the fascination with illegal steroids and other forms of recreational drugs.

Suggested Readers

- Men who challenge the assumption that gay men are incapable of settling down
- Gay men who are moving into midlife with pride and vitality
- Gay men who want to face the passage of time with maturity

Therapeutic Insights

- Gay men occupy every facet of American life.
- For gay men, a wide variety of social and sexual subcultures has developed and grown over the years.
- The new gay fast life is similar to the old one except for now the drugs are more potent and destructive, physical paradigms are more rigid, and the anxiety around AIDS is greater than ever.
- The gay urban scene today encompasses what is known as the *circuit,* a series of large dance parties that occur around the country.
- There appears to be a trend in black market steroid use.

That's Mr. Faggot to You: Further Trials from My Queer Life
Michael Thomas Ford
Consortium Books, 1999
234 pages

Book Byte

In his follow-up to *Alec Baldwin Doesn't Love Me,* syndicated columnist Michael Thomas Ford takes the reader even further inside his gay life. The essays in this wild and wide-ranging collection are often poignant and quite funny. Ford speaks with candor about feeling invisible at times as a gay man (the culmination of feelings and emotions that develop by being around straight people for too long), responsibilities to family, monogamy, romance, holidays, animals, and on-line relationships.

Suggested Readers

- Gay men who are in search of relationships
- Gay men who are more actively involved with their family of origin
- Gay men who want to laugh at themselves

Therapeutic Insights

- Sometimes, when talking to parents, it is important to cut and paste (in other words, to give only the essential details).
- Risk and relationships go hand in hand.
- For many gay men, being single is a constant source of sorrow.
- Homophobic episodes from early school years can stay with gay men for all of their lives.
- Often in relationships, gay men capitulate everything that is theirs.

LESBIANS

Don't Get Me Started
Kate Clinton
Ballentine Books, 1998
199 pages

Book Byte

Kate Clinton is the founding mother of lesbian comedy. She is out and proud. She uses family, politics, Catholicism, and lesbians as basic themes to prove her clever points. She has four comedy CDs to her credit, but this is her first book. Clinton's thoughts and observations range from gay marriage to Henry Kissinger. She is not afraid of anything.

Suggested Readers

- Anyone who wants to laugh out loud
- Lesbians who need affirmation and a reason to laugh at themselves
- Lesbians who are looking for comebacks to crazy questions from family

Therapeutic Insights

- Many retirement motor home parks are training sites for secret societies of older women, banding together to take over the world.
- Don't come out to a parent in a moving vehicle.
- A new addition to the Gay Games now includes an event called the sperm carry.
- Don't Ask Don't Tell might be a nice add campaign for *The Crying Game,* but it's no way to live a life in the military.
- Gays obviously did not design military fatigues, because they never would have stayed with the earth tones for so long.

Dyke Life: From Growing Up to Growing Old, A Celebration of the Lesbian Experience
Karla Jay
Basic Books, 1996
374 pages

Book Byte

This book contains a mix of the serious and the irreverent, a wide-ranging comprehensive view of the many rites and passages of lesbian life. Karla Jay has brought together essays written by a group of lesbian and bisexual women from every walk of life. They discuss trends, coming out, commitment ceremonies, and the community's intellectual and experiential diversity. This collection of writers celebrates the range and vitality of the lesbian community. This book also includes an excellent selection of further recommended readings.

Suggested Readers

- Lesbians who are coming out
- Lesbian and bisexual women who are creating families
- Lesbians who are encountering challenges in their relationships

Therapeutic Insights

- The homophobic climate plays a decisive role in many of the barriers to intimacy in lesbian couples.
- Regardless of the specific group to which they belong, lesbian women of color must manage the dominant culture's racism, sexism, and heterosexism.
- Passionate love between women is as old as time.
- The legal strategy most often used by lesbians is called *durable power of attorney*.
- Lesbians play a great price for being sexual outlaws.

Lesbian Couples, Second Edition

D. Merilee Clunis and G. Dorsey Green
Seal Press, 1993
274 pages

Book Byte

This is a popular guide for lesbians in couple relationships. It covers a wide range of topics, including living arrangements, work, money, separateness and togetherness, coming out to family and friends, resolving conflict, and understanding each other. The authors use a variety of helpful examples and problem-solving techniques.

Suggested Readers

- Lesbians who are in relationships
- Lesbian couples who are seeking to make their relationships mutually satisfying and long lasting
- Lesbians who want to create relationships and family

Therapeutic Insights

- There is a backlash that comes with increased visibility and attempts to further political goals.
- The desire for intimacy is a major reason for wanting a couple relationship.
- Couples move through stages, and each of these stages has its own particular characteristics, tasks, and difficulties.
- Commitment implies an expectation about the future, but it does not guarantee the future outcome.
- To have intimacy, each woman must allow her partner to be herself.

Lesbian Epiphanies: Women Coming Out in Later Life
Karol Jensen, M.P.H., Ph.D.
The Harrington Park Press, 1999
240 pages

Book Byte

Exploring identity development and gender orientation, this book contains important information about the experiences and difficulties of women who come out later in life. Karol Jensen interviews 24 women on psychological, erotic, and social processes of women who come out after a heterosexual marriage. She explores the societal limits placed on women and the cultural restraints that prevented these women from being aware of their sexuality.

Suggested Readers

- Women who identify as lesbian or bisexual later in life
- Families and friends who are supporting an older woman's coming-out process
- Women who want clarity and understanding in the context of leaving their marriages

Therapeutic Insights

- There is no evidence that a lesbian mother's sexual orientation has any adverse consequences on her child's development.
- Women who marry and later realize that they have significant attractions to women as primary partners have been out of touch with a major aspect of themselves.
- The family provides the earliest instruction on what sexual and other behaviors are acceptable for young women within a given context.
- Social constructions can limit a woman's knowledge of herself.
- Some women, who have denied their feelings toward women, consciously repress the importance of those feelings.

Lesbian Passion: Loving Ourselves and Each Other

JoAnn Loulan
Spinsters Ink, 1987
223 pages

Book Byte

This classic landmark book is found on many lesbians' bookshelves. Loulan has written about the joys of being a lesbian. She includes self-esteem, passionate friendships, intimacy in recovery, passion of long-term couples, survival after incest, and research on the lives and sex practices of 1,600 lesbians. Loulan believes that passion is a source of greatness within each lesbian. It is the life source that energizes people.

Suggested Readers

- Lesbians who are recovering from addiction
- Lesbians who are in long-term relationships
- Single lesbians who are looking for relationships

Therapeutic Insights

- It is often frightening for lesbians to tell their partners how they feel about their bodies.
- It is difficult to feel sexy, self-loving, and uninhibited in the bodies that the dominant culture has taught are too big or don't work right.
- Though friendships and romantic relationships overlap, friends are very different than lovers.
- The strain between family and friends can become intensified for lesbians, because friends are so integral to the emotional survival of many lesbians.
- Organized religion has done a great deal to oppress lesbians.

So, You Want to Be a Lesbian?: A Guide For Amateurs and Professionals
Liz Tracey and Sydney Pokorny
St. Martin's Press, Inc., 1996
223 pages

Book Byte

This book answers the essential questions, pokes fun at lesbian tradition, and provides a roadmap of where lesbians are heading for the millennium. The authors demystify recruitment, lesbians who want to be men, lesbians who have bad haircuts, and the observations that all lesbians wear flannel and that lesbians just really need one good man. They discuss parents, friends, sex, dating, lesbian culture, literature, and politics. For an extra bonus, they include a lesbian aptitude test.

Suggested Readers

- Lesbians who want to laugh
- Lesbians who want more information regarding their culture, history (herstory), or politics
- People who love lesbians

Therapeutic Insights

- Republican conventions are bad places to meet lesbians.
- For years, people have accused lesbians of deliberately setting out to get bad haircuts, thereby destroying the moral fabric of society.
- From Sleepytime to Lemon Zinger, lesbians are the only group of people well acquainted with the wide variety of decaffeinated teas.
- When coming out, one should be prepared to lose friends.
- Bonds forged during a relationship are strong and often don't end simply because the relationship has ended.

Unbroken Ties: Lesbian Ex-Lovers

Carol Becker, Ph.D.
Alyson Publications, 1991
218 pages

Book Byte

Going through a breakup can be a period of intense emotion and pain. Bonds forged during a lesbian relationship are strong. This book examines the phenomenon of friendship that remains after the relationship is over. In interviews with 40 lesbians of diverse backgrounds, Carol Becker traces the emotional trauma of the breakup, the stages of recovery, and the different ways that former partners stay in contact with each other.

Suggested Readers

- Lesbians who are in the process of ending their relationships
- Lesbians who are interested in maintaining a friendship after the relationship
- Lesbians who are in transition with their relationships

Therapeutic Insights

- There is great diversity and complexity in the range of lesbian breakups.
- Relationship endings are an opportunity to clarify interpersonal needs and desires.
- Moving from partner to friend means establishing new commitments and boundaries in the relationship.
- Ex-partners may remain an important part of a woman's evolving identity.
- Partnerships and breakups are often not given status and recognition by others.

SPIRITUALITY

Coming Out of Shame: Transforming Gay and Lesbian Lives

Gershen Kaufman, Ph.D., and Lev Raphael, Ph.D.
Main Street Books, 1996
287 pages

Book Byte

Most lesbians and gay men grow up learning that to be gay is deviant, sick, perverted, and unnatural. By adolescence, these attitudes have produced an overriding single emotion of shame, that feeling that who one is as a person is bad and defective. More specifically, it is one's gayness that makes him or her defective. Gershen Kaufman and Lev Raphael expose the role that shame has come to play in gay and lesbian lives, how it shapes identity, development, intimacy, and self-esteem. They offer strategies for restoring self-esteem, creating a positive gay identity, and healing shame.

Suggested Readers

- Gays and lesbians who are attempting to overcome the legacy of shame
- Gays and lesbians who are attempting to build self-esteem and intimacy
- Gays and lesbians who have internalized shame and self-loathing

Therapeutic Insights

- Parents and families inevitably struggle with shame when a loved one comes out to them.
- Guilt is very different than shame. Guilt is more connected to specific acts instead of the self as a whole.
- Shame creates exposure, which generates self-consciousness, which produces paralysis.
- Shaming gays and lesbians gives people a false sense of safety by making them feel superior, but it never creates inner security.
- Gays and lesbians need to celebrate their sexuality.

Coming Out Spiritually: The Next Step

Christian de la Huerta
Tarcher/Putnam, 1999
256 pages

Book Byte

This is a guide for gays and lesbians who want to reclaim a spiritual connection. Christian de la Huerta synthesizes the spiritual roles or archetypes that gays and lesbians have often assumed and continue to enact today: creator of beauty, consciousness scout, mediator, shaman, and healer. He also introduces readers to many of the world's religions, including Buddhism, Christianity, Hinduism, Judaism, Sufism, and Taoism, and he investigates the teachings of these traditions and their attitudes toward homosexuality.

Suggested Readers

- Gays and lesbians who are seeking to build a spiritual life
- Gays and lesbians who want to explore the deeper aspects of compassion, grief, joy, and gratitude
- Those who want to have more honesty in their lives regarding their sexuality

Therapeutic Insights

- When soul issues are ignored, addiction sets in.
- Spirituality cuts through denial and offers an alternative to self-hatred.
- When homophobia poisons a culture, spiritual leadership is lost and moralizing substitutes for spiritual living.
- People are created with their sexuality.
- What is lacking in the gay community, both among individuals and collectively, is a real sense of self.

Like Bread on the Seder Plate: Jewish Lesbians and the Transformation of Tradition
Rebecca Alpert
Columbia University Press, 1998
224 pages

Book Byte

Rebecca Albert, one of the first women to be ordained a rabbi, explores how lesbians can shape Jewish tradition to resonate with their own experience. She defines lesbianism in a multifaceted way that allows her to examine the shift of understandings of lesbians in Jewish tradition. She also suggests some new directions for reinterpreting and transforming Jewish texts from a uniquely lesbian Jewish perspective.

Suggested Readers

- Women who wish to increase their knowledge of Jewish lesbian history
- Lesbian Jews who are moving toward the transformation of Jewish tradition
- Lesbians who are making their presence felt in the Jewish world

Therapeutic Insights

- When Jewish lesbians made themselves visible, the community reacted with ignorance, silence, and homogenization.
- Liberal Jewish institutions, while more sympathetic than many, have not given Jewish lesbians full access to religious life.
- The absence of any severe prohibition against lesbians does not make it permissible—it merely renders it invisible.
- When multiple identities come into conflict, groups are then compelled to set out to define their own separate spaces.
- The Jewish community can help by making lesbian and gay commitment ceremonies a part of Jewish ritual life.

STRAIGHT SPOUSES, GAY PARTNERS

The Other Side of the Closet: The Coming-Out Crisis for Straight Spouses and Families

Amity Pierce Buxton, Ph.D.

John Wiley & Sons, Inc., 1994 (revised and expanded edition)

352 pages

Book Byte

For straight wives and husbands whose partners come out, the devastating impact of gay men and women's liberation on their lives cannot be minimized. Most heterosexual spouses endure the pain in silence on their side of the closet, whereas their gay, lesbian, and bisexual partners find support from their respective communities. Because the trauma for spouses can be so profound, the process of recovery and transformation is long and arduous. The stories and analyses in this book present a collective portrait of how spouses and children come to terms with such disclosures.

Suggested Readers

- Men and women who have been left by gay or lesbian spouses
- Families in which a parent has come out
- Friends and loved ones who are attempting to support spouses of gays, lesbians, or bisexual people

Therapeutic Insights

- Approximately 20 percent of gay men marry due to internalized homophobia and social pressures.
- Spouses face major issues, such as damage to their sexuality, negation of their marriage, and a breakdown of integrity and trust.
- The discovery that a spouse is gay acts like a confirmation to the spouse of his or her own sexual inadequacy.
- The habit of self-blame is hard to break.
- Anger and feeling victimized may last for months until spouses understand more about homosexuality.

When Husbands Come Out of the Closet

Jean Schaar Gochros, Ph.D.
The Haworth Press, Inc., 1990
267 pages

Book Byte

This book is for and about wives whose husbands are gay or bisexual. These are women who, often without a previous hint of such concern, are confronted with the reality that such an intimate part of their husband's life was completely secret from them. These are the stories of some couples who worked things out satisfactorily, and of others who remained devastated by the experience. This book will clear away myths and replace them with understanding.

Suggested Readers

- Women whose husbands have come out as gay or bisexual
- Families and friends of couples who want to be supportive and caring
- Helping professionals who need insight and information

Therapeutic Insights

- Wives of gay men experience great isolation.
- Sexual responses come from a combination of biological, intellectual, and emotional processes.
- The goals for wives are to help themselves remobilize, recognize, and utilize their own strength and independence as soon as possible.
- Almost all wives of gay men become moderately to seriously depressed after their husbands come out.
- Couples and families can recover from this crisis.

TRANSGENDER ISSUES

Trans Liberation: Beyond Pink or Blue

Leslie Feinberg

Beacon Press, 1999

160 pages

Book Byte

This collection of Leslie Feinberg's speeches on transliberation is immediate, impassioned, and stirring for anyone concerned about civil rights. She believes that the public has had caricatures of men and women drilled into them. She raises questions about the societal treatment of people based on their sex and gender expression. It is a transliberation movement of masculine females, feminine males, cross-dressers, transsexual men and women, intersexuals (hermaphrodites), gender benders, and other sex- and gender-variant people.

Suggested Readers

- People who feel oppressed because they do not fit into societal norms
- Men and women who do not feel aligned to either gender
- Trans people who are looking for support, information, and meaning

Therapeutic Insights

- Understanding gender expression cannot be done simply by determining one's sex.
- Trans people are still literally social outlaws.
- To refer to anyone's gender expression as exaggerated is insulting and restricts gender freedom.
- Trans people have been denied medical care due to bigotry and hatred.
- True gender lies not in the appearance of the body but the working of the mind.

True Selves: Understanding Transsexualism

Mildred L. Brown and Chloe Ann Rounsley

Jossey-Brown Publishers, 1996

271 pages

Book Byte

Mildred L. Brown, one of the country's most experienced clinicians in the field of transsexuals, and Chloe Ann Rounsley have written an authoritative and sensitive book about the transsexual experience. They discuss the myriad of conflicts that transsexuals face on a daily basis, and the courage they must summon every day to live their lives. The book breaks down common misconceptions about transsexuals, and it offers recommendations to family members and friends of these individuals. They address childhood, adolescence, and adult years, as well as therapy, workplace issues, and medical options.

Suggested Readers

- Transgender people who need information and support
- Transgender people who want to pursue medical alternatives
- Families and friends of transgender people

Therapeutic Insights

- Transsexualism is not a recent phenomenon; the first surgery was performed in 1931.
- Gender-dysphoric children and adolescents often feel like they have a monstrous dark cloud hanging over their heads.
- Transgender people often feel sad about the superficiality of many of their relationships, afraid to let people know their truth.
- Families will generally experience confusion, denial, fear, anger, depression, guilt, and shame in response to a child coming out as transgender.
- Not all transgender people go through surgery.

 **GRIEF AND LOSS**

GENERAL

Ambiguous Loss: Learning to Live with Unresolved Grief
Pauline Boss
Harvard University Press, 1999
192 pages

Book Byte

Pauline Boss has written a book about coping and moving on after ambiguous losses, such as the family of an Alzheimer's patient, parents of abducted children, and divorce. These losses are not clear cut and can often lead to complicated and unresolved grieving. Pauline Boss' book shows readers how they can move on and come to terms with their grief.

Suggested Readers

- Clients with complicated grieving issues
- Clients who are experiencing unclear losses
- Couples with infertility issues

Therapeutic Insights

- Unresolved grief is similar to post-traumatic stress disorder. When the loss is not resolved, a person can continue to experience it long after the traumatic experience.
- Ambiguous loss is often responsible for ambiguous feelings. Mixed feelings are normal.
- Denial serves a purpose. It is not something to avoid or something to advocate. In living with ambiguous loss, a person needs to have a combination of optimism and realistic thinking.
- To turn the corner and cope with the unclear losses, a client must first give up finding the perfect solution. A client's relationship with the loss must be redefined.
- How to bring meaning to an ambiguous loss is a critical issue. The answer will be different for each and every person.

Grieving: How to Go on Living When Someone You Love Dies

Therese Rando, Ph.D.
Lexington Books, 1988 (out of print)
312 pages

Book Byte

Therese Rando is a nationally known psychologist on bereavement issues. She dispels the myths of mourning and provides instead the information and support that will help others cope with their loss. She addresses the issues of loss circumstances separately, whether the death was sudden or expected: from accident, illness, suicide, or homicide, or acute natural consequences. She also considers whether the loved one was a parent, child, sibling, spouse, or friend. For each, she offers suggestions on what individuals can do to successfully come to terms with their grief.

Suggested Readers

- Those who are looking for guidance in adjusting to a new life without forgetting their treasured past
- Adults who have lost a sibling, parent, child, or spouse
- Individuals who are suffering from guilt, sadness, or regret because the relationship was not what they had hoped for

Therapeutic Insights

- Death of a first parent usually means some reorganization in the adult child's relationship with the surviving parent.
- Parental grief is particularly intense. It is unusually complicated and has an extraordinary up-and-down period.
- The developmental issues that a person must confront as an aging parent of an adult child can complicate his or her bereavement.
- When family configurations differ from the two-parent, several-children model, there can be an additional difficulty for family members mourning a loss.
- Children do grieve and need the help of adults to cope with a major loss.

Giving Sorrow Words: How to Cope with Grief and Get On with Your Life

Candy Lightner
Warner Books, Inc., 1990
230 pages

Book Byte

A hit-and-run drunk driver killed Candy Lightner's daughter in 1980. Galvanized by anger, Candy started Mothers Against Drunk Drivers (MADD) and went on to become the crusading force behind new tough drinking-and-driving laws. This book is the result of interviews with more than 100 people whose lives were changed by the death of a loved one. These stories illuminate the complexity of grieving.

Suggested Readers

- Those who are experiencing grief regarding sudden and unanticipated loss
- Individuals who have lost loved ones to AIDS
- Adults who are dealing with the loss of their child

Therapeutic Insights

- The bereaved typically feel ambushed by a mixture of sadness, fear, anxiety, agitation, anger, guilt, depression, and despair.
- To mourn fully is also to admit to the difficulties and disappointments in that relationship.
- Grief comes in waves. Another loss that needs to be mourned is the loss of the future as one had imagined it.
- Grief opens doors in the mind and in the heart that may have been shut.
- Fear is a natural component of grief. Once someone has experienced the death of a loved one, he or she may come to believe that the world is not a safe place.

The Healing Journey through Grief: Your Journal for Reflection and Recovery
Phil Rich, Ed.D., M.S.W.
John Wiley & Sons, Inc., 1999
264 pages

Book Byte

This is a unique journal/workbook to help clients work through issues of grief and loss. Written by an experienced psychotherapist, this book guides readers through the painful emotions, thoughts, and memories that result from losing someone close to them. *The Healing Journey through Grief* contains writing exercises to guide readers through the stages of the healing process and to take an active part in their own recovery.

Suggested Readers

- Clients with issues of loss
- Clients who are stuck or overwhelmed by the grief process
- Clients with unfinished grieving issues

Therapeutic Insights

- Mourning has no time limit. Grief work for some may be relatively short, and for others it may be a process that takes years.
- Grief work is unique and personal, but it has some general stages that are common to all. The stages include acclimation and adjustment, emotional immersion and deconstruction, and reclamation and reconciliation. The goal of grief work is not to avoid or bypass any one of these stages but to work through the emotions connected with each stage.
- When acclimating to a loss, there are several tasks and many accompanying emotions. These tasks include adjusting, functioning, keeping in check, and accepting support.
- During the stage of emotional immersion and deconstruction, the most active aspects of grief work are done. During this time, a person contends with reality, develops insight, reconstructs personal values and beliefs, and learns to accept and let go.
- Reclamation and reconciliation are the time when a person rebuilds and creates a new life, shifting from focusing internally to focusing externally.

Necessary Losses: The Loves, Illusions, Dependencies and Impossible Expectations That All of Us Have to Give Up in Order to Grow

Judith Viorst

Fireside Books, 1998 (reprint edition)

447 pages

Book Byte

Judith Viorst draws on her very special sensibilities to illuminate a subject that is central to everyone's life: loss. She examines the loss of childhood, expectations in relationships, and the loss of loved ones. In this landmark book, she uses a multitude of resources to synthesize an understanding of loss, including literature, vivid interviews, and her own compelling experiences. Viorst is witty, wise, sensitive, and has written a very comprehensive book.

Suggested Readers

- Individuals who are seeking to understand the difference between childish and grown-up love
- Those who are attempting to love deeply without becoming vulnerable to loss
- Those for whom separation has always been a terror-filled experience

Therapeutic Insights

- Severe separation in early life leaves emotional scars on the brain, because they assault the essential human connection: the parent-child bond, which teaches us that one is lovable.
- People repeat the past by superimposing parental images onto the present.
- By blaming oneself for losses, a person is saying that he or she would rather feel guilty and helpless than to not feel in control.
- Individuals have to live with a sense of transience, aware that no matter how passionately they love, whatever they love, they don't have the power to make it stay.
- In confronting the many losses that are brought by time and death, there are opportunities for transformation.

BOOKS FOR CHILDREN ABOUT GRIEF AND LOSS

Lost & Found: A Kid's Book for Living Through Loss

Rabbi Marc Gellman and Monsignor Thomas Hartman

Morrow Junior Books, 1999

144 pages

Book Byte

This is a book about the many losses that children experience in their lives, from the loss of a game to the loss of a life. It is designed to be read alone by children or with a caregiver. The authors believe that loss is an opportunity to gain new insights and wisdom. How hardships are handled shapes a person's life more than do the victories. The authors not only explore loss, but they also present opportunities for children to learn compassion.

Suggested Readers

- Children, between ages 8 and 12, who are experiencing loss through divorce
- Children who are experiencing loss through the death of a loved one
- Children who have lost confidence and trust in themselves or others

Therapeutic Insights

- Everyone has to think about death sometimes.
- Nothing, except death, is forever.
- Memories make the sadness hurt a little less.
- The way time heals our wounds is an up-and-down process.
- No one wants to die frightened or angry.

Saying Goodbye to Daddy

Judith Vigna
Albert Whitman & Co., 1991
32 pages

Book Byte

This is a beautifully written book about a young girl named Clare, whose father is killed in a car accident. Clare is devastated at the loss of her father, and she goes through the many emotions of grief, anger, fear, guilt, sadness, and disbelief. The story takes Clare through the death, funeral, and healing process of losing her father.

Suggested Readers

- Children, between ages 5 and 9, who have lost a parent
- Children who are experiencing grief over the loss of a family member
- Families in which there has been a significant loss

Therapeutic Insights

- A death is never the child's fault.
- A relationship with the person who died can continue.
- Children should be permitted to attend the funeral of a loved one.
- It is essential to help children remember stories and experiences with their loved one who has died.
- Allow children to create some of their own rituals as a part of their grieving process.

When a Pet Dies

Fred Rogers (*Mister Rogers's Neighborhood*)
The Putnam & Grosset Book & Activity Group, 1998 (reissue edition)
32 pages

Book Byte

Like others of Fred Rogers' books, this, too, was created to encourage family talk. As families look at the photos and read the text, it may make it easier for children to share their real feelings about a pet dying. For many children, the loss of a pet is like the loss of a family member. Children may experience the same emotions as if a loved one is ill or dies. Death can create fear, confusion, anger, and sadness for children.

Suggested Readers

- Children, between ages 4 and 8, who have experienced the loss of a pet

Therapeutic Insights

- It isn't always easy to talk about sad and angry feelings.
- Missing his or her pet can make a child feel lonely.
- Children often believe that they could have prevented the pet's death.

When Dinosaurs Die: A Guide to Understanding Death

Laurie Krasny Brown and Marc Brown
Little, Brown & Co., 1998
32 pages

Book Byte

For children, the death of a loved one can be especially confusing and turbulent. This is true whether the loss is a classmate, a friend, a family member, or a pet. These wise dinosaurs offer help and reassurance, and they dispel the mythology that is associated with death. The dinosaurs are perfect companions for children who are experiencing the death of a loved one. They talk about their feelings of anger, fear, and hurt, and the comforting around such emotions.

Suggested Readers

- Children, up to age 8, who have experienced a loss
- Children who are looking for ways to remember someone
- Children who want to know about other cultures regarding death

Therapeutic Insights

- Many families continue to honor the day long after their loved ones have died.
- It is natural for a child to be angry when he or she misses someone so much.

- Children may want time to themselves when a loved one dies.
- When someone dies, there is no right or wrong way to feel.
- Children who are worried that they, too, might die, should be reassured.

When I Die Will I Get Better?

Joeri and Piet Breebaart
NTC/Contemporary Publishing Group, 1993
29 pages

Book Byte

This touching story comes from a 5-year-old and his father, who are seeking to understand the sudden death of his younger brother. Unable at first to understand what has happened, the boy slowly begins to tell a story about animals to his father. In the story, one of the animals becomes sick and dies, and the boy describes to his father what that means to all the other animals. At a time of great loss and sadness, children need consolation more than they need explanation. This book provides that beautifully.

Suggested Readers

- Children, between 5 and 10 years old, who have experienced the death of a sibling
- Families who need help comforting children who are struggling with the death of a sibling
- Children who are looking for comfort and reassurance

Therapeutic Insights

- Children need to be encouraged to talk about their grief without revealing all of their vulnerability.
- When siblings die, there are generally complex feelings of loss and guilt.
- Children can never have too many loving people around.
- Emotional pain hurts as much as physical pain.
- Children are resilient.

CATASTROPHIC LOSS/SUDDEN LOSS

A Grace Disguised: How the Soul Grows Through Loss
Gerald L. Sittser
Zondervan Publishing House, 1998
192 pages

Book Byte

This book is about catastrophic loss and the transformation that can occur in our lives because of it. With a Christian perspective, Sittser believes that it is not the experience of loss that becomes the defining moment in our lives, for that is as inevitable as death, which is the last loss awaiting us all. How one responds is the defining moment that will largely determine the quality, the direction, and the impact of our lives. Gerald Sittser survived two car accidents that killed his wife, daughter, and mother. Of course, he had no way of anticipating the adjustments he and his surviving children would have to make or the suffering they would endure. Catastrophic loss wreaks destruction. It is unforgiving and unrelenting. Sittser speaks to his surviving such a loss and the meaning he gained from it. He believes that forgiveness in the end brings freedom to the ones who give it.

Suggested Readers

- Survivors of catastrophic loss
- Those who are attempting to find meaning in loss
- Individuals who are seeking a universal understanding of grief

Therapeutic Insights

- Experiencing loss can take a person face to face with the dark side of life as well as to the frailty of human nature.
- Loss deprives an individual of control.
- Loss has little to do with notions of fairness; justice is not always served.
- Unforgiveness should not be confused with healthy responses to loss.
- It takes tremendous courage to love when one is broken.

No Time for Good-byes: Coping with Sorrow, Anger, and Injustice After a Tragic Death, Fourth Edition

Janice Harris Lord
Pathfinder Publishing, 1990
160 pages

Book Byte

Grieving the loss of a loved one who has been killed violently and senselessly is unique. This book focuses on the needs of family and friends of a loved one who has been violently killed. Survivors may be angrier and sadder than they thought possible. They may fear they are going crazy. In criminal victimization, those who are left behind cannot assimilate the fact that someone chose to be negligent, or selected a victim to brutalize. It makes no sense. Families are never prepared, nor are they prepared to face the weeks, months, and even years of waiting until a criminal case is resolved. How one grieves such a tragedy depends on many factors: support, religious beliefs, quality of their relationship with the loved one who was killed, the circumstances of the death, and their success with the criminal justice system.

Suggested Readers

- Family or friend of a murder victim
- Family or friend of a loved one who has been killed by a drunk driver
- Family or friend who has survived the death of a loved one through violent means

Therapeutic Insights

- One not only misses the living presence of a loved one, but he or she will also deeply resent the fact that the killer did not respect life.
- If a child was killed, a part of each family member also feels dead.
- One of the most difficult losses to survive is a murder in which the offender was known.
- The fear and vulnerability of now knowing that tragedy can strike anyone at any time has an almost existential quality. "What is life anyway?"
- How a person acts on anger doesn't matter as long as he or she doesn't hurt him- or herself or anyone else.

CHILDREN'S LOSS ISSUES

Are You Sad Too? Helping Children Deal with Loss and Death

Dinah Seibert, Judy Drolet, and Joyce Fetro

ETR Associates, 1993

154 pages

Book Byte

This is a sensitive handbook designed to provide tangible suggestions, from spontaneous conversations to planned classroom activities, to assist children to explore and to accept their feelings about loss and death. This book helps prepare caregivers for common questions with appropriate answers for each development stage. It covers loss due to the death of a family member, death of a teacher or friend, death of a pet, and divorce. It is an excellent guide for teachers, nurses, school guidance counselors, parents, and other caregivers.

Suggested Readers

- Adults assisting children (up to the age of 10) who are experiencing grief and pain
- Adults who are attempting to increase their communication skills with children
- Helping professionals who want to be more effective in helping grieving children

Therapeutic Insights

- It is important to identify what children understand about loss and death.
- It is important to not interpret children's feelings but to accept them at face value.
- Sometimes just the act of sharing spreads the weight of the sadness between an adult and a child.
- Children's perspectives and relationships to the object lost or the person who died will influence their response.
- Children need memories close at hand.

The Grieving Child: A Parent's Guide

Helen Fitzgerald

Simon & Schuster, 1992

207 pages

Book Byte

Explaining death to a child is one of the most difficult tasks that a parent or a relative faces. Parents of children, from preschool age to the teen years, will find the needed guidance covering such areas as: visiting the seriously ill or dying, using language that is appropriate to the child's age level, selecting useful books about death, handling especially difficult situations including murder and suicide, and deciding whenever a child should attend a funeral.

Suggested Readers

- Parents of children (preschool to early teens) who are experiencing the death of a loved one
- Adults with unresolved grief from their childhood
- Helping professionals who work with children who have suffered losses

Therapeutic Insights

- Children need to be informed of important things that are happening to their loved ones.
- It is important to take stock of one's own "death history" and one's own feelings of death before beginning to talk to children about the death of a loved one.
- Far from an experience to be endured alone, the death of a loved one is an opportunity for bonding and connection.
- Children grieve more sporadically than adults, and they are more capable than adults at putting grief aside.
- As they grow up, children go through tremendous development changes; with each stage of development, children perceive death differently.

DEATH OF A CHILD

Andrew, You Died Too Soon: A Family Experience of Grieving and Living Again

Corinne Chilstrom
Augsburg Fortress Publishers, 1994
144 pages

Book Byte

In the most simple, straightforward language, this mother tells the story of her love for her son, the overwhelming grief, the embrace of a community, and the deep spiritual events that occurred for her and her family when her son Andrew took his own life. Corinne Chilstrom is a pastor for a Lutheran church; her husband is the presiding bishop of the Evangelical Lutheran Church in America. Well acquainted with sorrow, this author shares her grief, invites others into the circle of mourners, offers quiet counsel on grieving to others who need it and welcome it, and still succeeds in having written an affirmative book. Her story is offered primarily for parents who grieve the loss of a child. It is written from a Christian perspective.

Suggested Readers

- Parents who are looking for understanding and a Christian perspective in the wake of a suicide of their child
- For survivors of suicide in the midst of the grieving process who are looking for some practical tools in the face of tragedy
- Family and community who are seeking spiritual insights regarding suicide

Therapeutic Applications

- One can love completely without complete understanding.
- Nurturing, loving parents cannot always help their children pull free from self-destruction.
- Those that are loved by others sometimes make life-altering decisions with which many must come to terms.
- Having close friends and community support is an essential element in facing dramatic life changes.
- Spirituality offers the possibility that a tragedy can be more meaningful.

A Broken Heart Still Beats: When Your Child Dies

Anne McCracken and Mary Semel
Hazelden Publishing Group, 1998
295 pages

Book Byte

This book is a collection of poetry, fiction, and essays, compiled by a journalist and a social worker, who have both lost a child. Judith Guest, Dominick Dunne, Albert Camus, Anne Morrow Lindbergh, George McGovern, John Irving, and Robert Frost are among the many writers whose works explore the grief and shock of losing a child. This anthology of similar experiences is an excellent source of comfort and healing. These authors give voice to grief and teach us how to come to terms with loss. They speak of the transformation of suffering into strength.

Suggested Readers

- Those who are looking to literature to find comfort in other bereaved parents and siblings
- Families who are looking for more than a self-help book to guide them through the loss of a child
- Individuals who are seeking a full choice of voices to validate the feelings of the bereaved

Therapeutic Insights

- This book offers dozens of voices, which echo a collective anger and despair over losing a child.
- People can become strengthened through grief and find the courage to stay productive in their work.
- When a child is killed, there is no longer a sense of order in the universe.
- Tragedy is not reserved for others.
- Parents feel failure merely in remaining alive after the death of a child.

A Child Dies: A Portrait of Family Grief, Second Edition

Joan Hagen Arnold and Penelope Buschman Gemma
The Charles Press, Publishers, 1994
136 pages

Book Byte

The death of a child, whether expected or unexpected, is incomprehensible. Family members ache with the pain of powerlessness and vulnerability and live with emptiness. The family may never feel whole again. This book is an attempt to bring to the surface what has been silenced in many families in order to portray a child's death and a family's loss. There is a connectedness between the parent and the child that has its roots in the biological and emotional bonds and attachments that precede birth. The child is the parent's link to the future. A child's death is a penetrating, agonizing blow to the entire family system.

Suggested Readers

- Any family member who is grieving the loss of a child
- Those who are seeking to understand the alteration in the family structure after the death of a child
- Parents who are feeling isolated and alone in their grief

Therapeutic Insights

- The child who has died continues to be a family member after death. Parents are forever parents of a dead child, as well as of the surviving children.
- There is a social pressure against the prolonged and public expression of personal grief.
- Parents' self-esteem is shattered because the foundation of their significant role has been shattered.
- Death ends the child's life, but it does not sever the bond between the parents, the child, and the sibling.
- Others may want the bereaved parents to hide their agony, because it makes them feel uncomfortable and evokes in them their own fear of death.

How to Survive the Loss of a Child: Filling the Emptiness and Rebuilding Your Life

Catherine Sanders, Ph.D.
Prima Publishing, 1998
256 pages

Book Byte

The death of a child is an impossible grief. The death of a child is viewed as the greatest of all tragedies. How does a parent survive? The death of a child takes much longer to process because the factors involved are compounded by guilt, anger, and a future interrupted or stolen. Catherine Sanders experienced such a grief with the death of her son, Jim, who was killed in a water skiing accident. Sanders articulates wisely and sensitively the grief that parents suffer not only for the deprivation of being without their child, but also for those lost aspects of themselves. Her suggestions for recovery are important and significant for bereaved parents. She believes that the pain cannot be circumvented; rather, it must be brought forward in its full vengeance in order to heal. There is also a reference section on self-help organizations included in the book.

Suggested Readers

- Parents who have lost a child due to a traumatic accident
- Helping professionals who are seeking information regarding the death of a child
- Family members who are seeking to process their fear, anxiety, and rage

Therapeutic Insights

- Bereaved parents must let go of denial if they are to manage and process their grief.
- For closed families in which communication is perceived as a danger, grieving is more difficult than in open families in which survivors express their feelings.
- A marriage that experiences the death of a child is seriously jeopardized.
- Survivor guilt is a major negative emotion in sibling bereavement.
- The trauma of violence and death (murder, suicide) forced upon a child stays with parents for a lifetime.

On Children and Death: How Children and Their Parents Can and Do Cope With Death

Elisabeth Kubler-Ross
Simon & Schuster Trade Paperbacks, 1997 (reprint edition)
288 pages

Book Byte

Elisabeth Kubler-Ross is a renowned expert on death and dying. She confronts the difficulty faced by parents of dying children. Her message of hope, love, and living throughout the final period of the life of a child is loving and compassionate. In the book, Doctor Ross suggests how to communicate most easily when children are ready, which serves to help them and their families express their natural fears about death.

Suggested Readers

- Parents who are experiencing their child's death or terminal illness
- Support persons who assist with families when there is the death of a child
- Siblings who need to be taught how they can contribute to their sibling's peaceful transition

Therapeutic Insights

- Children are different from adults when they are faced with terminal illness.
- All children know not consciously, but intuitively, about the outcome of their illness.
- It is normal and natural to have to confront the fear of having more children.
- Sudden deaths leave parents and siblings in a desperate state of guilt, even deaths that occur after a long history of illness.
- Often, children are not afraid to die.

Saying Goodbye to Daniel: When Death Is the Best Choice

Juliet Cassuto Rothman

The Continuum Publishing Corp., 1995

180 pages

Book Byte

This story is a heart-rendering account of the final two months in the life of Daniel Rothman, told lovingly by his mother. The story speaks to Daniel's dignity, to the harrowing story of a family's experience with tragedy, and reflections on terminating care decisions. Daniel was 21 when a diving accident left him a quadriplegic and led to his death 10 weeks later. With the support of his family, Daniel decided to remove the ventilator, which quickly ended his life. This compassionate book includes an update on how the family coped with the loss of their son and brother emotionally and spiritually in the Jewish faith.

Suggested Readers

- Families who are experiencing a crisis of spirituality because of the death of their child
- Parents who have lost a child due to an accident
- Those who are looking for a list of resources dealing with spinal cord injuries

Therapeutic Insights

- Like many couples, spouses grieve differently.
- Grief is very slow to move through; often times, it takes a lifetime to resolve.
- Survivors want reassurance that their loved one exists somewhere.
- A life that is meaningful contains a variety of possibilities for action.
- One can only view another's quality of life through the lens of his or her own beliefs, expectations, and values.

When a Baby Dies: The Experience of Late Miscarriage, Stillbirth and Neonatal Death

Nancy Kohner and Alix Henly
Thorsons, 1998
256 pages

Book Byte

The death of a baby, whether at birth or in the weeks or months ahead, is no less death than any other. It is no less heartbreaking and no less significant than the death of an older child or adult. A baby's death is also the death of a person who would have been. It means the ending of dreams, hopes, and plans, the loss of the future. In this book, parents tell the story of their baby's death, what happened, how they felt, and what impact it had on them and their lives. These authors focused on loss through late miscarriage, stillbirth, and neonatal death (death within the first 28 days of life). They address quite adeptly many medical explanations for the death of children.

Suggested Readers

- Parents who have experienced the death of their baby
- Professionals who are seeking assistance in supporting parents and families after the death of their baby
- Families who are seeking recognition of their loss and the cause of their sadness

Therapeutic Insights

- The death of a baby is so contrary to the natural order of things, so unexpected, and so rarely spoken about.
- The intensity of the shock that is felt by families may be all the greater because of the suddenness with which they are cut off from the future that they had imagined and looked forward to.
- Many parents suffer a complete loss of confidence in themselves.
- Parents often feel to blame for their baby's death, particularly when no satisfactory medical explanation is given or can be found.
- Fears and worries not expressed regarding future children can cause unnecessary extra pain and difficulty to parents.

DEATH OF A PARENT

How to Survive the Loss of a Parent: A Guide for Adults
Lois F. Akner
William Morrow & Co., Inc., 1993 (reprint edition)
234 pages

Book Byte

We have all been conditioned to think that people get old and they die; most likely, we expect our parents to die before we do. However, for many, the loss of a parent can feel devastating, unimaginable, and debilitating. Lois F. Akner speaks in frank, compassionate tones about the complex emotional reactions to the death of a parent. The book duplicates the setting of an actual ongoing workshop. Akner shares invaluable advice on avoiding emotional sabotage of self, preserving memories of the parent, and recovering from the loss.

Suggested Readers

- Adults who have experienced the death of a parent
- Families who are forced to keep secrets regarding terminal illness
- Individuals who are entering the world of parental mourning

Therapeutic Insights

- Through the loss of a parent, one must assess his or her own role in creating the system in which the family operated.
- The loss of a parent represents not only the permanent removal of that person from one's life, but all the situations in the future that would have been different had he or she remained alive.
- The psychic pain of mourning is not unlike what a person may feel physically after surgery.
- The death of a parent is a life-altering event, and the lens through which one views the world has changed as a result.
- It is normal to feel torn in two by emotions and to be uncertain as to how to behave.

Longing for Dad: Father Loss and Its Impact
Beth Erickson, Ph.D.
Health Communications, Inc., 1998
280 pages

Book Byte

Beth Erickson's work is about the impact of a father's literal absence or emotional unavailability. She shows readers how to validate "father hunger" and heal the pain surrounding this very specific loss. Throughout men and women's lives, the effects of father loss often show up in numerous ways (e.g., fear of commitment, anxiety regarding intimacy, fear, professional failure, or inability to be emotionally available to those they love). Doctor Erickson wants to assist men and women in understanding the role that their father's presence or absence played in their lives. She explores how a child's reasoning can compound the damage of the loss, how each sex responds to such a loss (differently and similarly), and the issues that may occur in intimate relationships in adulthood. Lastly, Erickson offers strategies for healing for those who suffer from father loss.

Suggested Readers

- Men and women who have experienced the literal or emotional death of their father, either as children or as adults
- Men and women who are looking for connections between the trauma of the loss of their father and current relationship problems
- Adults whose father abandoned them after a divorce from their mother

Therapeutic Insights

- There are fathers who are resistant to relationships due to their own unresolved losses.
- There are numerous behaviorial expressions of an unresolved loss.
- Children who have been abandoned often feel unimportant and unlovable.
- Sources of father hunger include death, divorce, abuse, adoption, and addiction.
- Unaddressed father loss becomes a prime barrier to marital intimacy and competence as a father.

Losing a Parent: Passage to a New Way of Living
Alexandra Kennedy
Harper, Inc., 1991
160 pages

Book Byte

Six months after her father's death, Alexandra Kennedy began writing for her own healing about the events, both inner and outer, of his dying. Most people will have to deal with the death of a parent; few people are prepared to. The prospect of her father's death triggered a process that lead her out of the complacent routine of her own life and into the deep recesses of the psyche, which she refers to as the *shamanic world*. Her concern is not to merely narrate the personal experience of her father's death, but to make readers mindful of how unprepared most of us are to deal with the death of parents.

Suggested Readers

- Adults who have experienced the death of a parent
- Those who are interested in shamanism and its effect on healing grief, the use of dreams, visualizations, and metaphor
- Adults who are preparing for the death of a parent

Therapeutic Insights

- Death ends a life, not a relationship.
- A parent's death can shatter adult children, leaving lifelong scars or a shattered sense of self.
- For many, the shock of a parent's death serves as a needed role of providing a protective transition into the often-overwhelming intensity of the next step, acceptance.
- In grieving for a parent, it is possible to feel abandonment and release, terror and exhilaration.
- Resisting the inevitable tides of grief is like swimming upstream for days.

Losing a Parent: A Personal Guide to Coping with That Special Grief That Comes with Losing a Parent
Fiona Marshall
Fisher Books, 1993
168 pages

Book Byte

Losing a parent suddenly brings about a particular kind of grief and loss. One tends to believe that one's parents will never die. Even after a long illness may give one time to prepare, one can never be fully ready for the ramifications of such a loss. The need to find meaning in what has happened can transform pain into valuable insights. It is Fiona Marshall's intent through this book to help adult children face the death of a parent and to learn to view it as the beginning of a new strength and maturity. This book includes numerous case histories that touch on as many reactions as possible. The people interviewed were drawn from a wide range of ages and social backgrounds.

Suggested Readers

- Adult children who are experiencing the death of a parent
- Adult children who are in the midst of watching their parent die
- Adult children who have experienced the sudden death of a parent

Therapeutic Insights

- Generally, if a parent dies of a disease, a person may be likely to be anxious about any illness that strikes him or her.
- There is the tension of having to deal with an event as an adult, which can easily return one to child status.
- A parent's death can be seen as the beginning of one's own death, or as the beginning of an independent life.
- One feature of a sudden death is that it allows no time for winding up unfinished business.
- A major part of grief is coming to terms with the fact that one is no longer safe from death him- or herself.

Motherless Daughters: The Legacy of Loss

Hope Edleman
Dell Publishing, 1995
324 pages

Book Byte

If one were to speak with a woman whose mother has died, she would probably say that her life had been irrevocably altered. Hope Edleman interviewed hundreds of women who had lost their mothers, as well as chronicled her own brave search for healing. What she reveals through this journey is essential for motherless survivors. She explains how the absence of a nurturing hand shapes a woman's identity; why living beyond a mother's final year reminds a daughter of her own separateness; how present-day relationships are defined by loss; and how to understand this very personal grief. Edleman astutely describes the development stages of a daughter's life, the father-daughter dyad, sibling connections, and development identity.

Suggested Readers

- Adult women who have experienced the premature death of their mothers
- Fathers who need to understand the development issues facing their daughters
- Adult women who have lost mothers due to mental illness, death, emotional abandonment, and neglect

Therapeutic Insights

- The loss of a parent during childhood is one of the most stressful life cycle events an individual can face.
- Motherless daughters share many similarities in the development into adult women.
- Losing a mother can mean feeling stuck in one's emotional development, isolated from family, and a sharp awareness of one's own mortality.
- Early loss is a maturing experience that forces a daughter to age faster than her peers at both cognitive and behavioral levels.
- Adulthood is a significantly different experience for women who travel through it with a maternal void and the memory of a dramatic loss.

When Parents Die

Edward Myers

Penguin Books, 1997 (revised and updated edition)

240 pages

Book Byte

Edward Myers writes a very sensitive guide offering compassionate advice to those coping with the death of a parent. He explores the complexity of feelings that a son or daughter may experience, including the special issues raised by a murder or suicide. Practical matters, such as dealing with funerals and estates, are also discussed. Myers poses questions about the death of parents; he explores what happens more generally (i.e., the nature of loss); then, he examines the specific consequences of a loss of a parent. This book would also be useful to adult children during a parent's illness, as the illness may evoke many of the same fears and worries that arise in the aftermath of the death itself.

Suggested Readers

- Those who are looking for practical information, as well as a theoretical overview of what adults experience when a parent dies
- Adults who are grieving the loss of a parent
- Adults who are dealing with a parent's suicide or murder

Therapeutic Insights

- The grief process is highly individual, and every relationship with parents is unique.
- An individual doesn't owe anyone any particular emotional expression, set of words, or gestures during the course of the grief process.
- It is no one's right to decide what meaning a parent's life held for the child.
- Sadness is a normal and healthy response to any loss.
- If one's relationship with his or her parent has been conflictual, he or she may feel relief after the death.

DEATH OF A SPOUSE OR PARTNER

Companion Through the Darkness: Inner Dialogues on Grief
Stephanie Ericsson
HarperCollins Publishers, 1993
208 pages

Book Byte

Stephanie Ericsson defines grief as the "constant reawakening that things are now different." Combining excerpts from her own journal writing, she speaks vividly of the sudden death of her husband while she was two months pregnant. She suggests that grief is like a tidal wave that overtakes a person and smashes him or her into darkness. It is utter loneliness that transforms the rational mind. Ericsson knows firsthand that grief will make a new person out of someone, if it doesn't kill him or her in the making. She takes the gloves off and does not hold back.

Suggested Readers

- Adults who are grieving the unexpected death of a spouse
- Those who are facing life and parenting without their partner
- Widows and widowers who are facing pain, self-doubt, and fear

Therapeutic Insights

- Whatever one resists it will persist. That is, if we run away from our feelings, those same feelings will hunt us down.
- Loss, especially sudden unexpected loss, reprioritizes life.
- Anger is a natural protective armor for the grieving.
- Death of a spouse realigns and redefines the limits and boundaries of life.
- Doing grief demands leaps of faith with no road signs along the way.

How to Survive the Loss of a Love
Melba Colgrove, Ph.D., Harold Bloomfield, M.D., and Peter McWilliams
Prelude Press, 1993 (reprint edition)
212 pages

Book Byte

This revised edition encompasses not only the medical and psychological advances in the treatment of loss, but also the authors' own experiences. They bring together practical advice with sensitive poetry, to assist the survivors of loss in their recovery. They give permission to feel angry, lost, and vulnerable. These authors encourage the reader to expect to feel guilty, afraid, uncertain, and depressed. It is their intent to help the reader visualize a positive outcome: thriving, loving, and being loved.

Suggested Readers

- Adults who are experiencing loss of job, money, or divorce
- Adults who have experienced the death of a loved one
- Adults who are experiencing not-so-obvious losses (e.g., goals, ideals, or illness)

Therapeutic Insights

- It is difficult to look back on any gain in life that does not have loss attached to it.
- Losses—immediate or cumulative, sudden or eventual, obvious or not—create an emotional wound.
- The greater the loss, the longer it takes to pass from one stage to another.
- One must see pain not only as hurting, but also as healing.
- A person is much more than the emotional wounds that he or she is suffering.

I'm Grieving as Fast as I Can: How Young Widows and Widowers Can Cope and Heal

Linda Feinberg
New Horizon Press, 1994
180 pages

Book Byte

This book is important not only for its wisdom regarding grief, but also because it serves a smaller group of survivors—that of young widows and widowers. The normal grief experience at the death of a spouse is difficult enough, but the unique issues that arise with the death of a young person—single parenthood, financial insecurity, isolation—often seem unbearable. Linda Feinberg, a specialist in grief and loss therapy, uses interviews and professional experience to guide young people through a grieving process that is unique to them.

Suggested Readers

- Young widows or widowers who are seeking guidance and support
- Friends, family, and caregivers of young widows or widowers
- Widowed parents of younger children

Therapeutic Insights

- To lose a spouse is to be banished from coupledom.
- The proof that the grief process is more difficult for young widowed men lives in the mortality statistics.
- It does matter how the person died.
- Some people will shun a young widow because of their own fears about death.
- Children will have some of the same problems as the surviving spouse, but without having the vocabulary to express the feelings.

Living with Loss: Meditation for Grieving Widows
Ellen Sue Stern
Dell Publishing, 1995
365 pages

Book Byte

With empathy and understanding, wisdom and encouragement, this meditation gives voice to the widow's emotions and concerns as she lets go of her loved one at her own pace. It will validate and affirm the widow's loss and help her reach into her individual resources to cope. The journey through widowhood isn't all horrific; there can be positive aspects. The opportunity for growth is powerful.

Suggested Readers

- Adult widows who are moving through grief and loss

Therapeutic Insights

- To the widow, the world will seem as though everyone is coupled but her.
- Numbness is a natural way of helping a person remain functional in the early stages of mourning.
- A person comes to realize that nothing is permanent; life feels very uncertain.
- There is no such thing as normal.
- Nothing can erase memories. They are etched permanently.

When Your Spouse Dies: A Concise and Practical Source of Help and Advice
Cathleen Curry
Ave Maria Press, 1990
128 pages

Book Byte

Cathleen Curry has written a wise and articulate book on how to grieve and grow through the loss of a spouse. Her husband Jim died of a massive heart attack at the age of 47, leaving behind Cathleen and nine children. This story is written from the perspective of a Catholic woman. Curry speaks of being overwhelmed, with only the ability to see endless unlit tunnels ahead. She realized, through her sadness, that she had received gifts and abilities that she had never recognized before. These led not only to great changes personally and professionally, but also opened up a new world of spirituality. Curry covers everything, from prayer to a balanced diet, in assisting the reader in his or her journey through grief.

Suggested Readers

- Widows and widowers who are processing the death of their spouse
- Widows and widowers who are looking for a spiritual perspective
- Families who are attempting to see their way through the loss of a parent or spouse

Therapeutic Insights

- Venturing outside of couple-oriented societies can be terrifying.
- The stages of grief will not come in a neat order, moving from one to another on a given timetable.
- Telling God how one feels is another way to reduce anger and helplessness.
- It is not easy to distinguish between physical illness and depression in children.
- The need to overcome loneliness often results in feverish, rather than creative, activity.

Widow to Widow: Thoughtful, Practical Ideas for Rebuilding Your Life

Genevieve Davis Ginsburg, M.S.
Fisher Books, 1999 (revised edition)
240 pages

Book Byte

There are 13.8 million widows and widowers in the United States. Yet, each time it happens, it is uniquely individual sorrow, as though it had never happened to anyone ever before. Genevieve Davis Ginsburg lost her husband after he died while playing tennis. She understands quite acutely what grief is made of. Just as people differ in the way they approach life cycles, they also differ in the way they handle widowhood, and with consistent unpredictability. Ginsburg explores every aspect of challenges facing widows: shock, grief, surviving the special days, dating, sex, traveling and eating alone, making decisions, family relationships, emptying their spouse's closets, details of living and caring for your home, and how to start a support group.

Suggested Readers

- Widows and widowers who are moving through the grief process
- Those who are looking to expand their support system and establish new contacts
- Family and friends who are assisting widows and widowers in their grief

Therapeutic Insights

- When asked, 48 percent of widows in a survey said they had experienced the presence of their husband during the early stages of bereavement.
- Among widows, the subject of "my husband's clothes" ranks among the top 10.
- Making one-person decisions takes time, practice, an uncluttered head, and a willingness to make mistakes.
- When children of any age become fatherless, the widow tries to split herself down the middle to make up for the loss. She can't do it.
- When an individual is alive, he or she is entitled to make the best of it.

MEDITATION BOOKS

A Time to Grieve: Meditations for Healing After the Death of a Loved One

Carol Staudacher
Harper & Row, 1994
256 pages

Book Byte

This meditation book on grief honors the time of mourning. It is a helpful guide for those who are forced to face the death of someone they love. This book can accompany readers through a difficult period. The meditations contained in this book speak to the personal concern of all survivors. The book is divided into three sections, which correspond to the broad and fluid phases of grief:

1. Retreating
2. Working through
3. Resolving

Suggested Readers

- Any survivor of grief and loss who is experiencing isolation
- Grief and loss survivors who need a touchstone each day
- Grief and loss survivors who are working through the pain of loss

Therapeutic Insights

- The person who has died continues to be a family member after death.
- There is no time limit on grieving.
- Self-esteem and confidence can be shattered after the death of a loved one.
- Death ends a life, but it does not sever a bond.
- Grieving should not be done in hiding or secrecy.

MEN AND GRIEVING

When Men Grieve: Why Men Grieve Differently and How You Can Help

Elizabeth Levang, Ph.D.
Fairview Press, 1998
224 pages

Book Byte

The essays of 11 men—fathers, spouses, brothers, and friends—are found within the pages of this wise and tender book. Men do grieve, and they do care. They grieve differently, but equally. Although grief is inevitable, most people are unprepared for the storm and thoughts it brings. It creates a sense of chaos in all that is familiar. It tests the human spirit. Such an experience separates people, and it makes clear the dramatic difference in coping styles. Many women talk about their feelings with ease. Many men grow weary of tears and attempt to distract themselves from their grief in order to get on with the business of living. Men and women often have very different languages for grief: For men, intellect is often their guide; for women, it is emotion. Through love and care for one another, it is important for men and women to recognize and respect their common pain.

Suggested Readers

- Men who have lost a loved one
- Adults who are helping adolescent boys move through grief
- Men who are afraid or uncertain as to how to process their grief

Therapeutic Insights

- The incongruity between men's and women's ways of grieving clearly takes a toll on relationships.
- Grief has no claim on gender.
- Society expects men to be unemotional and to react less intensely to grief than women.
- For many men, feelings of panic and insecurity are frightening and even degrading to their masculinity.
- Men have learned from experience to push sensitive or painful issues out of their awareness.

SUICIDE

Straight Talk about Death for Teenagers: How to Cope with Losing Someone You Love
Earl Grollman
Beacon Press, 1993
146 pages

Book Byte

This book is for teenagers whose friend or relative has died. Earl Grollman explains to teens what to expect when they lose someone they love. He discusses normal reactions to the shock of death, how grief can affect your relationships, how participating in a funeral can help, surviving birthdays and anniversaries, and how to work through grief as a teen.

Suggested Readers

- Teenagers, between ages 13 and 18, who are dealing with the loss of a loved one
- Parents of teens who are struggling with the grief process
- Family members and other support systems for teens

Therapeutic Insights

- With death, teens will experience many crushing losses at once.
- The only cure for grief is to grieve.
- Some teenagers have described grief as a physical sensation, like an injury to the body.
- Teens must discover their own needs and not let others direct or control their grief.
- Numbness helps the teen initially work through the necessary details of death.

The Suicidal Mind

Edwin Shneidman
Oxford University Press, 1998 (reprint edition)
208 pages

Book Byte

Suicide is an exclusively human response to extreme psychological pain, a desperate solution for the sufferer who can no longer see any alternatives. This book is filled with insights into the suicidal impulse and with helpful suggestions for counteraction methods. The commonalties of suicide include seeking a solution, cessation of consciousness, unbearable psychological pain, hopelessness, ambivalence, and escape. Shneidman believes that each of us has an idiosyncratic disposition made up of psychological needs. One can say that the relative weights that a person gives these psychological needs is a window into his or her own personality. It reflects what makes him or her tick.

Suggested Readers

- Those who are looking for a comprehensive understanding of suicide
- Family members who are caring for suicidal loved ones
- Families who are seeking to understand and come to terms with a suicide

Therapeutic Insights

- The common cognitive state in suicide is ambivalence.
- The common stressor in suicide is frustrated psychological needs.
- The suicidal act is both a moving away and a moving toward, escaping pain and seeking peace.
- For most suicides, the goal is not about reunion with a loved one; the destination is simply to go away.
- Sometimes, the most difficult thing in the world is to endure life.

Suicide: The Forever Decision . . . For Those Thinking About Suicide, and for Those Who Know, Love, or Counsel Them

Paul G. Quinnett, Ph.D.
Crossroad Publishing, 1997 (expanded edition)
144 pages

Book Byte

This book is for those who have considered suicide and for others who know, love, and/or counsel them. Suicide is an unpleasant topic that most people do not like to talk about. No one wants to know that someone is so distraught that they are thinking about or planning on taking their own life. The silence, however, only contributes to the potential of self-destruction. Paul G. Quinnett believes that the more we know about dying, the more we know about living. One does not have to be crazy to think about or to attempt suicide. For many, it is the solution to their problems. What are the other possibilities? Substantial amounts of people have considered suicide at one time in their lives. Step by step, Quinnett examines the thought processes and emotions that may lead to suicide and attacks the logic of suicide.

186

Suggested Readers

- Those individuals who are contemplating suicide
- Families of individuals who have attempted suicide
- Helping professions who are counseling suicide survivors

Therapeutic Insights

- For those people who think of themselves as failures, there is a terrible price to pay—that is hopelessness.
- The feeling that whatever one does doesn't matter is at the heart of learned helplessness.
- To the hopeful, a problem is a challenge; to the hopeless, it is another opportunity of defeat.
- People who drink or use drugs are at a higher risk of suicide than those who don't.
- If an individual has attempted suicide, he or she is at a higher risk of attempting again and succeeding.

Why Suicide?
Eric Marcus
HarperCollins Publishers, 1996
201 pages

Book Byte

Suicide is many things to different people: tragic, shameful, shocking, stigmatizing, selfish, confusing, a cry for help, the last word, punishment, a relief, a weapon, unforgivable. Eric Marcus answers 200 of the most frequently asked questions about suicide, attempting suicide, and assisted suicide. He addresses questions regarding family legacy of suicide; religious implications; issues of hopelessness; methods that people employ in their attempts; and issues specific to young people, to the elderly, and to different genders. He speaks with compassion in his exploration of emotions, such as guilt, shame, self-recrimination, confusion, relief, isolation, fear, and depression.

Suggested Readers

- Those who are seeking to understand suicide and the silence that surrounds it
- Adults who have been touched directly by the suicide of a loved one
- Families and caregivers who are in relationships with suicide victims, or those deaths that are the result of assisted suicide.

Therapeutic Insights

- The suicide of a loved one can devastate individuals and destroy already strained and fragile familiar ties.
- For parents, the suicide of a child brings extra doses of guilt and self-recrimination.
- The suicide of a parent can be so overwhelming to a child that they may put off grieving until they are old enough to manage it.
- When children are lied to about suicide, they may come to the belief that adults cannot be trusted.
- End-of-life issues surrounding assisted suicide are not issues to be considered without information and feedback.

TERMINAL ILLNESS

Final Gifts: Understanding the Special Awareness, Needs, and Communications of the Dying

Maggie Callanan and Patricia Kelley
Bantam Books, 1997 (reprint edition)
239 pages

Book Byte

For more than a decade, hospice nurses Maggie Callanan and Patricia Kelley have cared for the terminally ill. In this compassionate book, they share their intimate experiences with patients on the edge of life. This book is a significant contribution for anyone who is working or living with a dying person. The authors have garnered wisdom and cultivated a keen observation that only the dying could teach. These stories will assist the reader in appreciating the near miraculous way in which the dying communicate their needs, reveal their feelings, and choreograph their own final moments.

Suggested Readers

- Families who are experiencing the final days of a loved one
- Caregivers who work with the terminally ill
- Those who are seeking to increase their understanding of the dying process

Therapeutic Insights

- Friends and family often engage in denial longer than a dying person does.
- Just before they die, and usually without warning, some patients can muster an unusual strength.
- There is often a realization of the need for reconciliation with the dying person.
- Given the choice, most people prefer to die at home.
- The concept of family members includes whomever the patient chooses as such.

The Measure of Our Days: A Spiritual Exploration of Illness
Jerome Groopman, M.D.
Penguin Books, 1998
238 pages

Book Byte

Jerome Groopman has established himself as an eloquent new voice in the literature of medicine and illness. In this book, he offers us eight moving portraits of patients who are facing serious illness. These stories are diverse; each takes a spiritual journey. Doctor Groopman is one of the world's leading researchers in cancer and AIDS. He translates the misery of terrible suffering into a celebration of the joys and sweetness of human life. His writings document a powerful commitment to his patients with genuine compassion and scientific excellence. He identifies the elements that give him hope and strength in the face of death: One is modern science, and the other is wisdom and solace found in faith.

Suggested Readers

- Those who are looking for a frank discussion about death in our society
- Adults with loved ones who are suffering from cancer or AIDS

- Those who are seeking both intellectual and emotional insights regarding illness

Therapeutic Insights

- Being ill can access compassion toward oneself.
- A patient's struggle to reclaim and reconstruct his or her life is a process that enhances the sanctity of that life.
- There is both a deep attraction and a powerful resistance to thinking about the emotional and biological circumstances of death.
- The details of a loved one's illness and death may preoccupy a person to such an extent that he or she is unable to think of nothing else.
- People must assimilate gradually when a diagnosis is first related to them.

Mortally Wounded: Stories of Soul Pain, Death, and Healing
Michael Kearney, M.D.
Simon & Schuster, 1997 (reprint edition)
192 pages

Book Byte

Michael Kearney is a physician and consultant in palliative care medicine in Dublin, Ireland. In this book, he reflects on his personal experiences of working with the dying, and he shows that it is possible to die well. He believes that fearing death is neither a sign of weakness nor a reason for shame. It is a part of what it means to be human. Those who have spent time in the company of people with mortal illness have learned from them that being a good listener is the most effective resource. Kearney describes the experience of "soul pain (primal fear of the unknown) which brings us face to face not only with the needs of the dying but our own."

Suggested Readers

- Those who are assisting people with terminal illnesses
- Families who fear the death of a loved one
- Individuals who are searching for peace and strength around death

Therapeutic Insights

- No matter what is done to make it easier, death remains the ultimate separation, the ultimate unknown.
- The "total pain" of the dying person is a multifaceted experience of social, emotional, spiritual, and physical dimensions.
- Effective loving care of the dying is essential.
- The process of deep inner healing becomes accelerated in the dying.
- If the dying person attends to the soul, the soul will respond a thousandfold.

 **INFERTILITY**

GENERAL

Choosing Assisted Reproduction: Social, Emotional and Ethical Considerations
Susan Lewis Cooper and Ellen Sarasohn Glazer
Perspective Press, 1999
400 pages

Book Byte

Written by two highly respected infertility counselors, this book discusses assisted reproduction technologies and third-party parenting options. Susan Lewis Cooper and Ellen Sarasohn Glazer address these issues with sensitivity of the medical, emotional, legal, and ethical aspects of these high-tech alternatives. The authors integrate their years of experience and research to provide the reader insight into the complex issue that is involved in building a family by choosing assisted reproductive technology.

Suggested Readers

- Clients who are faced with infertility
- Clients who are considering assisted reproductive solutions to infertility
- Clients who are considering third-party parenting options

Therapeutic Insights

- The decision to consider assisted reproduction is difficult and multifaceted. It involves medical, psychological, emotional, financial, ethical, moral, practical, and religious questions. It often involves a challenging exploration of a client's self and the world around her.
- There are high emotional stakes when proceeding with in vitro fertilization. Clients need an adequate balance between optimism and caution.
- Knowing when to stop in vitro fertilization is unique to each client. Continuing or ending treatment is an individual decision.

- Pregnancy losses are often part of the in vitro fertilization process. Often, clients are not clear that they are entitled to grieve these losses.
- When talking to children who were born out of a third–party arrangement, it is helpful to give them this information at a young age. These children will then be more comfortable with this information, and it will help them integrate the information with their unique identities.

Complete Guide to Fertility

Sandra Ann Carson, M.D., and Peter R. Casson, M.D., with Deborah J. Shuman
Contemporary Books, Inc., 1999
256 pages

Book Byte

Sandra Ann Carson and Peter R. Casson have written a book that integrates the expertise of thousands of members of the American Society for Reproductive Medicine. They focus not only on the many techniques that are available, but also on the emotional issues that infertile men and women are facing. In easy-to-understand language, they explain the latest technological advances and include a complete glossary of terms. They also examine ethical issues, emotional issues, and physician-patient issues. Doctors Carson and Casson do this with the information and advice from some of the best and brightest genetic experts and reproductive biologists in the world. The American Society for Reproductive Medicine is a nonprofit medical organization with 10,000 members, physicians, scientists, and health professionals.

Suggested Readers

- Women with issues of infertility
- Men with issues of infertility
- Adults who want specific information on medical techniques for treating infertility

Therapeutic Insights

- For reproduction, multiple events must occur. Some factors, such as lifestyle factors, may be under a client's control; however, other medical conditions may not be within a person's control and will require physician-directed medical solutions.

- Asking the right questions and making choices are actually skills. These skills can be learned and improved. A client makes the best decisions when he or she first accesses his or her foundation on which decisions are made. A person's foundation includes his or her personal values, realistic goals, and the resources available.

- When working with a fertility clinic, ask for the clinic's success rates. Success rates can be measured in several ways and can give a different picture of the effectiveness of the procedures performed.

- Despite all the techniques now available, there are still causes of infertility that are unknown. Knowing when to stop treatment may be when clients have exhausted their financial, physical, or emotional resources.

- Alternatives to pregnancy—adoption or foster parenting—may not be for everyone. If the client and his or her spouse reach this point, communication between the two is imperative.

Infertility: Your Questions Answered

S. L. Tan, M.D.; Howard S. Jacobs, M.D.; and Machelle M. Seibel, M.D.
Citadel Press, Carol Publishing Group, 1997
232 pages

Book Byte

This book, written by three internationally recognized infertility experts, answers some of the common questions posed by couples who are facing infertility. In a general question-and-answer format, they cover the main causes and treatments for infertility. This is a user-friendly resource for couples who want specific information about infertility in an easy-to-read format. The authors also address causes and treatments of recurrent miscarriages.

Suggested Readers

- Adults with questions regarding infertility or recurring miscarriages
- Clients who want a user-friendly resource for common questions regarding infertility
- Couples who are considering infertility treatment

Therapeutic Insights

- Knowledge is power when addressing infertility issues.
- Understanding the cause of infertility is the first step in considering any type of treatment.
- Consider speaking to an infertility counselor. Counseling will make it easier to express the feelings that accompany infertility.
- Scientific evidence that stress causes infertility is weak.
- RESOLVE is the largest national support group for clients with infertility issues, providing information, advice, and support. The national headquarters is located in Somerville, Massachusetts.

The Unofficial Guide to Overcoming Infertility
Joan Liebmann-Smith, Ph.D.
MacMillan General Reference, 1999
398 pages

Book Byte

Joan Liebmann-Smith has written a book for readers who want an unbiased guide to the many different infertility treatments. She gives readers an appraisal of what works and what does not. Doctor Liebmann-Smith gives recommendations with money-saving and time-saving tips, and she does this without influence from any company, product, or organization. This is a how-to book for women who wish to know all of their options regarding infertility.

Suggested Readers

- Women with a diagnosis of infertility
- Couples who are considering infertility treatment
- Adults who want unbiased information on medical and nontraditional therapies for infertility

Therapeutic Insights

- It is rare for there to be no hope of getting pregnant. The field of reproductive medicine is evolving so quickly that what was not possible at one moment may be entirely possible six months later.
- Stress has not been proven by research to be a common cause of infertility. Evidence of this is anecdotal only.
- There are many different tests and procedures that can uncover the cause of a woman's infertility. Infertility diagnosis should involve both partners.
- If a woman is specifically denied coverage of infertility treatment by her insurance carrier, she may get many of the tests and procedures covered if she files for them separately.
- Mourning one's infertility losses is important for getting on with one's life. RESOLVE, a support group, is one of the best ways to get help and support for infertility issues.

GRIEVING

Longing for a Child—Coping with Infertility
Bobbie Reed, Ph.D.
Augsburg Fortress Publishers, 1994
127 pages

Book Byte

Bobbie Reed examines the feelings that parents may experience when they are childless. She explores the frustration, guilt, anger, and emptiness that often go along with infertility. Reed also looks at the choices that couples may have, including adoption, foster parenting, or trying new and expensive medical options. Although dated, regarding medical options, Reed's exploration of the psychological ramifications is excellent. Her book focuses heavily on the role of Christian faith and spiritual struggles, which are often part of coming to terms with infertility.

Suggested Readers

- Clients of Christian faith with infertility issues
- Childless adults
- Couples who are considering adoption or assisted reproductive solutions

Therapeutic Insights

- Working through the loss of fertility often takes longer than grieving a deep personal loss. Disbelief, anger, guilt, isolation, and depression are some of the feelings that clients may experience.
- Anger or loss of trust in God are natural reactions to infertility. Spiritual faith at this time can give clients the strength to cope and move on.
- Coping with infertility in the course of daily living requires that clients plan ahead and make personal decisions about specific social situations they may encounter.
- Clients may need to face the question of whether they can be fulfilled without having a child. Often, clients get stuck and stop living while they are waiting for conception.
- Resolution comes when clients accept their infertility and make the choice of moving forward with their lives. Choosing not to let the infertility control them helps clients begin to take control of their lives.

Sweet Grapes: How to Stop Being Infertile and Start Living Again

Jean W. Carter and Michael Carter
Perspective Press, 1998 (revised edition)
160 pages

Book Byte

Written by an infertile couple, Jean and Michael Carter explore the psychological process in dealing with the loss of fertility. They believe that even with this loss, there is potential for gain. In moving beyond infertility, a couple can find that choice remains. This choice may be found in living childless, or in forming a family by donor insemination, surrogacy, or adoption. Jean and Michael Carter give hope to the infertile couple as they share their own experiences and insights.

Suggested Readers

- Couples who are facing infertility issues
- Childless women
- Couples who are considering other choices after a diagnosis of infertility

Therapeutic Insights

- There is hope in "no longer" being fertile. This comes when couples leave behind the dreams of having a biological child and turn to the possible choices they have.
- *Living childfree* versus *living childless* is living without children in a positive way. It is viewing one's life positively and embracing the benefits of living without children.
- There is always potential for gain in loss. This transformation from loss to gain requires work, time, and communication.
- The power of choice comes when a person decides to end his or her infertility and to move forward looking at his or her choices.
- Being infertile does not mean that couples must define their lives by that loss. Being no longer fertile means that couples have the choice in how they wish to define their lives.

Unspeakable Losses: Understanding the Experience of Pregnancy Loss, Miscarriage, and Abortion
Kim Kluger-Bell
W. W. Norton & Co., Inc., 1998
171 pages

Book Byte

This book speaks to all women who have experienced a miscarriage, an abortion, or a pregnancy loss. The author brings significance to these often unacknowledged losses by naming them as tangible and real. By emphasizing the reality of these losses, readers can begin the process of mourning, healing, and moving on. Kim Kluger-Bell helps both genders face the loss, the disappointment, and the pain while moving them toward acceptance of their situations.

Suggested Readers

- Women or couples with a history of miscarriages or pregnancy losses
- Women or couples with a history of abortions
- Women or couples with a history of pregnancy loss and infertility

Therapeutic Insights

- Breaking the silence surrounding pregnancy loss begins the process of healing. Feelings of hopelessness, anger, disappointment, and envy are not uncommon.
- Death before birth is against our belief in how the life cycle works. The death of an unborn child can be devastating to a couple's or a mother's identity as a parent. They feel that they have failed to keep their vulnerable child safe.
- The grief process is facilitated by seeing, touching, and holding ultrasound photos of the child if possible. Also, funerals, memorial services, or other ceremonial rituals help the grieving process.
- Men are often left out of the grieving experience. Culturally, it is not okay for men to show intense feelings. Their grief often goes unresolved.
- The longing that a couple feels for children never goes away. Learning to live with the longing does happen little by little.

When Empty Arms Become a Heavy Burden: Encouragement for Couples Facing Infertility
Sandra Glahn and William Cutrer, M.D.
Broadman and Holman Publishers, 1997
240 pages

Book Byte

This book, written by patient and physician, brings encouragement for couples who are facing infertility. With detailed information and facts, William Cutrer and his patient, Sandra Glahn, explore the possible medical treatments along with the social and spiritual challenges of infertility. Both authors stress the role that God plays in giving support and helping patients face the possibility of infertility. The book is written from a Christian perspective.

Suggested Readers

- Adults with infertility issues
- Christian adults who are questioning their faith when faced with infertility
- Infertile couples who need encouragement

Therapeutic Insights

- Men and women handle crises differently. Infertility amplifies these differences. Men are less likely to express themselves verbally.
- Sexual difficulties are not uncommon with a couple who is experiencing infertility. Communication is the key to strengthening a couple's relationship during this time.
- Grieving over infertility may drag on for years. Infertility is a process, not an event, whereby a person grieves the loss and moves on. By identifying feelings, a client feels less crazy in the process.
- Family and friends often say the wrong thing. Clients need supportive people who will validate their feelings and be sensitive to them while being honest with them.
- Anger with God is natural. Questioning His purpose is also natural. The mystery of God's ways is beyond a person's grasp. Trusting God brings strength.

Without Child: Challenging the Stigma of Childlessness

Laurie Lisle
Routledge Publishing, 1999
288 pages

Book Byte

Laurie Lisle explores in-depth the subject of childlessness. Using her own and others' personal histories, she presents childlessness in a positive light. She touches on the facts and fallacies of being childless and the challenges of the stigma in our society. This book is excellent in exploring this forbidden topic and in reassuring women that they are not alone.

Suggested Readers

- Women who are infertile
- Women who choose not to have children
- Women who by age, circumstance, or chance have not had children

Therapeutic Insights

- Choices are usually not made with complete freedom; often, they are the result of smaller decisions, circumstances, and chance.
- Many childless women have fantasies about an imaginary child. These can often be highly romanticized. Getting in touch with their own childlike characteristics, such as curiosity and creativity, can help.
- Many women without children establish more important ties to the world of work.
- *Childless* versus *childfree* may be rhetoric for some; however, it can express how a woman views her life and how she changes it from a negative connotation to a positive one.
- True womanhood is not necessarily defined by being a mother.

MEDICATIONS AND ALTERNATIVE TREATMENTS

ALTERNATIVE MEDICINE

Beat Depression with St. John's Wort
Steven Bratman, M.D.
Prima Publishing, 1997
224 pages

Book Byte

Steven Bratman is a physician who practices a blend of alternative and conventional medicine. He believes the scientific data as well as his clinical experiences support the use of this herb in treating mild to moderate depression. During the period of explosive growth of Prozac use in the United States, St. John's Wort became the dominant antidepressant treatment in Germany, and is widely used across Europe. Realistically, depression is the result of a combination of influences. Traumatic childhood, biological amines, repressed memories, brain chemicals, negative self-talk, and receptor sites are all probably important and mutually influencing. In a study from 1993, 81 percent of patients taking St. John's Wort improved significantly. Only one patient reported any adverse side effects. St. John's Wort is a natural plant rather than a synthetic chemical. It is widely available in health food stores, natural food stores, and in some pharmacies. A typical dosage generally costs from $15 to $25 a month. Bratman cites several good sources of St. John's Wort, including Enzymatic Therapy, Nature's Plus, Source Natural, Native's Herb, Yerba Prima, or Nature's Way.

Suggested Readers

- Those who are seeking alternative treatment for depression
- Adults who want to use natural herbs to manage their depression
- Individuals who distrust drugs and are more comfortable with natural herbs

Therapeutic Insights

- Depression plays a role for many people who suffer from extreme emotional reactions.

- St. John's Wort is not appropriate for severe depression, especially when suicidal ideation is present.
- Depression is not easy to self-diagnose.
- The chances of results with St. John's Wort are reported to be high for mild depression.

Healing and the Mind
Bill Moyers
Doubleday, 1995
370 pages

Book Byte

This book is a companion to Bill Moyers' public television series, *Healing and the Mind*. It is an illuminating exploration of the healing connection between our minds and our bodies. This work by Moyers has shaped the debate over alternative medical treatments and the role of the mind in illness, and recovery in a way that has no precedent. In a series of fascinating interviews with world-renowned experts and lay people alike, Moyers looks at the mind-body connection from a host of angles. He examines how breakthroughs in mind-body medicine are being used to treat stress, depression, chronic disease, and neonatal problems in many American hospitals. He probes the chemical basis of emotions and their potential for making us sick and making us well.

Suggested Readers

- Those who are looking for alternative methods to understand and treat illness
- Medical professionals who want to change their medical paradigm
- Families who are attempting to take control of their lives and redefine healing and the quality of life

Therapeutic Insights

- To facilitate healing, one must understand the person within his or her family and community.
- There is a large capacity for self-healing through emotions.

- When a person experiences any emotion, there are effects on his or her immune system.
- The mind-body connection is as much spiritual as it is physical.
- Loneliness shows up as a significant factor in lowered immune response.

Healing Words: The Power of Prayer and the Practice of Medicine
Larry Dossey, M.D.
HarperCollins Publishers, 1997
288 pages

Book Byte

Larry Dossey had begun his research regarding the power of prayer believing it would turn up very little. What he found was an enormous body of evidence: over one hundred experiments exhibiting that prayer brings about significant changes in a variety of living beings. Why has this not been more visible in the literature? Because, as Dossey states, "a body of knowledge that does not fit with prevailing ideas can be ignored as if it does not exist, no matter how scientifically valid it may be." Scientists, including physicians can have blind spots in their vision. The power of prayer, it seems, is an example. Prayer can take many forms. In many experiments, a simple attitude of prayerfulness, an all-pervading sense of holiness and a feeling of empathy, caring and compassion for the entity in need, seems to set the stage for healing.

Suggested Readers

- Adults who are interested in pursuing other methods of care and treatment
- Individuals who feel comforted by the use of prayer
- Those who are seeking to redefine their ideals of space, time, energy and causation

Therapeutic Insights

- Prayer is a neglected area of medical science.
- Other people can participate in creating our health reality and we can participate in creating theirs.

- More people are becoming convinced that some things should be off limits to science, and that the scientist's wall of truth should extend only so far.
- Prayer-type healing may occur outside of conscious control.
- The lack of replicability of healing phenomena and their irregular occurrence in clinical settings is often used as justification to reject scientific studies out of hand.

KAVA—The Ultimate Guide to Nature's Anti Stress Herb
Maggie Greenwood-Robinson, Ph.D.
Dell Publishing, 1999
256 pages

Book Byte

Maggie Greenwood-Robinson is a certified nutritional consultant and the author of over 10 books on nutrition. She believes and supports the revival of the use of herbs to treat physical and emotional illnesses. Kava is one of the most extensively studied herbs with healing properties that can confer remarkable benefits. Her research suggests that Kava can relieve everyday stress, manage long-term anxiety, induce relaxation, improve alertness memory and reaction time, and significantly reduce menopausal symptoms such as depression and anxiety. Kava, although it is new to the United States, has been used in Europe since the 1920s. Kava comes in several forms: capsules, extracts, dried ground root, tea and multiherb formulation.

Suggested Readers

- Individuals who want to alleviate anxiety symptoms
- Adults who suffer from insomnia
- Those who are seeking alternative remedies for emotional well-being

Therapeutic Insights

- People should not take Kava if they are currently taking sedatives, antianxiety drugs, tranquilizers or other antidepressant, or if they are allergic to pepper.
- Kava is absorbed faster when taken with a little oil or fat.
- Stressful events in life can also trigger depression.

- Many people are choosing Kava over traditional antianxiety medications, which are often addictive.
- Kava has no withdrawal symptoms.

10 Natural Remedies That Can Save Your Life
James F. Balch, M.D.
Doubleday, 1999
256 pages

Book Byte

There continues to be a conflict between medical practitioners who seek natural remedies for their patients and members of the pharmaceutical industry. For thousands of years, people of all nations and cultures have used the resources of the world around them in order to remain healthy. James Balch believes we cannot rely upon only modern medicine to deal with problems of depression and stress. He has focused on 10 remedies he believes will improve the quality of life both physically and emotionally. He also offers a 25-point exam that isolates the biological stresses in our everyday lives.

Suggested Readers

- Those who are willing to use natural remedies as a preventative measure
- Adults who are concerned about their health issues
- Individuals who need to change their lifestyle

Therapeutic Insights

- Thousands of men have chosen to use saw palmetto instead of Viagra.
- Garlic, ginseng, and Ginkgo biloba have become very popular among those in the alternative medicine community.
- Full-spectrum lighting may be used as an alternative to drugs for depression.
- Natural hormone maintenance may safely alleviate the symptoms of menopause.
- Osteoporosis can be prevented or slowed down by doing regular exercises, especially with weights and consuming adequate quantities of calcium.

ANTIPSYCHOTIC MEDICATIONS

Breakthroughs in Antipsychotic Medications: A Guide for Consumers, Families, and Clinicians

Peter J. Weiden, M.D., Patricia I. Scheifler, M.S.N., Ronald J. Diamond, M.D., Ruth Ross, M.A.

National Alliance for the Mentally Ill, 1999

207 pages

Book Byte

For people with schizophrenia and other psychotic disorders, antipsychotic medications are the key to recovery. During the last decade, new kinds of antipsychotic medications have become available, which have several advantages over the older medications and are transforming the lives of many people. This book will help consumers and families weigh the pros and cons of switching medications. With clear language, these authors will answer frequently asked questions about medications, and they will guide readers through the process of switching. An extensive glossary of terms, resources, and handouts are included.

Suggested Readers

- Adults who are seeking effective medications for schizophrenia and other severe illnesses
- Patients who are trying to find out what to expect from switching medications
- Adults who want to learn about the difference between antipsychotic medications

Therapeutic Insights

- Antipsychotic medications work to stop or block unusual changes in a person's perceptions, thoughts, feelings, and behavior.
- Medications that stop or block dopamine in the brain decrease psychotic symptoms.
- Psychotic symptoms are caused by a chemical imbalance in the brain.
- Mediations cannot cure schizophrenia.
- Mental illness is isolating and makes it very difficult to connect with another person.

ELECTROSHOCK

Electroshock: Restoring the Mind

Max Fink, M.D.,
Oxford University Press, 1999
157 pages

Book Byte

Electroshock therapy (ECT) has long suffered from a controversial and bizarre public image, a reputation that has effectively removed it as a treatment option for many patients. In this book, Max Fink draws on 45 years of clinical and research experience to argue that ECT is now a safe, effective, painless, and sometimes life-saving treatment for emotional and mental disorders. Many disorders such as depression, mania, catatonia, and schizophrenia respond well to ECT.

Suggested Readers

- For those who are suffering from severe mental or emotional disorders
- Adults who are looking for a safe and effective alternative to ineffective medication
- Elderly, systemically ill, and pregnant women who need alternatives to medications

Therapeutic Insights

- Electroshock therapy has undergone dramatic and fundamental changes since its introduction 65 years ago.
- Electroshock therapy differs from other psychotic therapies in its breadth of action.
- Electroshock therapy is a procedure that induces an epileptic seizure in the brain.
- Electroshock therapy is advisable when other treatments have failed, when normal life is compromised, and when medications elicit unpleasant or dangerous symptoms.
- Almost every patient requires more than one treatment of ECT for a lasting beneficial effect.

PROZAC AND ANTIDEPRESSANT MEDICATIONS

Listening to Prozac: The Landmark Book About Anti-Depressants and the Remaking of Self
Peter Kramer
Penguin Books, 1997
425 pages

Book Byte

Since it was introduced in 1987, Prozac has been prescribed to millions of Americans. Prozac has proven itself as an effective, successful treatment for depression and other emotional difficulties. Kramer believes that Prozac's popularity comes not just from the treatment of emotional disorders, but because it also has the ability to alter personalities. What he saw in some patients was a quick alteration in ordinarily intractable problems of personality and social functioning. He wonders aloud if we as a society are ready for "cosmetic pharmacology." Would people prefer pharmacologic to psychological self-actualization? Now that questions of personality and social stance have entered the arena of medications, Kramer argues that we as a society will have to decide how comfortable we are with using chemicals to modify personality in useful, attractive ways.

Suggested Readers

- Those who are contemplating the use of Prozac for treatment
- Individuals who are seeking to understand the effects of Prozac on their lives
- Adults who are looking for options in treating their depression, OCD, or anxiety

Therapeutic Insights

- Psychotherapeutic drugs have the power to remap the mental landscape.
- Insomnia could be the solitary symptom of what, in biological terms, is chronic amino-depression.
- The stress that some children are exposed to is encoded physiologically as altered neurotransmitter systems.
- It is possible to come to depression through stress, temperament, or both in combination.

- Inability to achieve goals or find access to resources, space, friends, and mates has direct adverse psychological and physiological consequences.

Prozac and the New Antidepressants
William S. Appleton, M.D.
NAL/Dutton, 1997
200 pages

Book Byte

Much has been written and debated about Prozac and the other new antidepressants, but much of the information focuses on the ethical and societal implications of the drugs. William S. Appleton, a Harvard Medical School professor, speaks simply about Prozac, Zoloft, Paxil, Wellbutrin, Effexor, Serzone, and Luvox. A 1992 study found that only 11 percent of those needing an antidepressant drug get it. While headlines suggest we live in the "Prozac Nation," the fact is for a variety of reasons, most depressed people are not treated. One reason for this is the belief that psychiatric illness is due to lack of moral strength. This could not be further from the truth. Depression is often times masked in illness, fatigue, relationship, or job issues.

Suggested Readers

- Those depressed individuals who are uncertain about whether they should start on antidepressant medications
- Adults who are attempting to understand their emotional difficulties
- Individuals who have tried diet, exercise, vitamins, and vacations to manage their depression

Therapeutic Insights

- Antidepressants have been successful in treating depression, anxiety, PMS, bipolar disorders, chronic fatigue, bulimia, and panic disorders, to name but a few.
- Why some people are vulnerable to depression and others possess a greater resiliency is not clearly understood.
- About 15 to 20 percent of people who take antidepressants cannot tolerate them due to side effects, and they are not effective at all in 30 percent of people.

- Most antidepressants take a month to be fully effective.
- The relationships of depression to life events can be difficult to establish.

RITALIN AND PSYCHIATRIC MEDICATIONS FOR CHILDREN

Beyond Ritalin

Stephen W. Garber, Ph.D., Marianne Daniels Garber, Ph.D.,
and Robyn Freedman Spizman
Harper Perennial, 1997
242 pages

Book Byte

Based on hundreds of sources and more than 30 years of research, *Beyond Ritalin* may be the first book to explain in clear detail exactly how Ritalin affects individuals' social and organization skills, distractibility, activity level, academic performance, and other areas of behavior. These authors discuss what medication can and cannot do for children, adolescents, and adults. They identify the 10 most common myths surrounding Ritalin, as well as alternative medications and therapies. Lastly, they discuss why Ritalin does not solve social problems.

Suggested Readers

- Parents who want information concerning stimulants as a treatment for their child's attention deficit disorder (ADD) or attention deficit hyperactivity disorder (ADHD)
- Adults who are looking for strategies regarding ADD
- Teachers who are looking for tools to reinforce academics in the face of a distractible impulsive child

Therapeutic Insights

- There are several drug-related side effects that parents should be aware of and should carefully monitor.
- Antidepressants are slower-acting medications that have been shown to be effective in decreasing inattention, hyperactivity, and aggression for some children.
- Medication is never the first choice of treatment for ADD or ADHD.

- People with ADD miss crucial details of what is going on around them, which increases their sense of failure and alienation.
- ADHD youth do not recognize how their behavior affects others.

Ritalin Free Kids: Safe and Effective Homeopathic Medicine for ADD and Other Behavioral and Learning Problems

Judyth Reichenberg-Ullman, N.D., M.S.W., and Robert Ullman, N.D.
Prima Publishing, 1996
283 pages

Book Byte

People with ADHD manifest their distress differently depending on their unique constitutions. At least 2 million children in the United States are currently taking stimulant medications (including Ritalin, Dexedrine, and Aderal) for ADD. In 1990, the number of children diagnosed with ADD was 750,000. These authors believe that homeopathic medicine is a safe, effective, and natural treatment for ADD, and that it is a better alternative to stimulants. Homeopaths bring the individual into balance. For a homeopath, what needs to be treated is the specific pattern of symptoms that an individual presents. They use natural nontoxic medicines which last for months or years rather than hours.

Suggested Readers

- Parents who are looking for alternative treatments for ADD for their children
- Adults who want to use natural, nontoxic medicines
- Those who are looking for a different philosophy and approach than conventional medicine

Therapeutic Insights

- Patients must stay with homeopathic treatment for at least a year.
- Homeopathy will not make children depressed or dull.
- Homeopathic medicines often result in growth spurts in children and never suppress their development.
- There are over 2,000 homeopathic medicines.
- There are many conditions that mimic ADD, such as dyslexia, other learning disabilities, and vision and auditory problems.

Running on Ritalin: A Physician Reflects on Children, Society, and Performance in a Pill

Lawrence H. Diller, M.D.

Bantam Books, 1999

400 pages

Book Byte

In 1998, nearly 5 million people in the United States, most of them children, were prescribed Ritalin. Use of this drug has increased by 700 percent since 1990. Ninety percent of the world's Ritalin is used in America. Is this cause for alarm, or simply the case of an effective treatment meeting a newly discovered need? Lawrence H. Diller draws upon his wide-ranging experience with the treatment of attention deficit disorder (ADD) to address this crucial debate. Diller is among the most eloquent in his skepticism about the use of Ritalin for children who are not severely disabled. He believes there is chaos in the current ADHD diagnosis, which is blaming children's problems entirely on an unproved brain deficit.

Suggested Readers

- Parents of children who are making treatment decisions regarding their child's diagnosis of ADD or ADHD
- Teachers who address student issues in the classroom
- Helping professionals who make treatment recommendations

Therapeutic Insights

- A powerful group with a high investment in ADD and Ritalin is the pharmaceutical industry.
- The family of drugs to which Ritalin belongs is stimulants.
- There exists no complete understanding of exactly how Ritalin works in the brain.
- In normal low-dose usage, Ritalin generally produces a quick response and remains in the blood stream only a few hours.
- The effects of culture on ADD are difficult to demonstrate scientifically.

Straight Talk about Psychiatric Medications for Kids
Timothy E. Wilens, M.D.
The Guilford Press, 1998
279 pages

Book Byte

Psychiatric medications are being used with increasing confidence to treat a variety of common child and adolescent disorders, including depression, anxiety, bipolar disorders, ADHD, and Tourette's syndrome. As a parent, however, deciding whether to allow your child to take medication for emotional or behavioral problems is an extremely difficult decision. Timothy E. Wilens provides up-to-date information that will enable readers to fully understand what their doctors are recommending and what their options are. He provides an overview of the issues involved in the medicating process, information on common symptoms, biology, causes, and detailed descriptions of the major classes of medications used to treat psychiatric disorders. The back of the book includes a list of national resources, addresses, and web pages.

Suggested Readers

- Those who want more information regarding disorders of childhood
- Parents of children who are being treated with medications
- Helping professionals who work with children with psychiatric disorders

Therapeutic Insights

- There are many people today who still harbor misconceptions about psychiatric disorders.
- Each human carries a unique set of experiences and vulnerabilities that combine to make the person more or less susceptible to psychiatric disorders.
- Parents must consider the range of benefits and consequences before agreeing to a medication.
- A family and developmental history of the child is essential.
- In general, psychotherapies are reasonable considerations as first-line treatments in many disorders.

What You Need to Know about Ritalin

James Shaya, M.D., James Windell, and Holly Shreve Gilbert
Bantam Books, 1999
209 pages

Book Byte

This book contains general reference information about attention deficit hyperactivity disorder (ADHD), and it presents studies about the potential efficacy of various medications, particularly Ritalin, that have proven effective in treating attention disorders and related illnesses. In the past 20 years, Ritalin has become the drug of choice in treating ADD and ADHD. Experts estimate that as many as 12.5 million Americans suffer from various degrees of this condition characterized by three primary symptoms: inattentiveness, hyperactivity, and impulsivity. Ritalin is a short-acting stimulant medication, which will usually begin to work within a half hour after ingestion.

Suggested Readers

- Parents of children who have been diagnosed with ADD or ADHD
- Adults who have been diagnosed with ADD or ADHD
- Health professionals who assist in the treatment of those with ADD or ADHD

Therapeutic Insights

- Ritalin helps people sort and prioritize the constant stream of information that bombards them every second.
- People do not grow out of ADD or ADHD.
- Ritalin can enhance learning ability by improving concentration, short-term memory, vigilance, impulse control, and fine motor skills.
- This disorder is caused by an imbalance in the brain chemistry.
- Ritalin can have side effects, such as nausea, lack of appetite, and headaches.

 **MENTAL ILLNESS**

ANXIETY

The Anxiety Cure: An Eight-Step Program for Getting Well
Robert L. Dupont, M.D.; Elizabeth Dupont Spencer, M.S.W.; Caroline M. DuPont, M.D.
John Wiley & Sons, Inc., 1998
244 pages

Book Byte

This book, written by the founding president of the Anxiety Disorders Association of America and his two daughters (who are clinical practitioners), gives step-by-step methods for dealing with anxiety. *The Anxiety Cure* focuses on the six main types of anxiety, including panic disorder, agoraphobia, generalized anxiety disorder, specific phobias, and obsessive-compulsive disorder. The book highlights an eight-step program for managing anxiety along with action plans for friends and family. This is an excellent how-to book with specifics for confronting and taming anxiety.

Suggested Readers

- Adults with generalized anxiety disorders
- Clients with panic disorder, agoraphobia, or obsessive compulsive disorder
- Family, friends, and support people of individuals with anxiety disorders

Therapeutic Insights

- Acceptance is the universal antidote for anxiety disorders. Acceptance does not mean accepting one's limitations, but accepting the feelings and thoughts that accompany anxiety.
- To understand anxiety, one must understand one's thoughts. The main problem of all anxiety disorders is the fear of the fear or the fear of the anticipatory anxiety itself. The issue is not the outside event, but rather the inside thoughts one has about the event.
- Family and friends can help by not supporting the anxiety disorder. Trying to minimize anxiety symptoms by giving in to the illness and limitations can only prolong and intensify the symptoms.

- Use the Silver Five method as an armor against anxiety attacks. This method teaches people to accept the feelings they are having and to recognize that they are not dangerous, but rather normal, bodily functions. It also teaches individuals how to function in their "discomfort zone" while noticing achievements.
- People struggling with anxiety should have a support person to whom they are accountable. They should set goals for reducing or managing anxiety and practice once a day or at least once a week.

The Complete Idiot's Guide to Conquering Fear and Anxiety
Sharon Heller, Ph.D.
MacMillan, Inc., 1998
362 pages

Book Byte

Fears are frightening. Some 20 million Americans suffer from anxiety disorders, and 30 percent suffer from phobias—and this doesn't count the millions with chronic anxiety. This book covers specific phobias, social phobias, panic disorders, generalized anxiety, obsessive compulsive disorder, post-traumatic stress disorder, and separation anxiety. Sharon Heller takes the reader through all disorders in a clear and concise way, offering help for each kind of anxiety. She appreciates how debilitating anxiety can be and believes that people can conquer this malady.

Suggested Readers

- People with specific phobias, such as flying, stage fright, and agoraphobia
- People with social phobias, preventing relationships with others
- Those who are looking for solid skills to unlearn that which has made them anxious

Therapeutic Insights

- After a string of failures, people risk developing "learned helplessness" and the feeling that nothing they do makes any difference.
- The most successful treatment for many of these disorders appears to be cognitive behavioral therapy and medication.

- Of the people who experience panic attacks, about 50 percent will develop agoraphobia, unless they are treated medically.
- While Xanax and Klonopin are helpful in treating panic attacks, they are physically addictive.
- Breathing, relaxation, and meditation are essential for overcoming anxiety.

Finding Serenity in the Age of Anxiety
Robert Gerzon
Bantam Books, 1998 (reprint edition)
337 pages

Book Byte

In this book, Robert Gerzon approaches the age-old problems of anxiety, stress, and fears from a new perspective. He believes this approach can lead to personal and spiritual growth. He does not believe that anxiety is bad, and in fact sees it as natural and sacred. There are three distinct strands of anxiety:

1. Toxic anxiety
2. Natural anxiety
3. Sacred anxiety

Anxiety must be welcomed as readily as serenity. Gerzon believes that it is the lack of clarity regarding the three types of anxiety that is at the root of one's difficulty in dealing with anxiety.

Suggested Readers

- Those who are looking for serenity in the age of anxiety
- Adults whose anxiety is self-destructive in its manifestation
- Individuals who feel threatened by challenges and change

Therapeutic Insights

- Anxiety and tranquillity, conflict and peace are all essential to growth.
- Toxic anxiety is experienced as worry, self-doubt, panic, and hopelessness.
- Natural anxiety is a part of the challenge and uncertainty of everyday life.

- Sacred anxiety concerns the ultimates of life, death, life after death, and the meaning of our lives.
- Anxiety is inherent in human consciousness.

If You Think You Have Panic Disorder
Roger Granet, M.D., and Robert Aquinas McNally
Dell Publishing, 1998
198 pages

Book Byte

Panic disorder is the severest form of anxiety. Anxiety can be defined as tension, agitation, angst, or nervousness. Anxiety can be psychic, such as dread, fright, or impending doom. It can also be somatic, which includes sweating, trembling, palpitations, difficulty breathing, and chest pains. A panic attack is a direct episode of extremely intense anxiety that comes out of the blue. Panic attacks are devastating and can ruin lives, destroy careers, and shatter families. Panic disorder is more likely to precipitate alcohol and drug abuse. This book includes an up-to-date glossary, suggested readings, web sites, and a list of groups and organizations to support people with panic disorder and acute anxiety.

Suggested Readers

- Adults or adolescents who suffer from panic disorder
- Those with panic disorder who want to better understand this disorder
- Adults who want to understand the role of medication in treating panic disorders

Therapeutic Insights

- Women suffer from the disease two to three times more than men. It can also run in families.
- Ninety percent of people with panic disorders can improve significantly through treatment, with both medication and psychotherapy.
- The possible causes may be divided into biological, psychological, cognitive, behavioral, and sociological.

- Psychotherapy may shorten the time that one needs to stay on medication.
- Caffeine, chocolate, and recreational chemicals can induce panic attacks.

BIPOLAR DISORDER

Moodswing: Dr. Fieve on Depression, Second Edition
Ronald R. Fieve, M.D.
Bantam Books, 1997
322 pages

Book Byte

Bipolar disorder (manic depression) is a spectacular disease because of its bizarre, excruciating, sometimes detrimental, and at times beneficial and even ecstatic symptoms. It is spectacular because people who suffer from this illness in its milder form of moodswing tend to be magnificent performers, magnetic personalities, and true achievers. Although most people recognize that the exuberant drive is extraordinary, this same energy is very costly. It often results in personal disasters, such as losing a job, being divorced, being isolated from one's family, or even breaking the law. There is also a painful and dangerous low, sometimes enough to result in suicide. This book also includes chapters on depression, addiction, and suicide.

Suggested Readers

- Those who suffer from bipolar disorder
- Adults who want to understand the mood spirals of their loved ones who are bipolar
- Individuals who want to better understand the role of lithium in treating bipolar disorder

Therapeutic Insights

- Bipolar disorder, alcoholism, and substance abuse go hand in hand.
- Lithium is now the standard treatment for bipolar disorder and for many other forms of depression.
- Genius and insanity have been keeping company for at least 2,000 years.
- Reactive depressions due to stress are normal and can occur in anyone.

- Only when patients' symptoms are alleviated can they make rational decisions as to whether they want to further investigate their personalities.

We Heard the Angels of Madness: A Family Guide to Coping with Manic Depression

Diane and Lisa Berger
William Morrow & Co., 1992
256 pages

Book Byte

When 18-year-old Mark returned home from his first semester at college, his family thought he was on drugs. In fact, he was suffering from bipolar (manic depression) disorder. His mother and sister share both the intimate and inspiring story of how their family coped with Mark's illness and the information they gathered about this illness over the course of his treatment. This includes up-to-date facts on drugs, doctors, therapy, insurance, and other resources. They reveal how to identify the symptoms of the illness and how to avoid a false diagnosis.

Suggested Readers

- Close friends or relatives of someone who is suffering with bipolar disorder
- Professionals who work with individuals diagnosed with the illness
- Individuals who need information regarding treatment options

Therapeutic Insights

- The causes of bipolar disorder are a tangle of heredity, biology, and environment.
- This illness does run in families and through generations.
- Medication compliance is extremely difficult for those with bipolar disorder.
- Up to 15 percent of bipolar patients commit suicide.
- Not everyone responds to lithium. About 30 percent of bipolar patients need additional or alternative medications to control their illness.

CHILDREN AND DEPRESSION

The Childhood Depression Sourcebook
Jeffrey A. Miller, Ph.D.
Lowell House, 1999
272 pages

Book Byte

The diagnosis of childhood depression can be confusing and often times difficult to identify. As a result, many children go undiagnosed. Consequently, they experience feelings of worthlessness, guilt, shame, and a diminished ability to think or concentrate. This sourcebook helps identify why children get depressed, and where to find appropriate treatment. Jeffrey A. Miller examines how depression manifests during the developmental stages of early childhood, late childhood, and early adolescence. He also discusses the specific facets of childhood depression, as well as counseling, antidepressants, and treatment settings.

Suggested Readers

- Parents of depressed children
- Family members, school personnel, and teachers who work with depressed children
- Support systems that assess children

Therapeutic Insights

- Physical aggression, delinquent actions, eating or sleeping problems are cries for help.
- Faulty thinking that involves distortion, misinterpretation, or overreaction can cause depression.
- Anxiety frequently accompanies depression.
- Childhood depression is an underreported disorder.
- Some children need to be hospitalized for their depression.

Growing Up Sad: Childhood Depression and Its Treatment
Leon Cytryn, M.D., and Donald McKnew, M.D.
Norton, 1998
218 pages

Book Byte

In the last decade, clinicians and researchers have made significant advances in the diagnosis, treatment, and prevention of mood disorders in children and adolescents. Research has also found that depressive episodes are often followed by multiple recurrences. It is marked by sadness, a feeling of worthlessness, and a conviction that nothing one can do matters. These authors describe important advances that have been made in the last decade, such as new classes of antidepressants, new light on the continuity of mood disorders across the life span, and research that has clarified the coexistence of depression with other mental disorders.

Suggested Readers

- Parents of depressed children
- Helping professionals that support children's issues
- Those who want to understand childhood depression

Therapeutic Insights

- The best treatment for children and adolescents combines psychotherapy and medication.
- Depressed children often have deficiencies in their abilities to relate to other people and handle their emotions.
- There has been an assumption that children are protected from depression by their innocence.
- Two danger signs for children are when they not only feel sad and irritable, but they also lack interest in activities that once brought them pleasure and satisfaction.
- Other signs of depression are poor appetite or excessive eating, sleep disturbances, loss of energy, diminished ability to think, or recurrent thoughts of death.

Lonely, Sad and Angry: A Parent's Guide to Depression in Children and Adolescents

Barbara D. Ingersoll, Ph.D., and Sam Goldstein, Ph.D.
Doubleday, 1995
225 pages

Book Byte

This is the parents' guide to depression in children and adolescents. All children experience occasional feelings of loneliness, sadness, and anger. However, when these feelings are so strong and so prolonged that they appear to overwhelm the child, the possibility of depression must be considered. This book teaches parents how depression differs from normal ups and downs, what kind of behavior signals depression in children and adolescents, options regarding medical and psychological treatment, and guidelines for coping with crisis situations.

Suggested Readers

- Parents who are looking for a place to turn
- Parents who want to understand childhood depression
- Parents and teachers who want to act with confidence in dealing with childhood depression

Therapeutic Insights

- Depression involves not only changes in mood, but in every area of children's lives.
- Children's depression is seen in loss of energy, physical restlessness, diminished interest in pleasurable activities, and depressed or irritable mood.
- The diagnostic process is complex in children and adolescents.
- Depression can distort the way children see the world.
- Parents who are themselves depressed seem to have specific parenting problems.

DEPRESSION

The Beast: A Journey Through Depression

Tracy Thompson
Plume Books, 1996 (reprint edition)
288 pages

Book Byte

Tracy Thompson was an attractive woman and an outstanding journalist. Behind that facade, however, was a woman who struggled with episodes of bleak depression. The Beast, as she later came to call it, began stalking her in the 1960s and followed her into a busy newspaper career. Just as she took a leap forward with a new job at *The Washington Post,* she found herself locked in a psychiatric ward under a 24-hour suicide watch. She tells how she came to terms with this mental illness and found a new life at work and home.

Suggested Readers

- Those who want to understand the isolation of depression
- Adults who are unable to articulate their suffering from depression
- Adults who are unable to feel any sense of accomplishment

Therapeutic Insights

- Chronic depression can affect memory.
- There are techniques that can assist depressed people in unlearning bad habits.
- Depressed people can inflict enormous damage on those they love.
- Self-confidence and depression are mutually exclusive.
- Depressed people often feel inherently defective.

Breaking the Patterns of Depression
Michael D. Yapko, Ph.D.
Main Street Books, 1998
362 pages

Book Byte

Depression is a disorder that can strike anyone at any age. It strikes across all barriers, making its victims miserable and robbing them of joy and satisfaction. Its strength lies in its ability to make people feel that nothing they do will ever bring back a sense of peace or satisfaction with life. Michael D. Yapko believes that depression is a wolf in sheep's clothing. He believes that depression can be treated effectively and that the difference can last a lifetime. He assists readers in identifying their patterns for organizing their internal experience, and then he notes how they cause or contribute to their depression.

Suggested Readers

- Adults who have a fear of success and failure
- Individuals who want to shift from focusing on symptoms to focusing on learnable skills
- Adults who suffer from depression

Therapeutic Insights

- Good motivation does not compensate for poor strategies.
- Patterns that people develop can bring happiness and satisfaction, or they can lead to bad choices and form inadequate responses to life's problems.
- When people face ambiguous situations, they project meaning onto it according to their background or frame of reference.
- Certain styles of thinking and particular belief systems can cause or worsen depression.
- Personalization refers to the tendency to take things personally that are not at all personal.

Depression: The Way Out of Your Prison, Second Edition
Dorothy Rowe
Routledge Publishing, 1996
239 pages

Book Byte

According to Dorothy Rowe, depression is a prison in which the victim is both the suffering prisoner and the cruel jailer. It is this peculiar isolation that distinguishes depression from common unhappiness. It is not simply loneliness; it is an isolation that changes the victim's perception of his or her environment. Rowe believes that depression is not a genetic fault or a mysterious illness that descends on people; rather, she believes it is something that people create for themselves, and just as they create it, so can they dismantle it. This is a cognitive approach to depression.

Suggested Readers

- Adults who believe they have built a prison of depression for themselves
- Adults who hold critical opinions of themselves
- Adults who dislike themselves and expect others to dislike them, too

Therapeutic Insights

- How can people love or be loved when they are certain that at their core they are evil?
- Fearing, hating, and envying others robs people of what little self-confidence they might otherwise have.
- Depression is a state of mind that invites paranoia.
- To beat depression is to have the courage to face the pain and the courage to accept change.
- Historically, depression has been seen as a lack of wisdom in living and a lack of self-knowledge.

On the Edge of Darkness: Conversations About Conquering Depression

Kathy Cronkite
Dell Publishing, 1994
331 pages

Book Byte

They have made the impossible climb into the spotlight and attained their brightest dreams. However, for Mike Wallace, Kitty Dukakis, William Styron, Joan Rivers, and countless other people who struggle against the debilitating effects of depression, life's most challenging battle is waged in the darkest recesses of the mind. Kathy Cronkite gives voice to dozens of celebrated professionals who have endured and conquered chronic depression.

Suggested Readers

- Depressed adults and their families
- Adults who want new information on effective treatments
- Adults who suffer from chronic depression

Therapeutic Insights

- Between 93 and 95 percent of suicides suffer a psychiatric illness.
- In hiding battles of depression, many people fear what disclosures might have on their professional lives.
- Some people have a biologically, genetically based vulnerability to a mood disorder.
- Ten percent of depressions have some underlying medical cause.
- It is not uncommon for patients to go off medications a number of times, testing their limitations.

Undoing Depression: What Therapy Doesn't Teach You and Medication Can't Give You

Richard O'Connor, Ph.D.
Berkley Publishing Group, 1999 (reissue edition)
368 pages

Book Byte

Whether the roots of depression are from the past in childhood, or in the present in the brain, Richard O'Connor believes that recovery can only come about through a continuous act of will and self-discipline applied to emotions, behavior, and relationships in the here and now. People with depression must learn new emotional skills. Unwittingly, people get good at depression. Depressed people are their own worst critics. They interpret interactions in the world differently from other people, and lastly, depressed people have negative expectations of the future.

Suggested Readers

- Individuals with chronic depression
- Adults who are unable to stop their self-defeating behavior
- Adults who consistently expect the worst

Therapeutic Insights

- Depression leads to a negative self-consciousness, a tendency for people to magnify their own part in things.
- Depressed people often think in terms of good or bad, black or white.
- Depressed people are rarely good at being assertive.
- Depressed people have an obsessive quality that doesn't allow them to detach or let go.
- Depressed people tend to store up grievances and then burst forth in an explosion of accusations and generalizations.

MALE DEPRESSION

I Don't Want to Talk About It: Overcoming the Secret Legacy of Male Depression
Terrence Real
Fireside Books, 1998 (reprint edition)
383 pages

Book Byte

Terrence Real believes that depression is a silent epidemic in men and that men hide their condition from family, friends, and themselves to avoid the stigma of depression's "unmanliness." Problems that are typically thought of as male (including lack of intimacy, workaholism, abusive behavior, and rage) are actually attempts to escape depression. Terrence Real reveals how men can unearth their pain, heal themselves, and restore their relationships.

Suggested Readers

- Men who are depressed and unable to talk about it
- Women who are partnered with depressed men
- Men who are looking for guidance in pushing through their depression

Therapeutic Insights

- Depressed men use chemicals to keep their demons at arm's length.
- Men are less used to voicing emotional issues, because they are taught that it is unmanly to do so.
- Boys don't hunger for fathers who will model traditional mores of masculinity; they hunger for fathers who will rescue them from it.
- Men cannot recover from depression and remain emotionally numb at the same time.
- Relational impoverishment creates an insecure base that haunts many men.

OBSESSIVE-COMPULSIVE DISORDER

Passing for Normal: A Memoir of Compulsion
Amy S. Wilensky
Broadway Books, 1999
256 pages

Book Byte

This compelling book by Amy S. Wilensky is an emotionally charged account of her lifelong struggle with two very misunderstood disorders, obsessive-compulsive disorder (OCD) and Tourette's syndrome. A powerful witness to her own dysfunction, she describes the strain on her relationships with people she thought she knew best: family, friends, and herself. She describes her symptoms, diagnosis, and treatment with courage and a healthy dose of humor, while gradually coming to terms with the absurdities of life beset by irrational behavior.

Suggested Readers

- Those who are suffering from OCD
- Those who are suffering from Tourette's syndrome
- Family members and loved ones who are in relationships with a person with OCD or Tourette's syndrome

Therapeutic Insights

- Obsessive-compulsive disorder usually begins to surface in the late teenage years and early 20s.
- Once OCD symptoms begin they usually become increasingly more pervasive over time.
- Tourette's is a lifelong disorder and is controlled by the brain.
- There is a large continuum of behavior within Tourette's disorder.
- The symptoms of Tourette's and OCD can be compounded by isolation and embarrassment.

Stop Obsessing! How to Overcome Your Obsessions and Compulsions

Edna B. Foa, Ph.D., and Reid Wilson, Ph.D.

Bantam Books, 1991

247 pages

Book Byte

Obsessive-compulsive disorder (OCD) is manifested by unwanted, disturbing thoughts, or feeling compelled to perform rigidly set actions to reduce stress. It can be as mild as one wondering if he or she turned off the iron before leaving the house, or as severe as washing one's hands 50 times a day. Regardless of its intensity, it can disrupt one's life and destroy significant relationships. Edna B. Foa and Reid Wilson have developed a revolutionary self-help program that can relieve disabling obsessions and compulsion.

Suggested Readers

- Individuals with obsessions and compulsions
- Individuals who are suffering from thoughts, images, or impulses that provoke distress
- Individuals who feel compelled to place objects in special patterns

Therapeutic Insights

- Obsessions are thoughts, images, and impulses that come again and again and are distressing and frightening.
- Compulsions or rituals are any actions or thoughts that reduce the stress of the obsession.
- Approximately 5 million people in the United States suffer from OCD.
- The eight most common types of OCD are as follows:
  1. Washers
  2. Cleaners
  3. Checkers
  4. Repeaters
  5. Orderers
  6. Hoarders
  7. Thinking ritualizers
  8. Pure obsessionals
- Recovery also depends on a strong support system.

Tormenting Thoughts and Secret Rituals: The Hidden Epidemic of Obsessive-Compulsive Disorder
Ian Osborn, M.D.
Dell Publishing 1999
336 pages

Book Byte

Ian Osborn is a specialist in obsessive-compulsive disorder (OCD), and he is a sufferer himself. He has written a comprehensive book on his experiences, diagnosis, and treatment of OCD. He reveals recent discoveries about the disease as a biological physical disorder. He also outlines the exciting new therapies that have dramatically changed the future for OCD sufferers. This book includes tests for self-diagnosis, medication recommendations, early signs of OCD in children, guidelines for families, and a list of national organizations and support groups.

Suggested Readers

- Those who suspect they may have OCD
- Adults who are interested in the new behavior therapies
- OCD sufferers who want information regarding new medications

Therapeutic Insights

- Behavior therapy is the premier treatment for OCD.
- The meat of behavior therapy is in the tasks and homework assignments in which patients must expose themselves to obsessional situations while preventing themselves from performing compulsions.
- An obsession is not a phobia. An obsession is a focus on certain thoughts.
- Prozac, Paxil, Zoloft, Luvox, and Anafranil all work to lessen obsessions and compulsions.
- Obsessive-compulsive disorder is a biological medical brain disorder with both genetic and environmental determinants.

SCHIZOPHRENIA

Is There No Place On Earth For Me?
Susan Sheehan
Vintage Books, 1983
352 pages

Book Byte

Sylvia Frumkin, a highly intelligent young girl, became a schizophrenic in her late teens and spent most of the next 17 years in and out of mental institutions. Susan Sheehan, a reporter, followed Sylvia for almost a year, talking with and observing her, listening to her monologues, sitting in on consultations with doctors, and even for a period sleeping in the bed next to her in a mental hospital. Sheehan brought relentless intelligence and compassion to bear in this book, which also earned her a Pulitzer Prize for nonfiction.

Suggested Readers

- Those who have spent time in psychiatric hospitals
- Families who are caring for a schizophrenic loved one
- Those who are seeking to be understood in their illness

Therapeutic Insights

- The most extreme forms of negative symptoms are seen in catatonia.
- Volition is a state in which patients lack the will to act at all, and there is no concern for the world around them.
- Lack of self-care can be taken to great extremes.
- The most common forms of schizophrenic delusion are those involving thought insertion, thought withdrawal, or thought broadcasting.
- Hallucinations can be visual, auditory, persistent and unpleasant smells, persistent pains, or unpleasant tastes.

The Quiet Room: A Journey Out of the Torment of Madness

Lori Schiller and Amanda Bennett

Warner Books, Inc., 1995

288 pages

Book Byte

At 17, Lori Schiller was the perfect child, the only daughter of an affluent close-knit family. Six years later, she made her first suicide attempt, then wandered the streets of New York City dressed in ragged clothes, tormented by voices in her head. She had entered the terrifying world of full-blown schizophrenia. Against all odds, though, she survived. This is her own very personal account, taking readers not only into her own private world, but also drawing on the words of her doctors and family.

Suggested Readers

- For those who suffer from schizophrenia
- For family members who love and support someone with schizophrenia
- Helping professionals who want more clarity in understanding the world of schizophrenia

Therapeutic Insights

- A schizophrenia diagnosis requires the presence of massive disruptions in thought, perception, emotions, and motor behavior.
- Disruptions may take several forms, such as delusions or hallucinations.
- One person in every 100 will become schizophrenic.
- A supportive family system increases the reality of a positive prognosis.
- Paranoid ideation prevents schizophrenics from being medication compliant.

Schizophrenia: The Facts, Second Edition

Ming T. Tsuang and Stephen V. Faraone
Oxford University Press, 1997
167 pages

Book Byte

Schizophrenia is one of the most traumatic psychiatric conditions both for patients and for their families. The disorder usually manifests itself through significant periods of hallucinations and bizarre delusions, but patients are generally not violent and do have periods of remission. It is often difficult, however, for them to maintain a regular lifestyle and normal relationships. This book provides a concise and up-to-date account of the underlying causes and symptoms of the disease.

Suggested Readers

- Family members who have a loved one who is schizophrenic
- Individuals who have been diagnosed with schizophrenia
- Helping professionals who work with schizophrenic patients

Therapeutic Insights

- There is a more positive prognosis for those who develop schizophrenia later in life.
- Schizophrenia cannot be cured, but its symptoms can be managed.
- Certain forms of social interactions are liable to precipitate serious symptoms such as delusions and hallucinations.
- Families can unwittingly provide obstacles to recovery by being overly engaged in their loved ones' problems.
- Lengthy hospital stays can exacerbate symptoms and cause the institutionalization syndrome.

Surviving Schizophrenia: A Manual For Families, Consumers and Providers, Third Edition

E. Fuller Torrey, M.D.
Harper Perennial, 1995
409 pages

Book Byte

Since its first publication in 1983, this book has been the standard reference book on the disease. In clear language, E. Fuller Torrey describes the nature, causes, symptoms, treatment, and course of schizophrenia. He also explores living with it from both the patients' and families' points of view. This edition includes the latest research findings as well as the newest medications. Torrey also includes a list of the 15 best books written on schizophrenia (as of 1995), useful videotapes, useful resources, and contacts (state by state) for the Alliance for the Mentally Ill.

Suggested Readers

- Families and patients with schizophrenia
- Those who are looking for clear and concise language to understand this disease
- Professionals who want the latest research findings

Therapeutic Insights

- Many schizophrenics are associated with a flattening of emotions, apathy, slowness of movement, underactivity, lack of drive, and poverty of thought and speech.
- Depression and an exaggerated sense of feelings are very common early in the disease; however, often times, these are overlooked.
- Schizophrenic people have a difficult time processing emotional communication.
- People who do not respond to medications are more likely to be sick longer, to have more neurological abnormalities, and organic brain damage.
- Early treatment may lead to a better clinical outcome in schizophrenia.

SEASONAL AFFECTIVE DISORDER

Winter Blues: Seasonal Affective Disorder: What It Is and How to Overcome It
Norman Rosenthal, M.D.
The Guilford Press, 1998 (revised and updated edition)
354 pages

Book Byte

Surveys have shown that most people experience some alteration in mood or behavior with the changing seasons; for as many as one in four persons, these changes are a problem. There are those people for whom seasonal transitions trigger extreme changes in mood and energy, producing sadness and despair. In this book, Norman Rosenthal describes the types of marked responses that people experience and also how to respond to these problems and treat them. The strategies that he suggests include light therapy, antidepressants, and three dietary regimens.

Suggested Readers

- Those who experience depression or loss of energy when the seasons change
- Adults who feel less control of their appetites during seasonal change
- Those who want treatment options for seasonal affective disorder

Therapeutic Insights

- People experience many sensations in response to light therapy.
- For most people, light therapy's effects are felt after three or four days.
- Summer depressives ascribe their symptoms to the summer heat; winter depressives attribute their symptoms to the lack of light.
- Some people have both regular summer and winter depression.
- Children can also suffer from seasonal affective disorder.

 **MONEY**

The Complete Idiot's Guide to Making Money Through Intuition
Nancy Rosanoff
Alpha Books, 1999
371 pages

Book Byte

The biggest roadblock to creative decision making is not having the guts to heed a gut feeling. Nancy Rosanoff provides ample fodder for readers to trust their intuition and to follow those faint, but often unmistakable, signals that seem to come from some distant echo chamber deep in the subconscious. It takes courage to rely on those interior messages because they usually defy explanation. Rosanoff arms readers with the courage that it takes to trust their intuition and to turn it into a valuable tool. Moreover, she demonstrates to readers how to hone their intuition and put it to practical use when making a career change, investing their money, overcoming a personal or business obstacle, or even in developing their spiritual self.

Suggested Readers

- Those who are interested in improving their intuition
- Adults who want to learn how to get out of their own way
- Individuals who want to remove the mental blocks they have for making money

Therapeutic Insights

- Intuition is like a sleeping watchdog that remains perfectly dormant and uninvolved until something triggers it.
- People must recognize and eliminate emotional signals that interfere with intuition.
- It is important that people learn to use analytic skills to complement their intuition skills.
- People must be able to see and to articulate conflicting views.

■ When people intend something, they actually step into a desired state and decide that it's theirs.

The Courage to be Rich: Creating a Life of Material and Spiritual Abundance
Suze Orman
Riverhead Books, 1999
370 pages

Book Byte

Suze Orman is a best-selling author and financial expert. This book addresses the rites of passage that we must all face: marriage, divorce, death, spending on life's necessities and luxuries, and taking care of our financial tomorrows today. Orman's deep belief is that only when we learn to value and respect money in the most expansive sense, will we be able to change our financial destiny. She demonstrates this through exercises, examples, and case studies on how to create a rich and abundant life, starting today. Lastly, she takes on the seldom-explored subject of money and greed, the rewards that wealth bestows, and the responsibilities it demands.

Suggested Readers

■ Those who are attempting to change their financial destiny
■ Adults who are looking for the strength to begin asking themselves hard questions
■ Individuals who live with the trappings of wealth, but who have no money

Therapeutic Insights

■ People make room for more by knowing what they have, by not owning anything they don't want or need, and by valuing everything they own.
■ The emotional obstacles to wealth are shame, fear, and anger.
■ If people feel "less than," they'll spend more in order to feel like more.
■ Thoughts of poverty can dwell in everyone, no matter how much or how little money they have.
■ People must use words and thoughts that encompass wealth, bounty, and abundance.

Don't Worry, Make Money: Spiritual and Practical Ways to Create Abundance and More Fun in Your Life
Richard Carlson, Ph.D.
Little, Brown & Co., 1998
223 pages

Book Byte

Richard Carlson, author of *Don't Sweat the Small Stuff,* has written a book on the spiritual and practical ways to create abundance in our lives. He believes in opening the mind to new possibilities. Instead of approaching financial life with fear, he approaches it with wisdom. He suggests taking more personal risks and asking better questions. Carlson strongly believes in our potential, that we are resilient creatures, and that each one of us has the capacity for great joy, compassion, and wisdom. He prods us to take the first step in realizing our dreams. He borrows from other great thinkers, such as Deepak Chopra, Stephen Covey, Jack Canfield, and Mark Victor Hansen.

Suggested Readers

- Those who are attempting to learn the notion of nonattachment
- Adults who are looking to create passion in their financial lives
- Individuals who want to improve their ability to be more reflective

Therapeutic Insights

- People can make excuses, people can make money, but they can't do both.
- Successful people step out of their comfort zone.
- The implications of moods, as they relate to money, are significant.
- Cynics, critics, and doubters are clouded by their own destructive self-defeating filters.
- It is critical to know that there is plenty of success to go around.

Everything You Know About Money Is Wrong

Karen Ramsey
HarperCollins Publishers, 1999
224 pages

Book Byte

For most people, money is a taboo subject that is rarely discussed with friends, family, or significant others. Most people think that everyone knows more about this subject than they do. They fear that it is their lack of knowledge that leads to faulty ideas that drive lifestyle decisions often in the wrong direction. Karen Ramsey shatters myths like these and shows people how to take control of their finances and realize their dreams. She takes on the 21 biggest money myths. This is not a book about investing; rather, it is about how people can become prosperous using what they already know. It is about people transforming their relationship with money so that it can become a friendlier presence in their lives. Money not only represents security, control, prestige, and power, but it also represents some of the greatest fears of being without, of being powerless, and of not being worthy.

Suggested Readers

- Those who want to raise their awareness regarding the choices they make about money
- Adults who feel frustrated and less satisfied with the role of money in their lives
- Individuals who associate money with fear and anxiety

Therapeutic Insights

- People have been conditioned to think that money is the solution to all of their ills.
- Money has become synonymous with personal identity and selfworth.
- People are more likely to find an alternative to a bad job if they are open and receptive to the possibility.
- A key to personal financial well-being is, Be Clear About What You Want.
- Until an individual has a plan, life is not going to change.

Financial Peace: Restoring Financial Hope to You and Your Family

Dave Ramsey
Viking Penguin, 1997 (out of print)
235 pages

Book Byte

Why do Americans need financial peace? Because in 1996, 1 in 100 households declared bankruptcy; over 62 percent of Americans retired on annual incomes below $10,000; nearly 70 percent of all consumers lived from paycheck to paycheck; and 55 percent of all Americans "always" or "sometimes" worried about money. Dave Ramsey is a businessman and an entrepreneur who accumulated a 4-million-dollar real estate portfolio, only to lose it all and nearly everything else that he owned due to getting too far into debt. Through the turmoil of his financial nightmare, he discovered a new way of life. Written from a Christian perspective, Ramsey teaches the importance of communicating with a spouse about money. Filled with personal anecdotes and inspiring insights from his spouse, they tell of a road map to personal control and financial peace.

Suggested Readers

- Those who need guidance in eliminating destructive debt
- Couples who find it difficult to discuss financial issues
- Adults who are feeling hostage to their financial situation

Therapeutic Insights

- Often, a person must lose his or her money to learn how to hold on to it.
- Avoid the worship of "stuff."
- Take time to prioritize daily life.
- Sacrifice now so there can be peace later.
- A person should find where he or she is naturally gifted, enjoy his or her work, and work hard.

God Wants You To Be Rich: How and Why Everyone Can Enjoy Material and Spiritual Wealth in Our Abundant World
Paul Zane Pilzer
Simon & Schuster, 1997
239 pages

Book Byte

This book is an original, provocative view of how to accumulate wealth and why it is beneficial to all humankind. Paul Zane Pilzer belongs to a group of economists who believe that the world does *not* contain a limited amount of physical resources. Quite to the contrary, he believes that the world is a virtual cornucopia of resources. The erroneous economic belief in scarcity leads directly to the mistaken theological belief that God does not want people to be rich. This belief is further premised on the notion that achieving wealth can only occur by taking wealth from another. Pilzer believes that those beliefs have been incorrectly taken out of context and have been used for two millenniums to criticize the accumulators of economic wealth. Pilzer has served as an economic advisor for two presidents.

Suggested Readers

- Those who are afraid of accumulating wealth
- Adults who believe that wealth is selfish and selfindulgent
- Individuals who are seeking an understanding of personal and economic growth

Therapeutic Insights

- People must have faith in their abilities before they can achieve their goals.
- Individuals must make decisions based on real facts rather than on what the media requires to keep their attention.
- Technology controls both the definition and supply of physical resources.
- The rate at which a society's technology advances is determined by the relative level of its ability to process information.
- Technology is the major determinant of wealth.

How to Live within Your Means and Still Finance Your Dreams

Robert A. Ortalda, Jr., CPA
Simon & Schuster, 1990 (reprint edition)
350 pages

Book Byte

In this book, Robert A. Ortalda, Jr., presents a realistic, step-by-step system for people to get the things they want. He has developed a program that helps people define their goals, take a financial snapshot of their assets and liabilities, predict future earning power, and design their own financial future. He believes that budgeting is not "financial dieting," but a decision-making process. It focuses not on accounting or self-discipline; rather, it focuses on people making decisions about their lives and choosing specific plans to make them real. He identifies three stages of financial maturity:

1. *Adolescent.* One who spends tomorrow's earnings today.
2. *Young adult.* One who spends today's earnings today and repays overspending from the adolescent stage.
3. *Mature adult.* One who finances tomorrow's spending today.

Suggested Readers

- Baby boomers who are unprepared for retirement
- Those who enjoy the good life on credit
- Adults who are trying to change their spending habits

Therapeutic Insights

- More money rarely results in financial certainty.
- Neither the materialist nor the minimalist are effective ways of achieving balance. Both deny the fundamental human opportunity and responsibility: choice.
- The key to financial success for the future is simplicity in the present.
- Debt is like a dangerous and destructive romantic relationship that is both passionate and painful.
- Debt is the financial version of a regrettable fling.

How to Turn Your Money Life Around: The Money Book For Women

Ruth Hayden
Health Communications, Inc., 1992
126 pages

Book Byte

This is a book about women and money. Many women were never taught appropriate, useful monetary beliefs, attitudes, or skills. In fact, many women were taught that handling money was the exclusive province of men. Consequently, women who are uncomfortable with money find themselves at a distinct disadvantage. This book helps women identify attitudes of fear and shame about money, develop useful self-management skills, and learn to change their money behavior.

Suggested Readers

- Women who are trying to make changes in their personal finances
- Women in financial crises
- Women who want to understand why they have a problem with money

Therapeutic Insights

- Beliefs about money and the way individuals manage money are reflections of what people have been taught since childhood.
- Women must identify the specific money beliefs that have stopped them from changing their unworkable money behavior.
- Money beliefs are an emotional response to an experience.
- All change starts with a decision to change.
- Women must learn to set boundaries, and to estimate and to predict the consequences of their decisions.

Overcoming Overspending: A Winning Plan for Spenders and Their Partners

Olivia Mellan
Walker Publishing Co., Inc., 1997
216 pages

Book Bytes

For more than 20 years, Olivia Mellan has helped couples and individuals understand their attitudes and change their behavior toward money. In this book, she offers a dynamic, compassionate program to help adults understand their relationship with money and to tame out-of-control spending. This program includes self-assessment quizzes, innovative exercises and tips on controlling impulses to spend, communication exercises and dialogue to help spenders and their partners, and help in healing the relationship that is distressed by money conflicts.

Suggested Readers

- Couples who are facing harmful spending habits
- Individuals who live on the edge financially
- Those who are unable to control their spending and impulsive behaviors

Therapeutic Insights

- Like alcoholism, compulsive spending seems to be an affliction that willpower alone cannot overcome.
- When compulsive spenders are in denial, they reassure themselves that they are just having temporary money problems.
- The overspender will be denied the opportunity to grow and heal by taking personal responsibility if a spouse or partner regularly bails him or her out.
- Men and women have different defenses and vulnerabilities when they try to confront their destructive money behavior.
- Impulse purchases account for about one-half of all sales at grocery and hardware stores.

PARENTING/FAMILIES

GENERAL

Bradshaw on: The Family: A New Way of Creating Solid Self-Esteem

John Bradshaw
Health Communications, Inc. 1996 (revised edition)
303 pages

Book Byte

In this classic book on family relationships, Bradshaw explores the causes of emotionally impaired families. He focuses on the effect that these families have on an individual's self-esteem and, consequently, on society as a whole. His book shows readers ways to escape the unhealthy behavior passed from parents to their children. He also demonstrates how to make conscious choices to transform one's life and raise one's self-esteem. It is an excellent book on exploring the causes of low self-esteem and how to prevent it.

Suggested Readers

- Clients who are recovering from addiction
- Clients who are working on family-of-origin and self-esteem issues
- Adults who are recovering from childhood sexual or physical abuse

Therapeutic Insights

- Family rules that determine what it means to be a "human being" are the important rules in a family. A child's core belief system is formed by how he or she was parented.
- Parenting rules that are based on shame and abuse are destroying our children's self-esteem. Guilt differs from shame in that guilt says, "I made a mistake"; shame says, "I am a mistake."
- When a child's inner self is flawed by shame, he or she will develop a "false self" in order to survive. This false self makes it impossible to develop self-esteem.

- Shame fuels compulsivity, which causes people to be driven toward having more money, more sex, more food, more drugs, and more possessions. They grow up having insatiable needs.
- A child's beliefs about his or her parents actually come from the parent. If parents are abusive, the child will assume the blame, to make him- or herself bad and to maintain the system. For a young child, realizing the inadequacies of parents would produce unbearable anxiety.

The Early Childhood Years: The 2 to 6 Year Old

Theresa and Frank Caplan
Bantam Books, 1984 (reissue edition)
545 pages

Book Byte

This is a companion volume of *The First Twelve Months of Life* and *The Second Twelve Months of Life,* and it focuses on childhood growth and development. It is complete with growth charts and month-by-month specific developmental stages. It is geared to be somewhat of a minicourse in child development. It also covers such topics as day care, adoption, gifted children, and stepparenthood. Although somewhat outdated with these topics, it is an invaluable resource for how a child grows and learns.

Suggested Readers

- Parents of two- to six-year-olds with developmental questions
- Parents with discipline issues who would benefit from understanding a child's developmental stage
- Teachers and counselors who work with this age group

Therapeutic Insights

- Understanding a child's development can help parents avoid problems.
- Developmental functioning includes motor functioning, adaptive behavior, language behavior, and personal social behavior.
- The most formative years of a child's life are the first six years.
- A child's second through sixth years are an exciting and challenging time. It is a time in which a child begins to assert his individuality and move from clumsy coordination to refined motor skills.

- Two- to six-year-olds are, by nature, shy and not yet comfortable with a lot of people. They are transitioning from their private world of family to a larger world with strangers.

Good Enough Mothers: Changing Expectations for Ourselves
Melinda M. Marshall
Peterson's Publishing, 1994
321 pages

Book Byte

Melinda M. Marshall examines the myth of "the perfect mother." She looks at mothers as supreme compromisers. Examining the many conflicts of working versus stay-at-home moms, she explores the trade-offs inherent in each of them. She views compromise as a woman's strength, which in turn brings balance and fulfillment. The author gathers most of her information from her peers, who have compromised and found balance and fulfillment in their lives.

Suggested Readers

- Working mothers or caregivers
- Stay-at-home mothers or caregivers
- Mothers with overly high expectations of themselves, along with issues of guilt

Therapeutic Insights

- Women often feel inadequate because they do not perform their many roles perfectly. They expect more from themselves than from others.
- There are trade-offs with women who are stay-at-home moms, just as there are trade-offs with being a working mom. Achievement for women needs to be about balance. It is making acceptable choices and trade-offs.
- Letting go of the need to control is more difficult than trying to gain control, just as doing less is more difficult than trying to do it all.
- People trusting their own instincts are feeling confident in the choices they make for themselves and their families. This may mean striving for goals that no one else approves of.
- Just as there are only good-enough mothers, there are only good-enough child care providers. Mothers need to reevaluate not only the unrealistic expectations they have of themselves, but also of their child care providers.

How to Talk So Kids Will Listen and Listen So Kids Will Talk, 20th Edition

Adele Faber and Elaine Mazlish
Avon Books, 1999
272 pages

Book Byte

Adele Faber and Elaine Mazlish offer skills to parents that truly get results. Their method, which has led to nationwide successful parenting workshops, offers innovative ways to solve common problems. Problems they address include how to listen to and understand a child's concerns, how to build cooperation, how to find alternatives to discipline, and how to help a child have a positive self-image. This book is for parents and other caregivers with children of all ages.

Suggested Readers

- Parents who need better ways to communicate with their children
- Clients who are working on listening skills with their children
- Parents who want to enlist more cooperation from their children

Therapeutic Insights

- There is a direct connection between how kids feel and how they behave. We help kids feel right by accepting their feelings. Denial of feelings teaches kids not to know or to trust their own feelings and judgments.
- When dealing with children in distress, it is important to listen with full attention and to acknowledge their feelings with words, while naming their feelings and allowing them their wishes in fantasy.
- To have children cooperate, it is important to describe the problem, give information about the problem, talk about their feelings, and write a note to remind them.
- Problem solving begins with parents talking to their children, and it includes talking about their children's feelings and needs along with their own feelings and needs. Brainstorming suggestions together and writing them down is the next step.
- Encouraging autonomy with children helps them learn to make choices and to trust their own judgment.

The Mother Dance: How Children Change Your Life

Harriet Lerner, Ph.D.
HarperCollins Publishers, 1999
336 pages

Book Byte

From the author of *The Dance of Anger* comes a very unique book on mothering. Harriet Lerner writes about mothers and the transformation of their relationships with their children. She writes from the perspective of a psychologist as well as a mother while teaching the basic insights of motherhood. Lerner writes about a mother's lack of control in what happens to her children, along with how they love their mother with all her imperfections. This is an insightful and witty book about the "mother dance."

Suggested Readers

- New mothers who are questioning their own mothering
- Mothers of mothers
- All women who have experienced motherhood

Therapeutic Insights

- As women become mothers, they are presented with the opportunity of re-visiting their past and eliciting more stories from their own mothers and what it was really like for them. A woman begins to see her mother in a new light, more as a real person, thus helping her know herself better.
- New mothers should be careful of all the advice and opinions they get. It is good to be open to other points of view, but then they should follow what is best for them. New mothers should try not to be on automatic pilot, doing as their family or culture would do.
- A mother's children can love her with all her imperfections if she can do the same for them. What mothers worry about most usually does not happen.
- A mother is not unilaterally responsible for her child's behavior. She can do a good enough job, but she cannot control who her child is or how he or she thinks, feels, or behaves.
- How well kids communicate is determined by the family's emotional climate. Creating a calm, open climate makes children feel safe enough to ask questions and share feelings.

The New Peoplemaking, Second Edition

Virginia Satir
Science & Behavior Books, 1988
400 pages

Book Byte

A revised edition of her original book, which sold over 700,000 copies in 72 languages, Virginia Satir once again touches on the many aspects of "peoplemaking." This is a great parenting and family relationship book, and the author uses easy-to-understand language and examples. This is a book that brings family therapy into the public. In her revised edition, she includes chapters on adolescence, aging, peace, and spirituality. Her book is a classic for all parents and families.

Suggested Readers

- Parents
- Families
- All health clinicians who work with parents and families

Therapeutic Insights

- Feelings of self-worth can grow only in an environment that values individual differences, where love is openly shown, where mistakes are to be learned from, where communication is open, where rules are flexible, and where honesty and responsibility are modeled. This is the basis of a nurturing family. Low self-worth is learned; thus, it can be unlearned.
- Hope for change is always possible, because a person is always capable of learning new things.
- Communication is the single most important factor in determining the kind of relationships a person has.
- A good healthy fight in a relationship can bring trust and closeness.
- "Positive pairing" contains three parts: you, me, and us. All parts must be nurtured for a successful relationship to happen.

Parents Do Make a Difference: How to Raise Kids with Solid Character, Strong Minds and Caring Hearts

Michele Borba, Ed.D.

Jossey-Bass, Inc., Publishers, 1999

320 pages

Book Byte

Michele Borba, a former classroom teacher and internationally recognized educational consultant, brings to us a book specifically for building and strengthening self-esteem, achievement, and motivation. It is a how-to book for raising kids with solid character, strong minds, and caring hearts. She gives practical step-by-step advice with real-life examples for parents.

Suggested Readers

- Parents, teachers, or mentors of children between ages 3 and 12
- Parents of children with self-esteem and self-confidence issues
- Parents of children with motivation and achievement problems

Therapeutic Insights

- The eight skills of personal success for children are as follows:
    1. Positive self-esteem
    2. Self-awareness
    3. Understanding
    4. Self-reliance
    5. Cooperation
    6. Self-motivation
    7. Perseverance
    8. Empathy
- Parents can model positive self-esteem with an "I can" attitude and nurture children's innate strengths to develop their personal potential and enhance their individuality.
- Effective communication is one of the greatest gifts that a parent can give. Children need to learn effective communication skills as much as they need to learn to write, read, and do math.

- Teaching kids how to find solutions and how to resolve conflicts, in addition to getting along with others, helps build their self-esteem.
- Children can be more self-motivated if they are taught to set goals, to develop a plan to achieve them, and to persevere with the understanding that mistakes are not fatal.

P.E.T.: Parent Effectiveness Training
Dr. Thomas Gordon
Plume/Penguin Books, 1989
352 pages

Book Byte

This is a proven method for effectively parenting children so they grow up to be mature, healthy young adults. The parent effectiveness training (PET) system works for all ages and is a training program endorsed by schools, churches, and many youth agencies. Thomas Gordon promises tangible results, such as less fighting, closer relationships, more responsible children, and a genuine respect between parents and children. Although this book was written over 20 years ago, Gordon has produced a training system that will last over time.

Suggested Readers

- Parents of children all ages
- Parents with discipline issues with their children
- Parents with communication issues with their children

Therapeutic Insights

- Discipline can be brought back into the home by effectively managing conflict.
- Parents need to learn the skill of nonevaluative listening and honest communication of their feelings. Active listening can facilitate problem solving and influence children to be more open to listening to parents' thoughts and ideas.
- "I" messages with children can work only if they are used properly.
- Changing unacceptable behavior can sometimes be achieved by changing the environment.
- When parents use a no-lose method for resolving conflicts, no one loses in a conflict.

Raising Good Children
Dr. Thomas Lickona
Bantam Books, 1994
402 pages

Book Byte

Thomas Lickona, author of *Education for Character,* has written this book specifically for parents who wish to raise honest, decent, respectful children with positive values. Based on research in the area of moral development, Lickona describes the predictable stages of moral development from birth to adulthood. He does this in a very readable way by using parents' language and experience. Lickona offers good down-to-earth advice and guidance to parents. He integrates moral development into a consistent approach to child rearing.

Suggested Readers

- Parents of children from birth through the teenage years
- Parents who wish to instill positive values in their children
- Parents who are seeking practical advice on disciplining their children

Therapeutic Insights

- It takes more from parents to raise children than ever before. No longer is the community (school, church, neighbors, and grandparents) involved in supervising children. The social environment (including TV, movies, and music) can actually be hostile to the values that parents are trying to instill in their children.
- The peer group is much more powerful than parents in shaping children's thoughts and behaviors.
- "New morality" includes such beliefs as "Look out for number one," and "Do as you damn well please." Self-centeredness and self-indulgence are key aspects.
- The core of morality is respect—respect for ourselves, for others, and for life in general.
- Morality develops slowly. It does not arrive at a particular age.

The 7 Habits of Highly Effective Families: Building a Beautiful Family Culture in a Turbulent World

Stephen R. Covey
St. Martin's Press, Inc., 1998
390 pages

Book Byte

Stephen R. Covey, author of *The 7 Habits of Highly Effective People,* has written a book specifically for families that build on his original principles. He offers strategies for building a strong family culture in a turbulent world, and he gives advice on solving common family problems. He demonstrates how his original principles can build strong loving families and gives practical advice for doing so.

Suggested Readers

- Parents who wish to strengthen their family relationships
- Adults with broken family relationships
- Adults with parental discipline issues

Therapeutic Insights

- Family members are responsible for their own choices. They can choose to be proactive rather than reactive to change. They can shape their future by having a mental vision or by having a family mission statement.
- Families need to learn to put families first. Families must be a priority. They are driven by purpose.
- Families think in terms of "we," not "me." Members seek to understand first, then to be understood.
- By respecting individual differences, the whole becomes greater than its parts.
- Families become more effective when they focus on the four basic areas of life:
  1. Physical
  2. Social/emotional
  3. Spiritual
  4. Mental

Touchpoints: Your Child's Emotional and Behavioral Development

T. Berry Brazelton, M.D.
Perseus Books, 1994
481 pages

Book Byte

Touchpoints is a comprehensive child care reference for parents, offering a complete understanding of child development. It is a child care guide that focuses on the physical, cognitive, emotional, and behavioral aspects of childhood. Part one of the book is a chronological view of the basic developmental stages of childhood—from feeding to toilet training to self-esteem. Part two, "Challenges to Development," is an alphabetical reference of potential childhood problems. Part three, "Allies in Development," explains the important roles of parents, friends, family, and caretakers in the child's life. T. Berry Brazelton, a pediatrician, looks not only at the medical aspects, but also at the psychological aspects of child development. It is a great, all-inclusive reference to a child's emotional and behavioral development.

Suggested Readers

- Parents of children from birth to six years old
- Parents who are questioning potential problem behaviors of their children
- Caregivers and educators of young children

Therapeutic Insights

- Touchpoints are the predictable times that occur right before a rapid surge in growth. It is when a child's behavior falls apart. During this time, a child often regresses and becomes difficult to understand.
- During a child's touchpoint, his or her strengths and vulnerabilities appear. It is a great chance for parents to learn more about their child.
- If a parent can understand a child's times of regression, it is a great opportunity to understand the child more deeply and support his or her growth.
- Often, the behavior problems of a child are actually his or her struggle for autonomy.
- Every close relationship, from parents to grandparents to caregivers, contributes to a child's emotional and behavioral development.

ADD/ADHD AND OTHER BEHAVIOR PROBLEMS

The Broken Cord

Michael Dorris
HarperCollins Publishers, 1990
320 pages

Book Byte

This is a deeply moving story of Michael Dorris' search for answers to his son's behavior problems. His search brought him to the effects of prenatal alcohol consumption on children's development and behavior. This was a revolutionary book exposing the effects of fetal alcohol syndrome (FAS). Dorris explored the lifelong effects and the struggles of these children and their parents. This is a rare and stunning memoir filled with sadness and love and a crucial message regarding the prenatal use of alcohol on unborn children.

Suggested Readers

- Pregnant women with chemical dependency issues
- Parents of adopted children
- All health clinicians and social workers

Therapeutic Insights

- Prenatal alcohol consumption can cause serious mental and physical birth defects.
- When working with children with FAS, they need structure, consistency, variety, brevity, and persistence. Children with FAS lack the internal structure, so it needs to be provided externally.
- Repetition is important in the learning process due to their short attention span.
- Set limits and change rewards to keep the child's interest. Review and repeat the consequences of negative behavior.
- Avoid overstimulation and intervene before behavior escalates.

Driven to Distraction: Recognizing and Coping with Attention Deficit Disorder from Childhood Through Adulthood

Edward M. Hallowell, M.D., and John J. Ratey, M.D.
Simon & Schuster, 1995 (reprint edition)
319 pages

Book Byte

This is an excellent resource on attention deficit disorder (ADD). Edward M. Hallowell and John J. Ratey have written an easy-to-understand book based on their clinical experiences. It is a book about recognizing and coping with ADD; they show readers the many variations that ADD can take by exploring the diagnosis and treatment. It is informative and practical, and it shows readers what it feels like to live with ADD.

Suggested Readers

- Parents of children with ADD and/or attention deficit hyperactivity disorder (ADHD)
- Educators who work with ADD/ADHD kids
- Adults who suspect they may have ADD/ADHD

Therapeutic Insights

- The hallmark symptoms of ADD/ADHD are distractibility and impulsivity. These are also typical symptoms of children in general. There is no clear-cut difference between ADD/ADHD children and normal children.
- A diagnosis of ADD/ADHD is comparative. It depends not only on the presence of symptoms, but also on the duration and the intensity.
- The earlier the diagnosis is made, the less damage there may be on a child's self-esteem. Otherwise, the child could be labeled lazy, defiant, stupid, or bad.
- A common misconception is that all ADD has hyperactivity associated with it. This is not true. It can occur without hyperactivity.
- In adulthood, ADD/ADHD is a logical outgrowth of symptoms from childhood, including distractibility, impulsivity, and hyperactivity or restlessness. In addition, there are problems with moods, depression, self-esteem, and self-image.

How to Handle a Hard-to-Handle Kid: A Parent's Guide to Understanding and Changing Problem Behaviors
C. Drew Edwards
Free Spirit Publishing, Inc., 1999
216 pages

Book Byte

This book is written specifically for parents who are raising hard-to-handle kids. C. Drew Edwards explains first why some kids are more challenging than others, and he gives parents specific strategies for handling everyday problems. He begins his book with information on understanding the challenging child, and then he provides tips and skills to identify and correct the problem behaviors. Edwards has written a book with good insight and advice for parents who are struggling with hard-to-handle children and with ADD/ADHD children.

Suggested Readers

- Parents of kids with behavior problems
- Parents of kids with ADD/ADHD
- Teachers who work with difficult or hard-to-handle kids

Therapeutic Insights

- Parenting a hard-to-handle child can be exhausting. Irritability, anger, arguing, disobedience, and failing to accept responsibility for actions are common behaviors of hard-to-handle children. Parents can look at their own feelings and their reactions to their child as good indicators of the level of difficulty.
- Frequently, hard-to-handle kids are diagnosed with ADHD, which is a complex disorder of impulsivity, hyperactivity, and inattention.
- Strong aggression, stealing, chronic lying, cruelty, and setting fires are warning signs of severe problems. Professional help is strongly encouraged.
- Authoritative parents can provide direction and structure along with a lot of nurturing and support. It is a balance between responsiveness and requiring responsibility.
- A "home economy" system combines positive and negative feedback while making expectations and consequences clear to the child.

Raising Your Spirited Child: A Guide For Parents Whose Child Is More Intense, Sensitive, Perceptive, Persistent and Energetic

Mary Sheedy Kuschinka
Harper Perennial, 1998
302 pages

Book Byte

Spirited kids are often considered "strong-willed" or "difficult," and they can easily frustrate and overwhelm parents. They are actually more intense, more sensitive, more perceptive, more persistent, and more energetic. This author, a licensed teacher and parent educator, has now written a guide for understanding children with this type of temperament. She calls these children spirited and offers emotional support and specific strategies to parents.

Suggested Readers

- Parents of temperamental or strong-willed children
- Parents needing emotional support and specific strategies for parenting spirited children
- Educators who work with spirited children

Therapeutic Insights

- Spirited children are often labeled difficult children due to their intensity and energy.
- Labels can be devastating to children. It is important to positively reframe the labels used with spirited children.
- By recognizing the strengths of both introverts and extroverts, it is easier for parents to accept their style and their child's. Extroverts draw their energy from other people. Introverts get their energy from being alone.
- By managing children's intensity well, they have the potential to be extremely creative rather than to cause havoc and destruction.
- Recognize children's achievements rather than focus on what they have done wrong.

Your Kid Has ADHD, Now What?: A Handbook for Parents, Educators & Practitioners
Janette M. Schaub
Beavers Pond Publishing & Printing, 1998
396 pages

Book Byte

Janette M. Schaub has written an up-to-date book on one of the most common childhood disorders that is perhaps the most misunderstood. She brings to the readers a new understanding of this disorder based on current research and controlled studies. It is a handbook written for parents, educators, and practitioners that contains a wealth of information. Schaub does an excellent job of providing information to the readers on the diagnosis of ADHD as well as what parents and educators can do at home and at school to help their children.

Suggested Readers

- Parents of ADHD children
- Educators of ADHD children
- Practitioners who work with ADHD children

Therapeutic Insights

- School underachievement is the number one symptom of ADHD. The most effective treatment includes parent education, behavior management, medication, academic support, social skills training, and counseling for the child and the family.
- There are multiple causes of ADHD. Poor parenting, brain damage, sugar, or food additives are not causes.
- Symptoms of ADHD are usually inconsistent. The environment, the nature of the task, or whom the child is interacting with are all variables. A child's impulsivity is often the major problem underlying ADHD. Hyperactivity does not occur in all ADHD children.
- A parent or educator can redirect a child's behavior by telling him or her what to do, not what not to do. Giving specific positive feedback can reinforce the child's behavior.
- A parent can learn to stop the cycle of noncompliance by stopping the pattern of repeating, reasoning, arguing, or threatening. "1, 2, 3, Magic" is a discipline technique to help the parent do this.

DEVELOPMENTAL DISABILITIES

We'll Paint the Octopus Red

Stephanie Stuve-Bodeen
Woodbine House, 1998
44 pages

Book Byte

This is a children's book written for siblings of Down's syndrome children. The author has written it through the eyes of a young girl who has a baby brother born with Down's syndrome. The book addresses sibling rivalry and brings to light the many ways Down's syndrome children are just like other children. The author ends the book with a series of commonly asked questions and answers about Down's syndrome.

Suggested Readers

- Parents of Down's syndrome children between ages 3 and 6
- Siblings of Down's syndrome children between ages 3 and 6
- Families of Down's syndrome children

Therapeutic Insights

- In many ways, having a sibling with Down's syndrome is just like having any other sibling. Although different in how he or she looks and learns, the Down's syndrome sibling can still do many things with older brothers and sisters and is still very much part of the family.
- Elder children often fear losing their place in the family when a new baby is born. Once they understand the positive benefits of being an older sibling, they will adapt more easily.
- The Down's syndrome child looks different and learns at a slower pace, but he or she looks like other members of the family and has his or her own personality.

PARENTING TEENS

Get Out of My Life, but First Could You Drive Me and Cheryl to the Mall: A Parent's Guide to the New Teenager
Anthony E. Wolf
Noonday Press, 1991
204 pages

Book Byte

Anthony E. Wolf offers assistance and advice for parents of adolescents. He empathizes with parents but does not belittle teens. Wolf believes teens of today act differently than their parents did when they were teens; thus, parents must have new approaches to communicating with them. In his book, the author describes the difficulty between boys and girls and the psychological rules that dictate teens' behaviors.

Suggested Readers

- Parents of adolescents who are struggling with communication issues
- Therapists who work with adolescents and parents
- Parents who have conflictual relationships with their teens

Therapeutic Insights

- Adolescence is a time of transformation. There are distinct differences in how boys and girls go through this period of life.
- The main focus of the adolescent years is the emergence of their sexuality and the beginning of their separation from their childhood and parents.
- As teens establish their independence, a parent's main task is to let go while maintaining limits. Parents need to ride out the "storms" while giving the teens love.
- A parent's greatest error is believing that disobedience means a total loss of control. This belief can lead to negative consequences.
- Conflict is not necessarily bad, as it is a teen's struggle to become independent. Conflict is inevitable. How a parent handles it makes the difference.

Positive Parenting Your Teens: The A to Z Book of Sound Advice and Practical Solutions

Karen Renshaw Joslin and Mary Bunting Decher
Fawcett Books, 1997
448 pages

Book Byte

This is a handbook written for parents of teens that gives practical advice and solutions on a comprehensive list of problems. The authors teach techniques that emphasize active listening, cooperation, and mutual respect with the teen. They do this by pinpointing problems, providing solutions with sample dialogue, and guiding parents through each problem. It is an easy-to-use book for parents of teens, and it covers topics from homework to sex. The authors also detail preventive measures to incorporate into everyday parenting.

Suggested Readers

- Parents who are challenged by raising teenagers
- Adults who have a conflictual relationship with their teen
- Therapists who work with adolescents and parents

Therapeutic Insights

- Parents must love their teens unconditionally, letting them know that they are special and that the parents' love is not based on their behavior, but on who they are.
- Setting limits lets a teen know that he or she is responsible for his or her actions. The parents give the teen the message that they trust him or her and they know that he or she can handle situations. It also lets the teen know that if he or she makes mistakes, the parents will trust that he or she knows how to repair the mistakes.
- A teen's self-esteem is changing rapidly in many areas. This rate of change may not be identical to other teens. Parents need to respect their teen's uniqueness.
- Parents should focus more on what their teen does right than on his or her mistakes. All situations have some good involved. Build on the good.
- Parents' words and actions have influence on their teen. They need to model the behavior they wish to see from their teen. Parents need to build a bond of mutual respect, not by demanding it, but by reassuring and understanding.

Real Boys: Rescuing Our Sons from the Myths of Boyhood

William Pollack, Ph.D.

Henry Holt & Co., Inc., 1999

447 pages

Book Byte

William Pollack addresses society's expectations of manhood and explores why so many boys are sad, lonely, and confused, although they appear confident and tough. He examines the process by which parents treat young boys as men and raise them through a toughening process. This in turn drives their emotions underground. Just as *Reviving Ophelia* addresses the crisis facing adolescent girls, *Real Boys* looks at the real needs of our male children.

Suggested Readers

- Parents of male children
- Families with male children
- Educators and professionals who work with male children

Therapeutic Insights

- Our views of boys is distorted by society's myths of manhood. The stereotypes are limiting and false.
- Often, boys appear all right on the surface, but they are suffering from isolation and confusion. They mask their vulnerability with toughness.
- Studies have shown that boys are falling behind in the educational system and that they are more often labeled as learning-disabled than girls.
- Society judges boys' behavior against outmoded ideas. This in turn causes them to limit themselves emotionally. Boys learn to hide their emotions behind a mask.
- We can connect and support our boys by becoming aware of the stereotypes, recognizing the words they use when they are troubled, and learning to get our sons to talk by finding safe places where they can open up and be validated.

Reviving Ophelia: Saving the Selves of Adolescent Girls
Mary Pipher, Ph.D.
Ballentine Books, 1995 (reissue edition)
304 pages

Book Byte

Mary Pipher explores why American adolescent girls are more susceptible to depression, eating disorders, and addictions than ever before. She believes we are raising our girls in a looks-obsessed, media-saturated culture. Pipher, who has treated girls for more than 20 years, believes our culture has stifled young girls' creative spirits, thus destroying their self-esteem. This book is composed of stories of adolescent girls and their struggles.

Suggested Readers

- Parents who are raising daughters
- Teachers and educators of young girls
- Adolescent girls with low self-esteem

Therapeutic Insights

- Adolescence for girls is more difficult than it was 30 years ago and even more difficult than 10 years ago. Childhood keeps growing shorter.
- Girls have been trained to be feminine at all costs. They are trained to be image-conscious and look-obsessed. They are taught to be what our culture wants them to be, not what they want. They are taught to achieve, but not too much.
- Adolescence is a time of great change, and it's the most formative time in girls' lives. During this time, choices are made with long-term implications.
- It is difficult within families to find a balance between security and freedom, along with conformity and autonomy for adolescents.
- Worshipping the god of thinness can lead to bulimia, anorexia, and compulsive eating. Alcohol, drugs, sex, and violence are symptoms of young girls' grief at the loss of their selves.

The Roller Coaster Years: Raising Your Child Through the Maddening, Yet Magical Middle School Years

Charlene C. Giannetti and Margaret Sargarese
Broadway Books, 1997
308 pages

Book Byte

The Roller Coaster Years is a guide to mastering the ups and downs of the early teenage years. It is aimed at parents of 10- to 15-year-olds, and it draws information from parents, teachers, and teens themselves. The authors attempt to cover all facets of adolescence, including physical, social, emotional, and intellectual development. This is a user-friendly guide with great advice on these difficult years.

Suggested Readers

- Parents, teachers, and counselors of teens between ages 10 and 15
- Parents of teens who are struggling with self-esteem and body image issues
- Parents who are concerned about the effects of peer pressure on their teens

Therapeutic Insights

- The roller coaster of emotions is the biggest challenge in dealing with teens between the ages of 10 and 15.
- Young boys and girls often have distorted images of their bodies. There are strategies that parents can follow to help shatter these distortions.
- When a child says "leave me alone," he or she may simply want more privacy, not necessarily for the parent to go away.
- Parental involvement is key when helping children avoid tobacco, alcohol, and drugs. Teaching teens how to handle peer pressure is crucial.
- Good parenting that includes care, support, participation, and expectations develops resiliency in teens.

RAISING CHILDREN OF COLOR/MULTIRACIAL FAMILIES

I'm Chocolate, You're Vanilla: Raising Healthy Black and Biracial Children in a Race-Conscious World

Marguerite A. Wright

Jossey-Bass, Inc., Publishers, 1998

256 pages

Book Byte

Marguerite A. Wright has written a book for parents and educators of black and biracial children. She contends that young children are unable to handle racial prejudice and believes that shielding young children can increase their self-esteem. *I'm Chocolate, You're Vanilla* is filled with commonsense advice on practical issues facing black and biracial children in a race-conscious world. Her focus is on educating black and biracial children about race while maintaining their innate optimism and resiliency. She teaches parents and educators how to reduce racism's impact on children.

Suggested Readers

- Parents of biracial children
- Parents of black children
- Educators of black and biracial children

Therapeutic Insights

- Children are too immature to handle or cope with pervasive racial bigotry. It is better if parents shield kids from this information as long as possible. Love and security bring a high sense of self-worth to black and biracial children.
- Children come to understand race differently as they pass through developmental stages. As children develop from preschoolers to teens, they begin to face tough race-related issues.
- A preschooler's self-concept is formed by parents and caregivers. It is not so much what a child experiences, but how the important people around him interpret the world.
- Black and biracial children with low self-esteem experience problems as a direct result of the care given by caregivers and parents.

- By age 8, black and biracial children are beginning to learn about racial stereotypes. Stereotypes are learned from the media, television, and music. Some are positive, others negative.

Raising Black Children: Two Leading Psychiatrists Confront the Educational, Social, and Emotional Problems Facing Black Children

James P. Comer, M.D., and Alvin F. Poussaint, M.D.
Plume/Penguin Books, 1992
436 pages

Book Byte

In this book for parents and teachers of black children, James P. Comer and Alvin F. Poussaint address the specific and unique issues facing African-American children. They offer practical and commonsense advice on nearly 1,000 common child-rearing questions. In particular, they focus on building self-esteem in a white-dominated culture, which is often unconsciously racist.

Suggested Readers

- African-American families
- Educators of African-American pupils
- Clients of all races who want to gain sensitivity to African-American kids

Therapeutic Insights

- The economic hardships of many African-American families affect their children directly.
- African-American children are forced to learn to live in two cultures with two sets of rules. In the majority white culture, they are taught to contain their aggression, whereas it is expressed freely in the black culture. This often leads to black-on-black violence.
- Being well educated is one way to prepare black children for living in the white-dominated culture. Education can instill self-confidence, black pride, and appropriate assertiveness.

- I.Q. tests are often culturally biased and racist. Often, what appear as differences on psychological tests are the results of experience and training.
- Children need to be raised in homes with love and security, regardless of their economic level. Involvement by parents, grandparents, uncles, and aunts is crucial.

STEPPARENTING AND SINGLE-PARENT FAMILIES

Blending Families: A Guide for Parents, Stepparents, and Everyone Building A Successful New Family

Elaine Fantle Shimberg
Berkley Publishing Group, 1999
217 pages

Book Byte

Elaine Fantle Shimberg, a medical writer and mother of five, has written an insightful and practical guide to blending families. With the growing rate of divorces and second marriages, new family structures are being formed. Shimberg offers viable solutions to address the unique problems and needs of these families. With real-life stories, she explains the viewpoints of all involved and shows how to navigate the unique situations that these families face.

Suggested Readers

- Blended families
- Clients who are considering second marriages
- Stepparents

Therapeutic Insights

- Problems need to be acknowledged early. Discuss issues before the wedding takes place.
- Effective communication, which includes active listening, is one of the most important skills to develop in a blended-family situation.
- The stepparent and parent of the child need to discuss and agree upon which rules to enforce and how to do this. A stepparent should move slowly

when enforcing discipline. The biological parent should take the lead unless he or she is absent.

- Financial issues, next to discipline, are one of the most emotionally laden subjects. Single parents are used to making decisions independently. Remember to view the blended family as a team and, thus, discuss all major purchases.
- The marriage needs time and space. Often, all the energy and effort go into the children. Bonding with a spouse and strengthening the marriage will provide unity for the whole family.

The Complete Single Mother: Reassuring Answers to Your Most Challenging Concerns

Andrea Engber and Leah Klungness, Ph.D.
Adams Media Corp., 1995
411 pages

Book Byte

The Complete Single Mother is a comprehensive guide to answering the most challenging concerns of single mothers. This book is filled with practical information and commonsense advice on issues including finances, handling custody issues, work pressures, collecting child support, and much more. Written by the founder of the National Organization of Single Mothers, Andrea Engber, and the advisor to the National Organization of Single Mothers, Leah Klungness, the book offers expert information on a single mother caring for herself and raising good children.

Suggested Readers

- Divorced single mothers
- Widowed single mothers
- Single mothers by choice

Therapeutic Insights

- A single mother needs to acknowledge and handle her feelings about an involved father. It is a loss that must be accepted.

- Single mothers need to take time for themselves. They need to be careful not to become overwhelmed by all they have to do. They should prioritize what is really important.
- Being a successful single mother begins with her own self-esteem. This means appreciating her own worth and importance and being accountable to herself and then to others. She can cultivate feelings of self-worth by treating herself with patience, love, and encouragement.
- The essence of a single mother being a good parent is putting her own needs first. A child grows and develops according to the parent's growth and development.
- Answer daddy questions honestly, directly, and age appropriately.

The Enlightened Stepmother: Revolutionizing the Role

Perdita Kirkness Norwood with Terry Wingender
Avon Books, 1999
454 pages

Book Byte

This is a book written for stepmothers by a stepmother. Rather than looking at how children adjust in a blended family, Perdita Kirkness Norwood approaches the subject from the perspective of the stepmother. She covers such topics as getting off to the right start, understanding the stages that every stepfamily goes through, and avoiding feeling guilty about circumstances beyond the stepmother's control. This is a great user-friendly book with comprehensive information about being a stepmother.

Suggested Readers

- New stepmothers
- Veteran stepmothers
- Potential stepmothers

Therapeutic Insights

- Preparation is essential. Women should begin the relationship the way they wish for it to be in the future. Courtesy and respect are the basis for any good relationship.

- There are no job descriptions. Every stepmother is unique in her role. The stepmother is the female head of the household. Her role is pivotal within the stepfamily.
- Making the marriage a priority is essential. Providing a united front must come first before working on other relationships. Recognize and accept the bond that a husband has with his children. This bond will be forever.
- Affirm mutual respect and fairness, and err on the side of overdiscussion in the new family.
- By developing a working relationship with the mother of the stepmother's children, many potential problems can be avoided. It is a myth that women are natural adversaries.

Family Rules: Helping Stepfamilies and Single Parents Build Happy Homes
Jeanette Lofas, C.S.W.
Kensington, 1998
164 pages

Book Byte

Jeanette Lofas, C.S.W., has written an easy-to-read guide for divorced, repartnered, and single-parent households. Her book focuses on family rules that will create a well-run family team based on respect. With the goal of bringing stability and tranquility to these families, the author gives simple dos and don'ts for everyday living. Her book consists of 53 family rules covering topics from visitation to creating a good partnership. This is a straightforward, no-nonsense book on making blended families work.

Suggested Readers

- Blended families
- Single-parent homes
- Stepparents

Therapeutic Insights

- Quality parenting is about close talk and togetherness, along with taking charge of the household and using discipline appropriately.
- Parents must be in charge and manage the home as they would their careers. Having realistic expectations is important for success.
- The family is a team; the parents are the coaches. Children like structure, predictability, and consistency.
- Family rituals bring a family together and become times that are remembered.
- Rules for visitation must be clear. It is important to learn to coparent with your ex-spouse. It is good for the children.

Living in a Stepfamily Without Getting Stepped On: Helping Your Children Survive the Birth Order Blender

Dr. Kevin Leman
Thomas Nelson Publications, 1994
282 pages

Book Byte

Author of *The Birth Order Book,* Kevin Leman brings us insights and information on helping children survive a blended-family situation. With a focus on birth order, Leman explores the many changes that children experience when their place in the family unit changes. The author calls this the "birth order blender," when two families are brought together by marriage and there is a collision or rearrangement of children's birth order in the new family.

Suggested Readers

- All blended families
- Clients with children who are considering remarriage
- Stepmothers and stepfathers

Therapeutic Insights

- Blending a family may take years. Children often feel betrayed. Understanding the blend of the children's birth orders gives the new family a greater chance for survival.

- Perfectionism is the cornerstone of many firstborns and only children.
- Last borns need lots of attention in the stepfamily.
- Middle children often feel ignored and left out. They are usually very sociable, peacemakers, risk takers, and easy to get along with.
- The blending process can be successful with lots of love and knowledge of the children's birth order position and repositioning in the new family.

Parenting Keys: Keys to Successful Step-Fathering
Carl E. Pickhardt, Ph.D.
Barron's Educational Series, Inc., 1997
182 pages

Book Byte

Carl E. Pickhardt has written a very practical book with commonsense advice on how to be an effective stepfather. He teaches the practice of tolerance, compassion, and understanding while establishing oneself in the new family structure. Pickhardt believes a man can be effective as a stepfather while maintaining a healthy marriage.

Suggested Readers

- Stepfathers
- Men who are considering remarriage with children
- Parents of blended families

Therapeutic Insights

- Understand that children's feelings toward a stepfather may be very mixed. Stepfathers who try to compete with biological fathers are bound to lose. Going slow is important.
- A shift from romantic thinking to realistic thinking must happen if the new union is to make it. Clarifying expectations is the first step to realistic thinking. A remarriage with children can be very complex.
- How the children define the *step* in stepfather and the connotations that they attach to the word can create resistance from the beginning. Countering these often-negative definitions can lower the resistance.

- In the early part of the remarriage, the stepfather should assert his authority over small and routine matters. Larger decisions, including denying permission or correcting misbehavior, should be left to his wife. Start small in building a habit of consent from the children.
- There are many ways in which a stepfather can help take the woman out of the middle between him and the kids. One example is creating situations when just he and the kids are together, thus allowing his wife to get out with friends on her own or by herself.

The Second Time Around: Why Some Marriages Fail While Others Succeed

Dr. Louis J. Janda and Ellen MacCormack
Carol Publishing Group, 1991
352 pages

Book Byte

The Second Time Around addresses the challenges confronted by second marriages and examines why some succeed and others fail. People often go into second marriages with unrealistic expectations and a belief that their love and commitment will make this marriage different. Second marriages are actually a good chance for people to practice what they have learned from their first marriage. The authors have tried to present a comprehensive view of all aspects of second marriages, including romantic love, stepchildren, and finances. Their book is based on the experiences of men and women in second marriages, and it offers solid advice on how to make these marriages work.

Suggested Readers

- Clients who are considering remarriage
- Clients in second marriages
- Stepmothers and stepfathers

Therapeutic Insights

- People who are entering second marriages need to have realistic expectations. There are many potential complications. Anticipation of these challenges will help a second marriage be successful.

278

- There are many myths surrounding the notion of romantic love. Romantic love thrives on novelty and uncertainty. It does not necessarily last forever.
- Listening to what a prospective partner says about his or her first spouse provides important clues about the prospective partner's personality.
- Finances can be a major issue in second marriages unless they are faced squarely and honestly.
- To cope with an ex-spouse, the client must first understand the ex-spouse's frame of reference. Second, the client must understand the problem, and third, the client must put the pieces together. If possible, developing sympathy for the ex-spouse can reap rich rewards for the client.

The Single Father: A Dad's Guide to Parenting Without a Partner

Armin A. Brott
Abbeville Publishing Group, 1999
303 pages

Book Byte

The Single Father describes fathering without a partner. Armin Brott guides the divorced, separated, gay, widowed, and never married through all aspects of fatherhood. It is a wealth of information, from the emotional impact of divorce on children to child custody issues to stocking a kitchen and starting new relationships. Brott attempts to cover all possible issues faced by a single father and offers information, skills, tools, and support for being an actively involved parent.

Suggested Readers

- Newly divorced fathers
- Widowed fathers
- Gay, never married, or stepfathers

Therapeutic Insights

- Having a positive relationship with his children can help a father cope with his loneliness and grief and can do wonders for his self-confidence.

- By coming to grips with his own emotions, the single father will be a far better parent to his children.

- Getting professional help, building a strong support system, and being in touch with other men who are going through the same thing can make things easier.

- A father needs to be aware of sharing his grief with female friends. His vulnerability can lead to other things. This is not necessarily the time to start a new relationship.

- After a breakup, a father needs to care for himself, to not make major decisions, and to give himself a treat once in a while. With patience, his feelings and emotions will change with time.

Single Mothers by Choice: A Guidebook for Single Women Who Are Considering or Have Chosen Motherhood

Jane Mattes, C.S.W.
Times Books, 1997
243 pages

Book Byte

Jane Mattes, a psychotherapist and founder and director of Single Mothers by Choice, has written a guidebook for single women who have considered or have chosen motherhood. Mattes draws upon the experiences of thousands of women and presents the options they might choose in becoming mothers. She then examines the problems and benefits of these different options and the possible questions that might arise. She includes in her book lists of support groups, adoption agencies, and sperm banks that work with single women.

Suggested Readers

- Single women who are considering motherhood
- Single mothers
- Women with infertility issues

Therapeutic Insights

- Often, women don't make a decision in time to have a choice of options. A decision should be made while options are available, but the decision should not be made in haste.
- It is important to grieve the loss of your dream of bringing a child into the world with the support of a loving partner. This allows the woman to move past the loss and on to the next step.
- One way of lessening the intensity of single parenting is to share living arrangements with one or more families. This can be like an extended family, providing help to one another when needed.
- How a woman answers the daddy question may be more important than what she says. A woman needs to be comfortable with her own feelings so that she can answer the question calmly, as she would answer any emotionally charged and important question.
- It is particularly important for a child to have a positive male in his or her life if there is not an ongoing relationship with a dad.

Step Families: Love, Marriage, and Parenting in the First Decade

Dr. James H. Bray and John Kelly
Broadway Books, 1998
288 pages

Book Byte

This book answers the myriad of questions concerning stepfamily life. The authors based their book on one of the largest and longest studies of stepfamilies ever conducted. They reveal, through case studies of these families, how a strong, healthy stepfamily is as viable as a nuclear family. The book serves the purpose of bringing essential knowledge to stepfamilies and to their effect on the children involved.

Suggested Readers

- Blended families
- Stepparents
- Clients who are considering remarriage with children involved

Therapeutic Insights

- Over the years, a stepfamily blends into a family unit with its own natural life cycle.
- The greatest risk of failure happens in the first two years.
- There are three basic types of stepfamilies:
  1. The neotraditional
  2. The romantic
  3. The matriarchal

  The romantic is more prone to divorce.
- A healthy and strong stepfamily has three elements:
  1. The couple attends to their own adult needs.
  2. The couple develops a shared vision of marriage and family life.
  3. The couple parents by mutual consensus.
- The four basic tasks for a stepfamily to succeed are as follows:
  1. Integrating stepparents into the children's lives
  2. Creating a strong marriage, separate and distinct from the first
  3. Managing change
  4. Developing workable rules for noncustodial parents and former spouses

Stepmothering
Pearl Ketover Prilik
Forman Publishing, Inc., 1988 (out of print)
280 pages

Book Byte

Pearl Ketover Prilik provides a positive and practical approach to stepmothering. She covers such topics as first impressions, entering the new family, stepsiblings, the marriage relationship, and many more. She focuses on the many challenges that a stepmother faces and offers practical suggestions for those challenges. This is a well-organized and easy-to-read book in which Prilik takes on one of the most challenging roles. Although out of print, the book is available in local libraries.

Suggested Readers

- Potential stepmothers
- New stepmothers
- Veteran stepmothers

Therapeutic Insights

- Stepmothers are not alone. With the increase in late marriages and second marriages, the number is rising steadily. Lack of a defined role, negative stereotypes, and legal blurriness are some of the common problems. Stepmothers can become confident and successful in their roles.
- Expect stepmothering to be different from any other type of mothering. Expect confusion, resistance, and many challenges.
- Stepmothers should formulate achievable goals by first assessing their own unique situations, and second, by focusing on their stepchildren.
- Stepmothers can build relationships with their stepchildren as advisers and trusted adults. This can be done by being consistent, honest, and discreet.
- The confident stepmother remains in the present, plans for the future, respects herself, commits herself to her stepchildren, recognizes limitations, accepts responsibility, is active rather than passive, and can accept rewards gracefully.

 **RELATIONSHIPS**

ADULT CHILDREN AND PARENT RELATIONSHIPS

Forgive Your Parents, Heal Yourself: How Understanding Your Painful Family Legacy Can Transform Your Life
Barry Grosskopf, M.D.
Simon & Schuster Trade, 1999
279 pages

Book Byte

For a generation, psychology and psychotherapy have promised healing and self-fulfillment through examination of childhood stories. Adults have been encouraged to reclaim and to nurture the wounded inner child. Barry Grosskopf asks adult children to reframe their painful family legacies. He emphasizes the healing power and benefits of forgiveness and how to approach parents with an open heart, without recrimination or blame. He believes that adult children can repair their own character and relationships by respecting and understanding hurtful caregivers.

Suggested Readers

- Adults who want to restore relationships with parents, siblings, or partners
- Adults who want to forgive parents who have failed them
- Adults who want to reconcile childhood pain

Therapeutic Insights

- Many adults who were abused in childhood find it difficult to live in peace.
- Children do not understand that parents' rage comes from helplessness, not strength.
- Adults are not responsible for how their parents behave; however, as adults, they are responsible for how they reply to that behavior.
- The karmic justice of hurt children hurting parents only prolongs the pain cycle.
- Emotional growth occurs as a by-product of exploring new directions and new relationships, rather than continuing weary confrontations between old ones.

284

For Mothers of Difficult Daughters: How to Enrich and Repair the Relationship in Adulthood

Charney Herst, Ph.D., and Lynette Padwa
Random House, 1999
302 pages

Book Byte

Many daughters, often at the urging of their therapists, reason that their unhappiness has been caused by a bad childhood, which basically translates to bad mothering. No one has been there to speak up for Mom, and Charney Herst and Lynette Padwa are determined to do so. The authors state that mothers and daughters are individuals. The bond between them is sacred and indestructible, but they are still individuals, and each is responsible for her own actions and fate. By acknowledging this individuality, mothers and daughters can work through old resentments and build a new relationship together.

Suggested Readers

- Mothers and daughters who are in distant, dissatisfied relationships with each other
- Mother-daughter relationships that have gone awry
- Mothers and daughters who want to repair and rebuild their relationship

Therapeutic Insights

- Every woman has a mother story.
- A mother does not have to fix her daughter's problems to improve the relationship with her.
- There are two sides to every story.
- Dissatisfied daughters seem to have a warehouse full of musty old grievances.
- All mothers have, at one time or another, hurt their daughters.

Mothers to Daughters: Searching for New Connections
Ann F. Caron, Ed.D.
St. Martin's Press, Inc., 1999
288 pages

Book Byte

This book is about the differences and similarities between these two generations of women. Mothers and daughters speak freely and clearly about their joys, frustrations, disappointments, hopes, and dreams. One message stands above them all: In both stages of life, they are searching for connections. Their connections to each other may form the underpinnings of that search, but they react beyond that mutual bond. They search also for connections to other people.

Suggested Readers

- Mothers who feel loss when their daughters leave for college
- Mothers and daughters who are adapting to a changing relationship
- Mothers and daughters who are attempting to understand their differences

Therapeutic Insights

- Attachment to parents during college is positively related with stability of a young person's self-esteem and life satisfaction.
- When daughters reach their 20s, mothers may demand attention and may not appreciate the fact that their daughters need time for themselves.
- For mothers who are in midlife, acknowledging a need for support is more effective than projecting a stiff upper lip.
- Mothers need confidants of the same age, and so do daughters.
- It is difficult for many women to search for an intimate circle of friends with whom they can share the evolving emotions of midlife.

Women and Their Fathers: The Sexual and Romantic Impact of the First Man in Your Life

Victoria Secunda
Dell Publishing, 1993
483 pages

Book Byte

Victoria Secunda has taken a very serious look at women and their fathers. Drawing on research, the latest studies, and hundreds of interviews with men, the author explores the father-daughter relationship and the impact that this has on the daughter's romantic choices. Fathers have a profound impact on forming a woman's sexuality and identity. Secunda explores a spectrum of father types and the way that they shape their daughters, first as children, later as wives.

Suggested Readers

- Fathers of female children
- Women who want a better understanding of their choices of mates
- Men who are attempting to sort out their emotional legacies of childhood

Therapeutic Insights

- A father's emotional growth and needs may coincide and collide with a daughter's puberty.
- The greatest impact on a woman's romantic choices and her ability to feel comfortable in her own sexual skin is how her father treated her in childhood.
- A daughter needs a loving, available, predictable father or father figure who can be counted on, whether divorced or at home.
- It isn't just the physical presence of the father that matters; it's his engagement and involvement.
- Many fathers are not just uninvolved; instead, it is simply that their daughters are not a priority.

DATING

Guerrilla Dating Tactics: Strategies, Tips and Secrets for Finding Romance
Sharyn Wolf
Plume Books, 1998
336 pages

Book Byte

It's a jungle out there, and jungles are made for prowling. This book arms single people with everything they will need to survive in today's world of dating: the perfect icebreakers for parties, chance encounters, or anywhere single people see someone that they want to meet. Sharyn Wolf helps master the multiple levels of conversation with someone new with small talk, midtalk, or deep talk. She provides the key to cyberflirting, the latest advice on telepersonals, and last, true stories from the front line of those who have survived and thrived.

Suggested Readers

- Single men or women trying to get past the first date
- Adults who are looking for ways to make the right connections
- Men and women who want to attract new people

Therapeutic Insights

- Technological connections shouldn't be made to avoid making real ones.
- Enthusiasm can be contagious.
- Avoid making judgments, especially early in the process.
- Making eye contact is not the same as staring.
- Flirting is not flighty or irresponsible.

If the Buddha Dated: A Handbook for Finding Love on a Spiritual Path

Charlotte Kasl, Ph.D.
Viking Penguin, 1999
192 pages

Book Byte

This is a practical, playful, and spiritual book about creating a new love story in one's life. Drawing from Christian, Buddhist, Sufi, and other spirited traditions, this book shows the reader how to find a partner without losing him- or herself. It is also about creating love. It begins with bringing awareness, compassion, and loving kindness to oneself, including the parts that he or she tends to disown or wants to keep hidden. The reader will recognize long-held beliefs that have been shaping his or her behavior, and he or she will move beyond them and into a new awareness.

Suggested Readers

- Men or women who are seeking a vibrant relationship
- Adults who want to break through illusion and fear
- Adults currently dating who are looking for healthy, intimate relationships

Therapeutic Insights

- People must be free of their illusions so they can be in touch with their inner radiance.
- Bringing Buddhist consciousness to dating means offering compassion, care, kindness, and giving up control.
- When people are attached to the outcome, they are unable to be in the moment and to appreciate the "what is" of life.
- The causes of troubled relationships and fears about dating are born in the stories we tell ourselves.
- Staying loyal to the journey means loving with integrity, even when it hurts.

DIFFICULT RELATIONSHIPS

The Angry Marriage: Overcoming the Rage, Reclaiming the Love

Bonnie Maslin, Ph.D.
Hyperion Press, 1995
288 pages

Book Bytes

According to Bonnie Maslin, anger is a gift, and it can be one of the most effective and constructive forms of communication. Because anger is inevitable in a marriage, how couples use that anger can mean the difference between a fulfilling relationship and a destructive one. This book helps couples discover how to identify the six angry love styles, how to unearth hidden sources of anger, how to confront and conquer the invisible angry marriage, and how to replace even the greatest anger with compassion and goodwill.

Suggested Readers

- Individuals who want to learn how to channel their anger constructively
- Couples who want to end their destructive behaviors
- Couples who want to identify their angry styles

Therapeutic Insights

- Symbolizers are people whose anger appears in physical symptoms instead of words.
- Suppressors bury their anger by suppressing conflict. They will do anything to make sure that dissension doesn't appear in their marriage.
- Displacers are angry people who don't get angry with one another; instead, they divert their anger to targets outside of the relationship.
- Enactors distract themselves from anger by using action to prevent feeling.
- Venters let their anger out constantly.

Emotional Unavailability: Recognizing It, Understanding It, and Avoiding Its Trap

Bryn Collins, M.A.L.P.
Contemporary Books, Inc., 1998
304 pages

Book Byte

In this groundbreaking book, Bryn Collins opens up the discussion about life with an emotionally unavailable person. Using easy-to-understand concepts, case studies, quizzes, and jargon-free language, she profiles the most common types of emotionally unavailable partners, then offers practical skills that a person needs to change those painful associations. Collins offers ways to recognize "toxic types" before a person goes too far into the relationship. It is also worth noting that she believes people can change, if they are willing to commit to the work.

Suggested Readers

- Those who find themselves in a cycle of having emotionally unavailable partners
- Adults who are hooked by instant intensity with others
- Women and men who are attached to excitement and adrenaline

Therapeutic Insights

- There is a difference between unconditional love and boundary-free acceptance.
- Mama's boys and Daddy's girls were protected by their parents from all potentially painful and, therefore, learning experiences.
- People who don't connect often cease to believe that they are worthy of connections.
- Caretaking is doing something for people that they can't do for themselves.
- Many people can't connect with their partner's isolation and pain, because they can't connect with their own.

He's Scared She's Scared: Understanding the Hidden Fears That Sabotage Your Relationships

Steven Canter and Julia Sokol
Dell Publishing, 1995
352 pages

Book Byte

This is a guide for men and women who want to overcome their fear of commitment. Steven Canter and Julia Sokol assist the reader in discovering how to break the seduction-to-rejection cycle, how to avoid the quest for the perfect partner, and other mechanisms for evading commitment, what to do when the commitment problem is you, gaining a sense of closure when the relationship is over, and lastly, how to make and keep commitments.

Suggested Readers

- Adults who want to overcome their fear of commitment
- Adults who are looking for strategies to get beyond commitment phobia
- Couples who want to strike a balance between intimacy and space

Therapeutic Insights

- Forever is scary. Commitment represents an enormous responsibility.
- Men and women with unresolved commitment conflicts crave distance.
- If one chooses an unavailable partner, then he or she is choosing a relationship that already has a built-in sense of distance.
- The level of commitment anxiety typically emerges when the situation becomes overwhelmingly real.
- The first step in making a commitment is to acknowledge the conflicts and to make a commitment to manage them.

*Too Good to Leave, Too Bad to Stay: A Step-by-Step Guide
to Helping You Decide Whether to Stay In or Get Out
of Your Relationship*

Mira Kirshenbaum
Plume Books, 1997
288 pages

Book Byte

To make up or to break up? Whether a person is just getting serious or has a long-term commitment, no other question causes so much heartache and self-doubt. This book will help readers choose between leaving and staying. Mira Kirshenbaum gets to the heart of couples' problems. Which sins are forgivable and which ones are unpardonable? Does one partner's behavior create self-doubt in the other? Is the communication bad because the couple is not getting along, or is the couple not getting along because the communication is bad? This book is designed to help readers make the best choices for themselves.

Suggested Readers

- Individuals who are trying to make a decision regarding staying in a relationship
- Couples who are trying to figure out whether they fit together
- Adults who are looking for clarity in a time of crisis

Therapeutic Insights

- Staying ambivalent can cause tremendous damage.
- Physical abuse means love is dead.
- If a person looks like he or she is leaving the relationship and acts like he or she is leaving, then that person is leaving it.
- Crazy communication is where confused, unclear, misleading, misconceived words and gestures cause the problems.
- Mutual shutdown is a sure-bet way for a relationship to die.

What No One Tells the Bride

Marg Stark
Hyperion Press, 1998
307 pages

Book Byte

This is the humorous and compassionate inside scoop, the good and the bad, as to what it is really like to be married. Marg Stark and 50 women tell their stories, exposing the profound adjustment that brides often experience. This is a reassuring book; in many ways, it normalizes the fears and anxieties that women feel in their journey from singlehood to marriage. Feelings of ambivalence and bliss are a normal part of the process. This is a book for and by brides, so it may feel one-sided at times.

Suggested Readers

- Brides who are beginning the journey into married life
- Men who want to understand their mates
- Couples who are fearful of current difficulties in the engagement

Therapeutic Insights

- Articulating fears does not mean that one has chosen the wrong person.
- There is a fairy-tale myth that is imposed on newlyweds.
- It is normal to have trouble adjusting to being "someone's wife."
- Many newly married women miss the feistiness and independence that single life forged in them.
- For the bride who has someone to love her and someone who wants to devote the rest of his life to her, life is changing in and of itself.

INFIDELITY

After the Affair: Healing the Pain and Rebuilding Trust when A Partner Has Been Unfaithful

Janis Abrahms Spring, Ph.D.
Harper Perennial, 1997
258 pages

Book Byte

This is a book primarily for any two people who want to rebuild their relationship after one of them has been unfaithful. This includes married and cohabitating couples (heterosexuals and gays and lesbians). This book is also for people (whose relationships ended as a result of infidelity) who are unable to move beyond the experience, people who want to make sense of the infidelity that they experienced in their own families when they were growing up, professionals who treat individuals and couples affected by infidelity, partners who are thinking of having an affair, and partners who suspect their partners of being unfaithful. She then considers the three stages of healing:

1. Normalizing their feelings
2. Deciding whether to recommit or quit
3. Rebuilding their relationship

Suggested Readers

- Couples who are dealing with secrets, lies, and trust issues
- Couples who want to learn how to cope with the inevitable disenchantment of life before turning elsewhere.
- Couples who are attempting to restore trust and intimacy after an affair.

Therapeutic Insights

- An affair can either be the kiss of death or a wake-up call.
- Couples must attempt to decipher the meaning of the affair, and accept an appropriate share of responsibility in it.
- An affair can have both an emotional and physiological impact.
- Even if couples have made a decision to recommit, they may still feel overwhelmed by the hours of restorative work ahead.
- Not all couples can recover from an affair.

The Monogamy Myth: A Personal Handbook for Recovering from Affairs

Peggy Vaughan
Newmarket Press, Revised 1998
224 pages

Book Byte

The myths that reinforce the idea that affairs happen only because of personal failure have made it extremely difficult for people to recover their self-esteem and rebuild their relationships. Most people expect monogamy to be a normal part of a marriage or a significant relationship. Affairs have been understood only as a personal problem, a personal failure of the people involved. The person who has been cheated on becomes preoccupied with his or her perceived weaknesses and imperfections; he or she looks for his or her particular personal inadequacies that might have caused the affair. Peggy Vaughan helps couples uncover the many reasons why affairs happen. Her words assist couples in coping with pain, blame, shame, and anger, as well as strategies for rebuilding the relationship.

Suggested Readers

- Couples who want to understand why an affair happened
- Individuals who are devastated by an affair
- Adults who want to work through their shame and guilt

Therapeutic Insights

- A person needs to be able to talk about what has happened in order to recover a sense of equilibrium.
- An important factor in rebuilding self-esteem is breaking the cycle of secrecy and isolation.
- Attractions to others are natural; they are not a reason to suspect an affair.
- Failing to ask a direct question allows the other person to avoid a direct reply.
- The longer a person denies his or her suspicions, the harder it becomes to face them.

Surviving an Affair

Willard Harley, Jr., Ph.D., and Jennifer Harley Chalmers, Ph.D.
Fleming H. Revell Co., 1998
224 pages

Book Byte

Infidelity is one of life's most painful experiences for everyone involved—the betrayed spouse, the children, the extended family, and even the wayward spouse. The abandoned spouses feel completely victimized and unable to get off the most painful emotional roller coaster of their lives. Many question if it's possible to ever reconcile. Clearly, the path to recovery is very thin and narrow. Not all couples can maneuver such a path. Willard Harley, Jr., and Jennifer Harley Chalmers both believe that not only can couples survive an affair, but they can also thrive if they do the necessary work to recover. They discuss the common characteristics of affairs, the continuum in which affairs fall, and how to prepare for marital recovery.

Suggested Readers

- Couples who are experiencing the crisis of a current affair
- Couples who feel hopeless about the recovery process
- Couples who are finding it difficult to communicate their feelings

Therapeutic Insights

- To end an affair, a person must be willing to change jobs and to relocate, if necessary.
- Marital recovery cannot begin until withdrawal has ended.
- Affairs and dishonesty go hand in hand.
- Most affairs are based on fantasy and wishful thinking.
- An emotional affair can be just as threatening to a couple as a sexual affair.

IN-LAWS

The Ties That Bind . . . and Bind . . . and Bind: A Survival Guide to In-law Relationships
Sylvia Bigelsen
Element Books, 1999
255 pages

Book Byte

In-law relationships are the most challenging that a couple can face. Holidays, money matters, and the most trivial of squabbles can turn into major obstacles for any couple when the in-laws are involved. This book explains the life cycle of in-law relationships from all the players' points of view. Each chapter includes check-lists of tips for each family member. If an in-law problem festers, it can inevitably poison a couple's relationship. This book offers guidelines for all kinds of couples, including gay and lesbian couples.

Suggested Readers

- New families that have been created due to a marriage
- Couples who must challenge the behavior of their in-laws
- Couples with significant family-of-origin issues

Therapeutic Insights

- People can choose their friends, but they cannot choose their relatives.
- Unresolved family-of-origin issues, especially emancipation issues, can poison a relationship.
- Couples must recognize when compromise is not possible.
- It is helpful to articulate out loud the expectation of the relationship with the in-laws.
- Couples must be prepared to make decisions that won't please the parents or the in-laws.

INTIMACY

The Future of Love: The Power of the Soul in Intimate Relationships

Daphne Rose Kingma
Doubleday, 1999
221 pages

Book Byte

In this innovative book, Daphne Rose Kingma breaks down the popular myth of how love is "supposed" to be by introducing a broad spectrum of intimate connections. This best-selling author explains where people have gone wrong and how everyone can experience deeper, more loving relationships. She describes how well-intentioned couples often strive to create the perfect relationship, only to find themselves coping with disappointment and blame when they fail to live up to their unattainable goals. Kingma discusses ways to break the vicious cycle and ways to learn to relate on a higher level characterized by love and forgiveness.

Suggested Readers

- Couples who are attempting to move past their war zones
- Couples who want to achieve a deeper love
- Couples who experience chronic disappointment in their relationships

Therapeutic Insights

- People do not live in isolation. Entire lives are lived in a matrix of relationships.
- Relationships are fluid, vivid, mercurial, and constantly changing.
- Work, circumstances, and the passage of time all profoundly affect intimate relationships.
- Whatever the nature of one's childhood violations, they represent a theme in which one will spend a lifetime identifying, coming to terms with, and transcending them.
- Limitations of relationships invite one to evolve.

In the Meantime: Finding Yourself and the Love You Want

Iyanla Vanzant

Simon & Schuster Trade, 1999

336 pages

Book Byte

People know what they want in life, but what they want is nowhere in sight. Perhaps the vision is unclear, and the purpose undefined. On top of it all, romantic relationships may be failing. In this book, Iyanla Vanzant teaches how to move past the pains, hurt, past memories, and disappointments. She believes that this can be accomplished, and people can enrich the level of spirituality and intimacy in their relationships. Vanzant is an empowerment specialist, as well as an ordained minister.

Suggested Readers

- People who are in the midst of struggle and complicated relationships
- Individuals who are searching for answers and understanding in their relationships
- Adults with long histories of disappointment and hurt

Therapeutic Insights

- Disastrous relationships can teach people a great deal about themselves.
- When people are not happy with who they are, they are in the "meantime."
- The meantime is often a time of vagueness, a sort of limbo.
- What people believe about themselves is reflected in the people with whom they choose to align themselves.
- Once individuals become willing to grow, they will discover that they are not angry with others for doing something to them; instead, they are angry with themselves for allowing it.

Men Are From Mars, Women Are From Venus

John Gray, Ph.D.
HarperCollins Publishers, 1992
304 pages

Book Byte

This book is, in essence, a manual for loving relationships in the 1990s. It reveals how men and women differ in all areas of their lives. Not only do they communicate differently, but they think, feel, perceive, react, respond, love, need, and appreciate differently. They almost seem to be from different planets. This expanded understanding of the gender differences helps to resolve much of the frustration in dealing with and trying to understand the opposite sex. Misunderstanding can be quickly dissipated or avoided. Additionally, John Gray teaches practical techniques for solving problems that arise out of gender differences.

Suggested Readers

- Couples who are looking for tension-reducing strategies in relationships
- Couples who want to reduce the level of frustration in their relationships
- Adults who want to learn new ways to support the opposite sex

Therapeutic Insights

- It is a mistake to assume that if a person loves another, he or she will react and behave in certain ways.
- Men and women have different needs for intimacy.
- A man's sense of self is defined through his ability to achieve results.
- A woman's sense of self is defined through her feelings and the quality of her relationships.
- Men want space, whereas women want understanding.

The New Intimacy: Discovering the Magic at the Heart of Your Differences

Judith Sherven, Ph.D., and James Sniechowski, Ph.D.

Health Communications, Inc., 1997

320 pages

Book Byte

As the glitter of first attraction dims and the reality of differences between partners emerges, people who truly love each other often give up, rather than learn how to keep their love alive and thriving. They use the difficulties caused by their differences to sabotage the relationship. When two people are able to make a conscious decision to navigate their differences, only then can they achieve a deep, nourishing intimacy. These authors drew from case studies, contemporary culture, and their own lives to share with candor how to turn conflict into a rich opportunity for learning.

Suggested Readers

- Couples with difficulties
- Couples who are seeking more clarity in resolving conflict and disappointment
- Couples who find themselves sabotaging their relationships

Therapeutic Insights

- Most patterns of relationship failure originate in either the absence of love, the distortion of love, or in the disregard for differences.
- Adults can be unconsciously committed to self-sabotaging beliefs.
- Intimacy becomes real and tangible when individuals bring more and more of themselves to the relationship.
- Feelings are not, by themselves, trustworthy.
- If individuals depend on destiny or fate, they then abandon their own creative power, self-reliance, and personal initiative.

SEX

Couple Sexual Awareness: Building Sexual Happiness
Barry and Emily McCarthy
Carroll & Graf Publishers, Inc., 1998
304 pages

Book Byte

This is a practical, confidence-building book that was written to assist in enabling couples to enhance intimacy and to heighten sexual satisfaction by making sexual awareness a positive force in their relationship. Chapters on pleasuring, the marital bond, eroticizing marriage, equity between the sexes, sexual variation, conception, contraception and infertility, being a couple again, and sex after 60 provide excellent information accompanied by helpful illustrations. A sexual relationship will be more satisfying if it is based on solid information, awareness, comfort, communication, and a positive attitude.

Suggested Readers

- Couples who want to change their manner of relating
- Couples who are trying to reassess their expectations and communication skills
- Couples who are attempting to adopt a pleasure-oriented rather than a performance-oriented view of sex

Therapeutic Insights

- Being able to laugh and to accept idiosyncrasies and foibles is necessary; every person has weaknesses and irritating behaviors.
- Marital sexuality is a subject that is hidden behind self-defeating attitudes and myths.
- Many women resent having to be responsible for birth control.
- For many couples, after time, there is a decrease in communication and experimentation with sex.
- Couple time is crucial in keeping your intimate relationship vital.

The Erotic Edge: Erotica For Couples

Lonnie Barbach, Ph.D.
Plume/Penguin Books, 1996
269 pages

Book Byte

This is a graphically intense exploration of seduction, romance, and erotic fantasy. No taboos are put on shared pleasure or the imagination of desire. Lonnie Barbach has collected 22 erotic and arousing stories written by both men and women. In her commentaries, she examines the strong connection between men's sexual responses and visual stimuli, contrasted with the importance of foreplay and mental seduction for women. She offers advice on how to use particular stories as starting points for sexual encounters. These selections cover the full range of erotic themes, primarily heterosexual in nature.

Suggested Readers

- Couples who are attempting to improve their sexual relationship
- Women who are seeking literature with an erotic point of view
- Men and women who want to refresh their sexual relationship

Therapeutic Insights

- The desire for newness or variety does not necessarily indicate the existence of a sexual problem.
- It is helpful for couples to understand their inherent differences that may exist between their sexual natures.
- There has historically been a near-absence of erotica directed toward the unique needs of women.
- Many couples want to broaden their horizons as a way to further enhance their intimacy.
- It is important for men and women to understand and accept their differences.

Is There Sex after Kids?

Ellen Kreidman
St. Martin's Press, Inc., 1996
265 pages

Book Byte

Parents are lovers, too. And they should be. However, it is very difficult for couples to find time and energy for romance after they've had children. Ellen Kreidman offers sound advice for adults on how to rekindle the love with their mate for a lifetime of emotional and sexual fulfillment. She teaches how to have spontaneous sex, the magic of the 10-second kiss, 51 ways for a person to seduce his or her partner, what to do when one person isn't in the mood, and creative ways to go on a date with each other.

Suggested Readers

- Adults, who are also parents, who need to recreate the spark that brought the two of them together
- Couples who need more creative ideas to further their sexual intimacy
- Parents who need help in teaching their children to respect their privacy.

Therapeutic Insights

- Everyone wants some return on his or her effort.
- Couples must think of the bedroom as a room for romance rather than just a place to sleep.
- Couples must make a plan and commit to it.
- Each person must change his or her negative self-talk into positive self-talk.
- Schedule sex on the calendar.

Passionate Marriage: Love, Sex, and Intimacy in Emotionally Committed Relationships

David Schnarch, Ph.D.
Henry Holt & Co., Inc., 1998
408 pages

Book Byte

David Schnarch reveals in this book the notion that keeping passion and intimacy alive requires facing the anxiety of defining oneself while getting close to his or her partner. Using humor and compassion, he describes couples' explicit sexual encounters and dramatic therapy sessions to demonstrate how they found personal, marital, and sexual fulfillment far greater than they ever dreamed possible. He goes beyond addressing sexual dysfunction to help people achieve their sexual potential.

Suggested Readers

- Couples who want to invigorate their sexual relationships
- Adults who are looking for a new model for sexual intimacy
- Couples who want fundamental changes in their relationships

Therapeutic Insights

- Couples who are moderately differentiated are more willing to go through their dilemmas.
- Love is often confused with emotional fusion.
- Foreplay is where the boundaries of intimacy and eroticism are negotiated.
- Individuals must be willing to engage in self-confrontation to gain emotionally.
- One must own their own projections as an act of integrity.

Sex for Dummies
Dr. Ruth K. Westheimer
IDG Books, 1995
400 pages

Book Byte

For more than 20 years, Ruth K. Westheimer has traveled the world and has been bringing her message of sexual literacy to millions of people who need information on love, relationships, and sex, but have been too afraid to ask. This is an excellent down-to-earth, humorous, educational, comprehensive, and informative guide to heterosexual and gay and lesbian sex in the 1990s and beyond. This book teaches many things, such as how to keep the romantic fires burning, exploring family options, discussion of HIV and AIDS, making foreplay and afterplay a normal part of the couple's lovemaking, sex for the first time, infertility and impotency, maintaining an active sex life in the face of medical or physical disabilities, and exploring the topic of sex on-line. She also includes 10 things women wish men knew about sex, and 10 things men wish women knew about sex.

Suggested Readers

- Adults who are attempting to sort through the mass of sexual information and sexual imagery
- Couples who are caught between conflicting sexual views
- Those who have a less-than-satisfactory sex life

Therapeutic Insights

- Many issues contribute to a lack of a sexual relationship.
- Couples must commit to sex in the same ways they commit to other relationship needs and responsibilities.
- The pressures that society puts on gays and lesbians to keep their sexuality hidden causes untold damage.
- The ultimate intimacy is to totally give yourself to your partner.
- Each individual has different needs when it comes to enjoying sex to the fullest.

The Soul of Sex: Cultivating Life as an Act of Love

Thomas Moore
HarperCollins Publishers, 1998
336 pages

Book Byte

In this provocative and highly original work, Thomas Moore restores sex to its rightful place in the human psyche. Describing sex as an experience of the soul, he brings out the fully human side of sex: the roles of fantasy, desire, meaning, and morality. He then draws on religion, mythology, art, literature, and film to show how sex contains the most profound mysteries. Moore explains how spiritual values can sometimes wound a person's sexuality. He blends, rather than opposes, spirituality and sexuality.

Suggested Readers

- Those who want to appreciate the human body with both emotion and imagination
- Adults who want to deconstruct the myths of sexuality and spirituality
- Couples who want to become more deeply sexual and loving

Therapeutic Insights

- Sexual attraction is not at all a purely physical event.
- People are always living in a story surrounded by images, and they're always perceiving with imagination.
- Adults are often told in one form or another to resist the temptations of the world, the flesh, and the devil.
- One must invite the spirit of sex into the bedroom, or else sex will remain a secularized, egocentric, and exploitative endeavor.
- The very intensity and rigidity of some people's obsessions with sexual behavior betray their interest in it.

WOMEN AND SEXUAL DYSFUNCTION

I'm Not in the Mood: What Every Woman Should Know About Improving Her Libido
Judith Reichman, M.D.
William Morrow & Co., Inc., 1999
208 pages

Book Byte

If a man is suffering from a sexual disorder that leads to impotency, it's Viagra to the rescue. If a woman has sexual problems, the medical establishment's response and attitude are less than supportive or enthusiastic. Judith Reichman addresses the medical bias and provides important information for women experiencing a decrease or loss of sexual interest and desire. She removes the denial, embarrassment, and shame associated with sexual dysfunction. Reichman educates women about the factors that affect their libido, demystifies the sexual issues they are facing, and presents significant information on how women can reach their full biological sexual potential.

Suggested Readers

- Women who are experiencing loss of sexual interest and desire
- Women who want help in speaking to their doctors
- Women who want understanding and information as to the factors that affect their libido

Therapeutic Insights

- Hormones can control women's sense of well-being, passion, and sexual response.
- Race and religion appear to have little effect on fantasy, frequency of sex, or satisfaction.
- Even the most health-conscious women wait for the advent of menopause to discuss hormonal issues.
- Body image, relationship difficulties, medications, power issues, hormonal issues, and lack of chemistry all contribute to lack of sexual desire.
- Sexual difficulties must be talked about as well as worked at on a physical level.

Okay, So I Don't Have a Headache

Cristina Ferrare
Golden Books, 1999
177 pages

Book Byte

Cristina Ferrare is a very brave woman. Coming forward nationally on TV, she acknowledged her lack of sexual desire. When she went to the doctor, she found that a lack of testosterone in her body was the key reason for her lack of interest in sex. The doctor prescribed a testosterone crème that put her back in the mood. Spurred by her approaching menopause, she wanted to find out for herself how hormonal levels affect everything in our bodies—and how everything we do and eat affects our hormonal levels. This is a frank, funny, informative, and inspiring personal account of her experience and what she learned along the way.

Suggested Readers

- Women who are experiencing lack of sexual desire
- Women who are struggling with PMS
- Couples who are working through the issue of the loss of sexual interest

Therapeutic Insights

- Women must be aware of how alcohol affects them mentally and physically.
- There are natural herbs and vitamins that can help keep hormones in balance.
- Hormone replacement is attractive to many women, but it does not always work.
- Chronic stress is one of the threats to sexual health.
- Thirty-eight to 43 percent of women report loss of sexual interest during their adult life span.

 **SPIRITUALITY**

Awaken to Your Spiritual Self

M. J. Abadie
Adams Media Corp., 1998
238 pages

Book Byte

Author of *Healing Mind, Body, Spirit,* M. J. Abadie addresses the question of how to bring a sense of completeness and harmony into one's life in *Awaken to Your Spiritual Self.* She does this with step-by-step exercises and meditations that focus on a person's inner strengths. She brings to spirituality a road map with instructions for recognizing and assessing the blessings in one's life, which, in turn, can help a person increase his or her confidence, and he or she can experience a sense of completeness.

Suggested Readers

- Clients who want to achieve a more spiritual self
- Clients who are looking for a sense of completeness in their lives
- Clients who are searching for inner peace

Therapeutic Insights

- To reach spiritual harmony, a person must first prepare. Silence, solitude, breathing, and relaxation are modes of preparation.
- Prayer is powerful and potent. It is a very effective means for bringing a spiritual dimension to one's life. Prayer can come in many different forms.
- Living spiritually is an awareness of connections. It is an awareness of oneself and how he or she is in the world. It is a wholeness.
- Awakening one's spiritual self is a journey. It is a journey of transformation of which there is no turning back. Spirituality is not separate from a person's self; it is part of him- or herself.
- Forgiveness is essential when awakening one's spirituality. Forgiveness of oneself and of others releases the negative emotion that a person may be carrying inside.

Conversations with God: An Uncommon Dialogue

Neale Donald Walsh

Hampton Roads Publishing Co., Inc., 1998

392 pages

Book Byte

Neale Donald Walsh has written an inspiring and unique book about his dialogue with God. According to the author, during a very difficult time in his life professionally and personally, he turned to God for answers. He wrote many of his questions on paper, and one day his pen began to move on its own, and out came the answers to many of his questions. These answers are the essence of his books. The books are filed with thought-provoking and insightful ideas.

Suggested Readers

- Clients who are looking for meaning in their world
- Adults of all faiths
- Clients with issues of depression or anxiety

Therapeutic Insights

- Feeling is the language of the soul. If people want to know what is right or true for themselves, then they should look to how they are feeling about something. To know truth, people need to listen to their feelings, thoughts, and experiences.
- Prayer should never be about asking. It should be about gratitude and appreciation. Saying you want something produces wanting.
- God gave people free will and free choice. God does not create the conditions or circumstances of people's lives.
- Fear or love governs all human actions. All thoughts and actions are based upon love or upon fear. These are the prime forces that drive all human experiences.
- When people choose to live their lives from the energy of love, they choose to do more than survive. They can then experience who they really are and who they can really be.

A Course in Miracles, Second Edition

Foundation for Inner Peace, 1992
Text: 669 pages
Workbook: 488 pages
Manual for teachers, 92 pages

Book Byte

A Course in Miracles came about through the joint effort of Helen Shueman and William Thetford, professors of medical psychology at Columbia University's College of Physicians and Surgeons in New York City. Helen Shueman, three months prior to the writing of the book, began to have highly symbolic and descriptive dreams, along with recurring unusual images. She began to write in collaboration with Bill Thetford and, thus, *A Course in Miracles* came about. She refers to the information as dictation from a voice that came to her. The course deals with universes of spiritual themes, and is Christian based. It is a theoretical course, but it includes a workbook and insights for bringing the ideas into everyday practice. It emphasizes application and experience over theory and theology.

Suggested Readers

- Adults of Christian faith
- Clients who are seeking universal spiritual truths
- Clients who want practical application for experiencing spiritual truths

Therapeutic Insights

- Knowledge is real. It is truth. It is the law of God's love. Perceptions are unreal, based only on people's interpretations, not on facts.
- Miracles are everyday occurrences. They naturally occur as expressions of love. Love is received through prayer and is expressed through miracles.
- The world that people see is the projection of their internal frame of reference.
- Sin is a "lack of love." It is a mistake to be corrected, not punished as evil.
- Forgiveness corrects all the mistakes that people have made. By forgiving others, people receive forgiveness for themselves.

Expect a Miracle: The Miraculous Things That Happen to Ordinary People

Dan Wakefield

Harper Paperbacks, 1998 (reprint edition)

368 pages

Book Byte

Dan Wakefield, author of *Returning,* has written a book about miracles. He illustrates through stories a wealth of divine experiences. By learning to recognize and to increase awareness to the possibility of miracles, he believes that we can live more fulfilled lives with greater understanding and love. He demonstrates to us how miracles happen on a daily basis. This is an insightful and straightforward book with stories of people from all walks of life.

Suggested Readers

- Adults of all faiths
- Clients who are looking for greater meaning in their lives
- Clients who want a greater understanding of miracles

Therapeutic Insights

- Miracles are mysteries, not something that we can request. We can only create an atmosphere in which miracles are more apt to occur.
- A miracle is something beyond what we presently know to be possible.
- Miracles are more about our perceptions being made finer, so that in an instant, we can actually see and hear beyond what we know.
- Miracles happen when we are open to receiving the gifts of the universe.
- Miracles happen all the time. When our awareness is heightened and we experience one miracle, we then begin to experience them more often. Acknowledging miracles is acknowledging God.

Going to Pieces Without Falling Apart: A Buddhist Perspective on Wholeness

Mark Epstein, M.D.
Broadway Books, 1999 (reprint edition)
224 pages

Book Byte

Mark Epstein, a psychiatrist, has written a book with a Buddhist perspective on wholeness. He explains from this perspective how happiness does not necessarily come from material or spiritual acquisitiveness, but actually from letting go. With a blend of Buddhist and Western psychology, Epstein shows us how, in relaxing our ever-busy minds, we can experience the freedom that comes from surrendering control. By letting go, we can live a more spiritual and peaceful life.

Suggested Readers

- Adults of all faiths
- Clients with issues of anxiety and depression
- Clients who are looking for more peace in their lives

Therapeutic Insights

- By feeling and focusing on our emptiness rather than trying to wipe it out or fill it up, we can reach a state of wholeness and our character will become stronger.
- Only by surrendering into the void can we begin to know ourselves.
- Meditation empowers the observing mind and is the link from isolation and distancing to intimacy and connection.
- When we are so uncomfortable with our own sense of emptiness, there is no way that we can be open and vulnerable to another human being. We are too afraid or ashamed to reveal ourselves to another person.
- Mindfulness of feelings is the careful attention to all feelings; pleasant, unpleasant, or neutral. When we can be mindful of all of our feelings, we become more tolerant and accepting.

How to Want What You Have: Discovering the Magic and Grandeur of Ordinary Existence
Timothy Miller, Ph.D.
Avon Books, 1995
265 pages

Book Byte

Timothy Miller's book focuses on how to get past resistance and learn a new approach to being happy and content with one's life. He teaches readers how to practice the three disciplines (e.g., compassion, attention, and gratitude), while taming their desire and learning to live in the present. In an age of consumption and consumerism, Miller gives practical and insightful advice on the secrets of happiness.

Suggested Readers

- Clients with depression
- Clients with anxiety
- Adults who are dissatisfied with their lives

Therapeutic Insights

- By altering one's beliefs and habits of thought, a person can make changes in his or her life.
- Compassion is seeing no person as better or worse, or more or less important than oneself.
- Attention is living in the here and now without placing a value judgment on one's experiences.
- Gratitude is counting one's blessings daily and by the minute, without the feeling of needing more or needing different.
- When one wants what he or she has, compassion, attention, gratitude, and acceptance are all optimistic positions. One recovers from depression when his or her interpretation of the world changes from pessimistic to optimistic.

One Day My Soul Just Opened Up: 40 Days and 40 Nights Towards Spiritual Strength and Personal Growth

Iyanla Vanzant
Fireside Books, 1998
303 pages

Book Byte

Iyanla Vanzant brings to readers a daily inspirational and motivational program that will help them work through problems and awaken their spirituality. Through exercises and her own personal insights, Iyanla gives readers the tools to change their lives and tap into their inner strengths. The book is a 40-day journey with daily inspirations and spiritual insights.

Suggested Readers

- Adults of all faiths
- Clients with issues of depression or anxiety
- Clients who are looking for more meaning in their lives

Therapeutic Insights

- Believing in God means believing in our own Godliness.
- To really know God, we must have a deep desire based on nothing but that deep desire.
- When we remember daily that we are perfect and unique representatives of all that is God, we will be equipped to handle anything.
- By trusting the Divine and by learning to recognize and interpret signs and signals that we receive, we will then learn to trust ourselves.
- Prayer is communication between man and the Divine. It brings the mind, body, and spirit into alignment with what we need at all times.

Powerful Prayers

Larry King with Rabbi Irwin Katsof
Renaissance Books, 1999
256 pages

Book Byte

In *Powerful Prayer,* Larry King explores, through interviews with prominent people, the role of prayer in their lives. His daughter, Chaia, posed the question to him one day: "You're always having conversations with powerful people, why not ask them about their prayers?" King, who considered himself an agnostic, looked to his friend, Rabbi Katsof, for guidance; Katsof then became his guide and coauthor. The book became a spiritual journey for Larry King as he spoke to prominent people, from Muhammad Ali to Jack Kevorkian, about their intimate relationships with God.

Suggested Readers

- Adults of all faiths
- Clients who question the power and purpose of prayer
- Clients who want a closer relationship with God

Therapeutic Insights

- There are many different forms of prayer—different people, different cultures, same destination.
- God gives us the opportunity to communicate and connect with him through prayer.
- To know God, we must converse with him. God is a conversationalist. Prayer is not a one-way conversation.
- Once we open our minds to God, the universe opens. Surrendering to God brings freedom.
- Answers to our prayers are not always the ones we want. God's will, not the our will, will be done. When a door is closed, often, a window opens up.

Proud Spirit: Lessons, Insights & Healing from "the Voice of the Spirit World"

Rosemary Altea
William Morrow & Co., Inc., 1998
267 pages

Book Byte

Author of the best-selling book, *The Eagle and The Rose,* Rosemary Altea brings the reader further along the spiritual path. *Proud Spirit* brings insights and healing from the spirit world. *Proud Spirit* is the continuous exploration of life after death, and it goes beyond into insights for everyday living. Rosemary, along with her spirit guide, Grey Eagle, addresses many of the most controversial issues of our times, including abortion, homosexuality, and racism.

Suggested Readers

- Adults of all faiths
- Clients who are exploring the evidence of afterlife
- A client with a belief of spiritual guides

Therapeutic Insights

- There is life after death.
- Animals and pets that people have loved do survive death.
- In the spirit world, it is the survival of the soul that is important, not the physical self, which may be old and wrinkled. Each being is responsible for its own soul; not all souls are happy.
- On this earth, people have a responsibility to their loved ones in the spirit world, to their loved ones on earth, and to themselves to perform all acts with love.
- One should be kind, tolerant, and gentle to his or her own self first, then to all humankind.

A Return to Love: Reflections on the Principles of a Course in Miracles

Marianne Williamson
HarperCollins Publishers, 1996
300 pages

Book Byte

In Marianne Williamson's best-selling book, she shares her reflections on *A Course in Miracles*. In her book, she reveals insights on love and teaches the reader how to become a miracle worker by accepting God and expressing love rather than fear in one's life. She reveals how powerful love can be the key to inner peace. This book is a classic in addressing the issues of psychic pain in the areas of relationship, career, and health.

Suggested Readers

- Clients with a quest for spirituality in their lives
- Clients with issues of anger and fear
- Clients with relationship, career, or health issues

Therapeutic Insights

- God is love and love is real. We create fear, God does not. Returning to love is returning to who we really are.
- Events fall into natural order when we stop trying to control our lives. Surrendering to God is giving up our attachment to results.
- If the world is to change, we must change our minds about the world. Our state of awareness is reflected by the energy around us.
- The experience of miracles begins with forgiving the past. The present is the only time.
- Loving another person is seeing the face of God. It is seeing the innocence and love behind the mask we wear. Forgiveness in relationships transforms our thoughts from fear to love. It is the key to inner peace.

The Road Less Traveled and Beyond: Spiritual Growth in an Age of Anxiety
M. Scott Peck, M.D.
Touchstone Books, 1998
320 pages

Book Byte

Author of the *The Road Less Traveled* and *Further Along the Road Less Traveled*, M. Scott Peck brings to us a book on spiritual growth in an age of anxiety. At 60 years of age, and with a culmination of experience in counseling, lecturing, and writing, Peck speaks about decision making and the choices that people make in their everyday lives, home, and business. He explores good and evil, narcissism, love, the consequences of a person's actions and choices, along with death and dying. In Peck's final book in the *Road* trilogy, he brings to the reader an awareness of how to live fuller and richer lives in a world with so much stress and anxiety.

Suggested Readers

- Clients who want a deeper spiritual awareness
- Clients who are struggling with personal choices in a stressful world
- Clients who are questioning the purpose of their existence

Therapeutic Insights

- There are no easy answers. People need to learn to think better. Our society endorses simplistic thinking; individuals are responsible for thinking well.
- Consciousness comes from thinking well, and thinking well comes from consciousness. Consciousness is the foundation of mental and spiritual growth.
- Learning and evolving is the reason for human beings to be on the earth. The world, with all its uncertainties and vicissitudes, is an ideal environment for human learning. The ultimate goal of human learning is the perfection of the soul.
- Consciousness not only precedes choices; it is the most important choice that people can make. It does not make choices easier. Consciousness actually multiplies the number of choices available. Doing the "right thing" or the "good thing" may often seem ambiguous at the time. Evil, on the other hand, is committed by people who are certain of what they are doing.

- Religion is an organized set of beliefs with a specific creed and membership rules. Spirituality is a desire to be in harmony and to be connected to the unseen order of things. Spirituality is a developmental process with stages of growth. Not everyone is in the stage they may appear to be.

Saved by the Light: The True Story of a Man Who Died Twice and the Profound Revelations He Received

Dannion Brinkley with Paul Perry

HarperCollins Publishers, 1995 (reprint edition)

224 pages

Book Byte

Dannion Brinkley brings to the reader one of the most compelling accounts of a near-death experience. His book, based on two near-death experiences, is a profoundly moving story about his personal spiritual transformation, which resulted from these experiences. His story speaks to what it was like to die and, more important, what it is like to live.

Suggested Readers

- Adults of all faiths
- Clients who are questioning the existence of an afterlife
- Clients who are looking for more meaning in their everyday lives

Therapeutic Insights

- Many people who have experienced near-death speak of seeing deceased relatives and of having their life pass before them in review.
- A personality transformation is not uncommon after a near-death experience. People often cease to take nature and their families for granted.
- Psychic powers may come as a result of a near-death experience.
- Near-death experiences can be extremely difficult on couples. The personal transformation often becomes the focus of a person's life.
- Many people who have near-death experiences have similar visions while dead. These are of beings of light and glorious cathedrals.

The Seat of the Soul

Gary Zukav
Simon & Schuster Trade, 1989
256 pages

Book Byte

Gary Zukav explains how humans as a species are evolving spiritually. No longer are people pursuing power based on the perceptions of their five senses, but now on multisensory perceptions. He explains how humans' "survival of the fittest" theory has brought them close to destruction from wars and personal conflict. Zukav shows how a person's emerging spirituality changes and transforms his or her life. In his thought-provoking book, Zukav challenges a person's everyday perceptions of the meaning and purpose of life.

Suggested Readers

- Clients who are seeking more meaningful lives
- Clients with chemical dependency issues
- Clients with responsibility issues

Therapeutic Insights

- In the evolutionary process, the soul's energy continually incarnates and reincarnates into physical reality for the purpose of healing and balancing energy. The soul must balance its energy to become whole.
- A human being is actually multisensory. A multisensory human has access to wise and compassionate guidance. Insights, intuitions, hunches, or inspirations are communications from the soul.
- Choice is the center of the evolutionary process. The choice to remain unconscious comes from choosing not to choose. Responsible choice is conscious choice and takes into account the consequences of one's choices.
- Acknowledging an addiction is the first step toward reducing its power. A different life is created by responsible choice. Living a conscious life empowers a person. This power accumulates while the challenged addiction loses its power.
- A spiritual partnership is more than a marriage commitment. A spiritual partnership recognizes the soul's evolution. It is a partnership between equals with a purpose of spiritual growth.

The Seven Spiritual Laws of Success: A Practical Guide to the Fulfillment of Your Dreams
Deepak Chopra
Amber-Allen Publishing, 1995
115 pages

Book Byte

Deepak Chopra offers a new perspective on attaining success in people's lives. By understanding a person's true nature and his or her harmony with natural law, he or she can naturally bring about well-being, good health, satisfying relationships, and material abundance. He brings to the reader practical steps for being successful and for having the energy and enthusiasm to live life effortlessly. Deepak Chopra blends Eastern and Western philosophies to bring to the reader seven basic laws of nature.

Suggested Readers

- Clients with depression or anxiety
- Clients who are seeking more meaningful lives
- Clients who want practical steps to being successful in their lives

Therapeutic Insights

- Pure consciousness or pure potentiality is a person's spiritual essence. The experience of self is a person's internal reference point rather than his or her experiences.
- Giving and receiving are harmonious interactions in life. They are both needed to keep wealth and affluence circulating in a person's life. The intention behind giving and receiving should be to create happiness.
- Karma is cause and effect. Every action generates a force of energy, which returns a like kind of energy. When actions are motivated by love, there is no waste of energy. Do less and accomplish more; accept people and events as they are.
- If a person lives in the present-moment awareness, then perceived obstacles vanish. By learning to harness the power of intention, people can create all they desire.
- To acquire anything in the physical world, a person must first surrender his or her attachment to it. Relinquishing one's attachment to results brings that which one desires. All problems in people's lives also have seeds of opportunity.

The Spirituality of Imperfection: Storytelling and the Journey to Wholeness

Ernest Krutz and Katherine Ketcham
Bantam Books, 1994 (reprint edition)
293 pages

Book Byte

The Spirituality of Imperfection is a compilation of stories about spirituality. It is a book that focuses on the spirituality of imperfection and the profound truth of the statement "I am not perfect." The book draws on the wisdom of the Hebrew prophets, Greek thinkers, Buddhist sages, and Christian disciples. Understanding and accepting a person's imperfection is the first step in understanding him- or herself and humanity. Serenity and self-awareness come when people can accept their limitations and the inevitability of failure and pain. It is a book for clients who are trying to put meaning to their suffering.

Suggested Readers

- Clients with issues of perfectionism and low self-esteem
- Clients with depression or anxiety
- Clients who are in recovery from chemical dependency or eating disorders

Therapeutic Insights

- In defining spirituality, a person discovers his or her own limits. Spirituality, like love, is the way that people "be." Words alone cannot describe spirituality. Metaphors, images, and stories can help people see and feel spirituality.
- What people see, how they feel, and why they choose are the essential elements of the experience of spirituality.
- Human beings make mistakes and that's okay. They are not God; they cannot control everything. Addiction is an attempt to control. It is an attempt to fill a spiritual void with a chemical. It is an attempt to get a quick spiritual fix.
- Spirituality involves experiencing something in a new way. Release is often the first experience of spirituality. This can be described as a "light going on," or perhaps as a "weight lifted."
- When experiencing spirituality, people discover the feelings of release, gratitude, humility, tolerance, forgiveness, and being at home. These experi-

ences cannot be commanded; they are available to people when they need them, if they are open to acceptance.

There Are No Accidents: Synchronicity and the Stories of Our Lives
Robert H. Hopcke
Riverhead Books, 1998
260 pages

Book Byte

This book is a fascinating guide to those meaningful coincidences we often experience. *Synchronicity,* a term coined by Carl Jung, is the basis for this book by Robert H. Hopcke. He explores the role of synchronicity in our everyday lives through storytelling. *There Are No Accidents* offers a unique way to examine meaningful coincidences in our lives.

Suggested Readers

- Adults of all faiths
- Clients who are seeking more meaningful lives
- Clients who question the interplay of life events

Therapeutic Insights

- Perhaps people are actually characters in a story. How would they know? Strange plot developments or coincidences may make them feel that way.
- Synchronicity is not just coincidences, but meaningful coincidences.
- Meaningful coincidences can occur, causing people to reconsider the stories they have made up for themselves. Openness to changing their stories may give new opportunities to people. This is often true in relationships.
- There are many synchronicities in love and friendship. Meeting the right person at the right time and in the right circumstance is a unique, unrepeatable, once-in-a-lifetime experience.
- With a symbolic attitude toward their lives and a search for meaning, people will realize there are no accidents in the stories of their lives.

Tuesdays with Morrie: An Old Man, A Young Man and the Last Great Lesson

Mitch Albom
Bantam Doubleday Publishing Group, Inc., 1997
192 pages

Book Byte

Mitch Albom has written a moving account of his time spent with Morrie Schwartz, Albom's college professor from nearly 20 years ago, who he befriended in the last months of Morrie's life. He shares with the reader Morrie's many insights and wisdom, which only an older and wiser person can impart. This book is a treasure and a tribute to age and the aging. It is an intimate experience between student and mentor. It is a gift to the reader.

Suggested Readers

- Clients who are looking for insight and wisdom about life
- Young clients who are seeking wisdom from the experience of an older person
- Aging clients

Therapeutic Insights

- Learning to give out love and to let it in is the most important lesson in life.
- Being prepared to die at any time is a better way to live. One should live life without regrets.
- One should experience emotions fully and completely. It is only then that one can detach from them. Being afraid of emotions (fear, pain, love, etc.) prevents a person from detaching.
- Money cannot bring a person tenderness or love; it is only a substitute for these. People who are hungry for love are those who are caught up in materialism.
- Respect, compromise, openness, and a common set of values are the basis for a good marriage. The largest belief must be in the importance of one's marriage.

Wisdom of the Ages: A Modern Master Brings Eternal Truth into Everyday Life

Dr. Wayne Dyer
HarperCollins Publishers, 1998
268 pages

Book Byte

In this inspirational book, Wayne Dyer brings together a collection of poems, writings, and sayings by many of the greatest writers and thinkers of the past 25 centuries. In this collection, Dyer looks at what these wise scholars have to say to us today. From Buddha to Jesus to Michelangelo, Wayne Dyer brings to the reader wisdom from the ages.

Suggested Readers

- Adults of all faiths
- Clients who are seeking more meaningful lives
- Clients with issues of depression or anxiety

Therapeutic Insights

- Learn to be silent. It is with silence that the mind can learn to listen and absorb.
- When we can turn a problem over to a higher power, we can shift to knowing a state of patience.
- By living in the present, we can free ourselves from the past. We can detach ourselves from what we used to be.
- The practice of prayer brings true spiritual growth. It is an incredibly powerful force for transformation in our lives.
- As divine creations of God, we are entitled to prosperity, love, and health. Ask and we shall receive.

WORKPLACE ISSUES

CHANGE IN THE WORKPLACE

Winning at Work: Breaking Free of Personal Traps to Find Success in the New Workplace
Mel Sandler and Muriel Gray
Davies-Black Publishing, 1999
210 pages

Book Byte

Mel Sandler and Muriel Gray are workplace consultants who have been involved with thousands of individuals who are struggling to adapt to a changing workplace. What they discovered is that people who succeeded in this new work environment had certain qualities in common, along with certain attributes, styles, and behavioral responses. At the same time, they have identified the traps that people fall into in the workplace. Whereas many of these personal traps were operating and were tolerated before the organizational changes, after the changes they became magnified and perceived by others as a problem. This book presents methods to help individuals free themselves from their traps and succeed under the most difficult of circumstances, including trap-breaking methods.

Suggested Readers

- Those who focus on the messenger rather than the message
- Employees who feel insecure and unsure of their work
- Adults who are trying to reclaim their motivation and sense of competence

Therapeutic Insights

- The rules of the workplace have changed radically; rapid change has become the norm.
- Bringing outdated beliefs or expectations to the workplace can cause barriers to one's career or job functioning.
- Confusion about loyalty is a major reason that people have problems in the workplace.

- People with tunnel vision cannot cope in today's unstable and unpredictable workplace.
- Relational patterns at work are very similar to those experienced in one's family.

Working with Emotional Intelligence
Daniel Goleman
Bantam Books, 1998
316 pages

Book Byte

Emotional intelligence refers to the capacity for reorganizing our own feelings and those of others, for motivating ourselves, and for managing emotions well in our relationships. It describes abilities distinct from, but complementary to, academic intelligence and the purely cognitive capacities measured by IQ. Goleman believes that the talents inherent in emotional intelligence matter in work life. He includes five basic emotional and social competencies that are needed to be successful in the workplace:

1. Self-awareness
2. Self-regulatory
3. Motivation
4. Empathy
5. Social skills

These competencies are distinguishing characteristics that set star performers apart from average performers.

Suggested Readers

- Individuals who are seeking understanding of emotional intelligence
- Employers who are attempting to understand the contribution of emotional competence to excellence
- Individuals who are learning to be more emotionally intelligent

Therapeutic Insights

- At an individual level, elements of emotional intelligence can be identified, assessed, and upgraded.

- At an organizational level, emotional intelligence means revising the value hierarchy to make it a priority.
- Autonomy in the workplace can only work if it goes hand in hand with self-control, trustworthiness, and conscientiousness.
- Emotional competencies are twice as important in contributing to excellence as are pure intellect and expertise.
- Emotional intelligence skills are synergistic with cognitive ones—top performers have both.

CREATIVITY AND WORK

Creating a Life Worth Living: A Practical Course in Career Design For Artists, Innovators, and Others Aspiring to a Creative Life
Carol Lloyd
HarperCollins Publishers, 1997
320 pages

Book Byte

Creating a Life Worth Living is a practical, inspiring, and irreverent crash course in career survival. Carol Lloyd guides individuals through the process of creating their vision, and then she helps them rigorously invent the means to support their long-term dreams. Each chapter directs the reader through a week's worth of concrete tasks, writing exercises, artistic assignments, experiments, and thought games, which help flush out ideas. This book is for those who are actively searching for two things: (1) the creative life they want to lead and (2) the way to reach and maintain that life, so that they are as sane and/or happy and as financially solvent as they want to be. This book applies the artistic process of building a career, and engages readers in the process of strengthening their relationship to their dreams with rigorous daily habits.

Suggested Readers

- Those individuals who want to redefine their career goals
- Adults who are experiencing the problems of indecision and competing interests
- Individuals who want to build a new model to reinvent their workday

Therapeutic Insights

- Until one is committed, there is a tendency to draw back.
- Inspiration grows into full-scale creation through persistence and imagination.
- Life changes do not spring from thin air. People must make concessions, take risks, and learn new skills.
- People must have the courage to reinvent themselves.
- A creative process is a mixture of routine, attitude, and motivation.

No More Blue Mondays: Four Keys to Finding Fulfillment at Work

Robert Sheerer
Davies-Black Publishing, 1999
249 pages

Book Byte

For many working adults, the thought of starting another workweek is less than thrilling. Many people get depressed on Sunday evenings. Whether feeling stuck or victimized at work, self-employed or unemployed, job changer or loyalty-committed, Sheerer believes that people can empower their work and change it for the better. Combined with good advice and inspiring stories, this book is filled with practical and thought-provoking ideas. It is supported additionally by checklists, questionnaires, and suggested action tips. He suggests four keys to finding fulfillment at work:

1. Revealing what is true
2. Reclaiming personal power
3. Expressing commitment
4. Surrounding oneself with support

Suggested Readers

- Adults who are discovering who they are personally and professionally
- Employees who are seeking an empowering work environment
- Accomplished individuals who are looking to new and different goals

Therapeutic Insights

- Simply saying the truth can be transforming.
- Getting into action relieves fear and depression.
- Commitment is the glue to an empowered and fulfilling work situation and a satisfactory life.
- The first step in uncovering one's passion is to become an astute observer of oneself.
- Taking risks is one way to feel alive.

LEADERSHIP IN THE WORKPLACE

Management Challenges for the 21st Century
Peter F. Drucker
HarperCollins Publishers, 1999
207 pages

Book Byte

Peter Drucker is believed to be, by many, the most important management thinker of modern time. In his newest book, he discusses the new paradigms of management and how they have changed and will continue to change the basic assumptions about the practice and principles of management. He addresses the "New Information Revolution," discussing the information that an executive needs along with the information an executive knows. He shows that changes in the basic attitude of individuals and organizations, as well as structural changes in work itself, are needed for increased productivity.

Suggested Readers

- Those who are challenged daily and those who must prepare themselves for future challenges
- Those who are seeking information on the issues specific to management
- Managers addressing their own call to action

Therapeutic Insights

- One cannot manage change; one can only be ahead of it.
- The task is not to manage people, but to lead people.

- The goal is to make the strength and knowledge of each individual productive.
- Management has to be operational. It must be focused on results and performance across the entire economic chain.
- Management should be defined operationally, not politically.

Real Power: Business Lessons from the Tao Te Ching

James A. Autry and Stephen Mitchell
Berkley Publishing Group, 1999
219 pages

Book Byte

The *Tao Te Ching,* written according to legend by the sage Lao-Tzu in the sixth century B.C.E., is the world's oldest leadership manual, written to help anyone in a position of power to use that power wisely. Premier business consultant James A. Autry and translator Stephen Mitchell present a modern-day guide to business leadership drawing on the age-old insights of the Tao Te Ching. They believe that the wise leader knows that it is absurd to believe that he can plan for every contingency, and that there are great opportunities if he remains flexible and makes use of whatever happens. Businesses fail because managers put too much faith in systems and not enough faith in people. Without the commitment and engagement of people, not just at the top but throughout an organization, no system can succeed.

Suggested Readers

- Managers who are looking to change the command-control system of business
- Employees who don't want to be limited by the desire for a particular result
- Those in business who see themselves as a work in progress

Therapeutic Insights

- Real power begins on the inside with self-awareness and self-acceptance.
- Wise leaders make use of difficulties, seeing them as opportunities.
- People driven by crisis let circumstances define their lives.
- Managers talk too much because they think they are supposed to have all of the answers.

334

- Preoccupation with the big picture can seduce people into believing that all of the details are not worth their attention.

The 7 Habits of Highly Effective People: Powerful Lessons in Personal Change
Stephen R. Covey
Simon & Schuster, 1990 (reprint edition)
360 pages

Book Byte

In this book, Stephen R. Covey presents a holistic, integrated, principle-centered approach to solving personal and professional problems. Using insight and poignant anecdotes, he reveals a step-by-step path for living with fairness, integrity, honesty, and human dignity. The seven habits embody many of the fundamental principles of human effectiveness. Covey believes that we have many maps in our heads, which can be divided into two main categories:

1. Maps of the way things are (realities)
2. Maps of the way things should be (values)

We interpret everything we experience through these mental maps. We simply assume that the way we see things is the way they really are or should be. Powerful conditioning affects our perception, our paradigms. These paradigms are also the source of our attitudes and behaviors. The more we are aware of these paradigms, the more we can take responsibility for them, test them against reality, and be open to other perceptions.

Suggested Readers

- Those who are exploring new belief systems
- Those who are seeking other visions of themselves
- Individuals who have lost a sense of balance necessary for effective living

Therapeutic Insights

- Within the freedom to choose is self-awareness, imagination, conscience, and independent will.

- Proactive people are driven by values; reactive people are driven by feelings, circumstances, and conditioning.
- Management is doing things right; leadership is doing the right thing.
- People must organize and execute around priorities.
- Win/win is a frame of mind and heart that constantly seeks mutual benefits in all human interactions.

The 21 Indispensable Qualities of a Leader: Becoming the Person Others Will Want to Follow
John Maxwell
Nelson Publishing, 1999
157 pages

Book Byte

John Maxwell believes that it is the qualities of the individual that make people want to follow. This book is to help the reader recognize, develop, and refine the personal characteristics needed to be a truly effective leader—the kind of leader that people want to follow. Leadership develops from the inside out. How a leader deals with life's circumstances tells you many things about his or her character. Crisis doesn't make character, but it certainly reveals it. People create their character—it is a choice. Maxwell explores all of the pieces of leadership, from character to charisma, commitment, communication, passion, vision, competence, courage, focus, generosity, and many more facets of quality leadership.

Suggested Readers

- Those who are working to be attractive to others
- Individuals who are learning how to share themselves with others
- Men and women who are driven to produce and follow through on their goals

Therapeutic Insights

- Sometimes, people think that they are committed to something, and yet their actions show otherwise.

- Communication is not just the words that are said, but rather how they are said.
- Highly competent people keep looking for ways to learn.
- Courage in a leader inspires commitment from followers.
- Effective leaders who reach their potential spend more time focusing on what they do well than on what they do wrong.

WOMEN AND WORK

The Web of Inclusion: A New Architecture for Building Great Organizations
Sally Helgesen
Doubleday, 1995
288 pages

Book Byte

Sally Helgesen's first book, *Female Advantage,* examined how women's leadership styles transformed organizations. *The Web of Inclusion* is a quantum leap forward, presenting a broad, revolutionary approach to management for the postindustrial society. Building a web of inclusion means that ideas come from all employees, not just from the top down. What individuals do in their workplace depends on their talents, not on their titles, and additionally a premium is placed on flexibility. The edges of this web of inclusion connect with people who are outside of the organization, including customers, suppliers, partners, and mass media. Helgesen profiles five organizations that have achieved extraordinary success demonstrating the web of inclusion.

Suggested Readers

- Those who are seeking to speak of organizations in a more human language
- Employees who want to talk of culture, values, relationships, inspiration, and meaning
- Managers who want to involve creative solutions to complex problems

Therapeutic Insights

- Interactive charisma is a way of leading that derives power and authority from being accessible.
- Women tend to put themselves at the center of their organizations, rather than at the top, emphasizing both equality and accessibility.
- The leader of a weblike structure must manifest strength by yielding and securing his or her position by continually augmenting the influence of others.
- The rapid and profound changes that are inherent in organizations put the burden on the leaders to reconfigure themselves in ways that reflect how people actually do their work.
- Identity is inseparable from relationship.

WORK STRESS

Beat Stress Together
Wayne M. Sotile, Ph.D., and Mary O. Sotile, M.A.
John Wiley & Sons, Inc., 1998
208 pages

Book Byte

Beat Stress Together addresses the effects of our chronically hectic and busy culture on a couple's relationship. The authors show readers how trying to be all things to all people creates distance and tension between partners. The book teaches couples how to lower their stress levels and revitalize their relationships with easy-to-do exercises. This is an excellent book for overworked and stressed couples who are looking for a change.

Suggested Readers

- Couples with issues of distance and lack of passion
- Double-income couples who are looking to reduce their stress
- Couples who are looking for balance in their lives

Therapeutic Insights

- Superachiever couples find themselves drained by their lives, with little energy for passion, creativity, and tolerance.
- Beating stress together, BEST, is about creating a nurturing fence around the territory of one's life. The territory consists of the situations, the relationships, and the processes that structure each partner's days.
- Two jobs, along with children, can often leave parenting on autopilot. Hurried children often grow up too fast.
- The change process begins first with imagining how one would like to be, then by practicing the behavior until one's emotions catch up and one feels natural and authentic with the change. Imagine it, pretend it, and become it.

Calm at Work

Paul Wilson
Plume Books, 1999
334 pages

Book Byte

Invariably, the things that cause workplace stress fall into one of three categories: physical, emotional, and behavioral. Paul Wilson believes that whether workers are trainees or CEOs, part-timers, or burned-out workaholics, they can change their lives into a more tranquil place. He offers calm-inducing programs for leaders and managers: how to choose the right employee; how to control time, visualization, and affirmation to overcome anxiety; and lastly, how to put fun back into the workplace. Simply put, it is a book of calm solutions.

Suggested Readers

- Employees who feel stressed and underappreciated
- Those who are driven by fear in their workplace
- Workers who are uncertain about the causes of their anxiety

Therapeutic Insights

- Many rely on stress to provide the adrenaline, fears, and panic they need to complete their work.

- Stressed people often create more work for themselves because of the inefficiencies brought about by being in that state.
- Working smarter is more productive than working longer.
- Breathing deeply and slowly will have a calming effect.
- Today, change in the workplace is the only thing of which people can be certain.

Chained to the Desk: A Guidebook for Workaholics, Their Partners and Children, and the Clinicians Who Treat Them
Bryan Robinson, Ph.D.
New York University Press, 1998
280 pages

Book Byte

Men and women are trying to figure out how to integrate work and family in their lives. As they try to achieve this balance, lives become a tangle of commitments, errands, appointments, and other added responsibilities. To complicate things, the boundary between home and work has been erased. Many people are caught up in the frantic pace of today's world: too much to do, too little time. Regardless of job title, people are speed-reading, quick-firing, rush-houring, and fast-tracking themselves to death. Parents have continually downsized their home lives by convincing themselves that their spouses and kids don't need them that much. The work-family balance is perhaps one of the biggest challenges facing adults as we approach the twenty-first century.

Suggested Readers

- Workers who are caught in the workaholic lifestyle
- Partners of workaholics who feel lonely and isolated in their relationships
- Clinicians who treat work addictions

Therapeutic Insights

- Because of their self-absorbed preoccupation with work, workaholics often do not notice signals, which can be warning signs.
- Work addiction is widespread in its devastation.

- A chaotic home situation can be an enabler that makes it preferable for a family member to stay at work to avoid the unpleasantness.
- Technologies have erased the lines that once separated home and work.
- Case studies indicate that workaholics are physically and emotionally unavailable to their children.

Dealing with People You Can't Stand: How to Bring Out the Best in People at Their Worst
Dr. Rick Brinkman and Dr. Rick Kirschner
McGraw-Hill, Inc., 1994
199 pages

Book Byte

In many parts of life, there will be people that one can't stand. These are the difficult people who don't do what people want them to do, or who do what people don't want them to do. When these people are coworkers, supervisors, or colleagues, one is often left feeling trapped without choices. These authors direct their efforts in four ways:

1. They examine the forces that compel people to be difficult.
2. They examine essential communication skills that turn conflict into cooperation, emotion into reason, and hidden agendas into honest dialogue.
3. They focus on specific strategies for dealing with the 10 most difficult behaviors.
4. They advise what to do when one can't stand him- or herself.

Suggested Readers

- Those who are deal with unreasonable, explosive, sarcastic, and/or aggressive coworkers
- Employees who must confront supervisors who are too passive, indecisive, and/or ambivalent
- Adults who are seeking to command respect in the workplace

Therapeutic Insights

- Aggressive people require assertive responses.
- If one is willing to project good intent onto negative behavior, the negative people may come to believe it.
- A key to dealing with negative people is to have compassion instead of contempt.
- There are few outcomes in life that are as gratifying as when a negative person gains the courage to let go of fear and to begin to live.
- When dealing with a "No" person, the goal is to move from fault finding toward problem solving.

The Lemming Conspiracy: How to Redirect Your Life from Stress to Balance
Bob McDonald, Ph.D., and Don Hutcheson
Longstreet Press, 1997
240 pages

Book Byte

Millions suffer from stress and burnout because their careers consume them, but do not fulfill them. Why do people stay on the wrong paths? These authors believe it is because the system, which largely determines one's course in life (families, schools, friends, and work), also limits the options that are open to people. The Lemming Conspiracy refers to small Arctic mammals, known as lemmings, that band together from time to time, run in vast herds, and throw themselves over cliffs to their deaths. As a metaphor, Bob McDonald and Don Hutcheson use this example as a description for how too many people live their lives. This book includes a detailed self-analysis, culminating in a new vision for a new life.

Suggested Readers

- Individuals who want to create a personal vision
- Employees who want to operate outside of their paths of systems
- Adults who are attempting to change significant parts of their jobs

Therapeutic Insights

- Crisis in one's adult life doesn't have to be negative.
- Personal vision includes stages of development, abilities, skills, personality, interests, goals, and family of origin.
- Companies cannot dictate whole lives.
- The responsibility for having a fulfilling and satisfying life rests with the employee.
- Moving from the stress cycle to a balanced cycle does not mean turning a life upside down.

You Don't Have to Go Home from Work Exhausted: A Program to Bring Joy, Energy, and Balance to Your Life

Ann McGee-Cooper
Bantam Books, 1999 (reprint edition)
288 pages

Book Byte

Material on stress management has flooded the market over the past 10 years. Although stress can be a factor in low energy, controlling stress does not necessarily result in sustained high energy levels and increased peace of mind. Ann McGee-Cooper believes people have a choice whether they come home from work tired and exhausted. First, adults must unlearn some comfortable habits that are unproductive and that drain them of vital energy. She addresses the myths around increasing energy, the balance of work and play, the link between play and innovation, expanding one's definition of fun, brain dominance, the perils of perfectionism, and the cure for burnout.

Suggested Readers

- Perfectionists who want to break out of their molds
- Those who are looking for signals that they are becoming trapped
- Supervisors whose self-worth comes from controlling others

Therapeutic Insights

- Perfectionism is as much an addiction as overeating, workaholism, or alcoholism.
- There is an intrinsic link between an energy-reviving break and overall productivity and creativity.
- One can benefit from joy and fun without losing sight of the complex good judgment of adulthood.
- Driving one's self beyond endurance is detrimental to others, as well as to oneself.
- When one truly cares for him- or herself, it becomes possible to care far more profoundly about other people.

📖 Bibliography

Baruth, L., and Burggraf, M. (1984). The counselor and single-parent families. *Elementary School Guidance and Counseling, 19,* 30–37.

Coleman, M., and Ganong, L. H. (1990). The use of juvenile fiction and self-help books with stepfamilies. *Journal of Counseling and Development, 68,* 327–331.

Ellis, A. (1993). The advantages and disadvantages of self-help therapy materials. *Professional Psychology, Research, and Practice, 24,* 335–339.

Halliday, G. (1991). Psychological self-help books: How dangerous are they? *Psychotherapy, 28,* 678–680.

Matthews, D., and Lonsdale, R. (1992). Children in hospitals: Reading therapy and children in hospitals. *Health Libraries Review, 9,* 14–26.

Orton, G. L. (1997). *Strategies for counseling with children and their parents.* Pacific Grove, CA: Brooks/Cole Publishing.

Pardek, J. T. (1993). *Using bibliotherapy in clinical practice: A guide to self help books.* Westport, CT: Greenwood Press.

Starker, S. (1992a). Self-help books: Ubiquitous agents of health care. *Medical Psychotherapy: An International Journal, 3,* 187–194.

Starker, S. (1992b). Characteristics of self-help book readers among VA medical outpatients. *Medical Psychotherapy: An International Journal, 6,* 89–93.

Starker, S. (1994). Self-care materials in the practice of cardiology: An explorative study among American cardiologists. *Patient Education and Counseling, 24,* 91–94.

About the Authors

Janice Maidman Joshua, Psy.D., is a Licensed Psychologist with 15 years of clinical experience. She obtained her Masters and Doctorate degrees from the University of St. Thomas and currently has a private practice in Edina, Minnesota. She specializes in the treatment of major depressive disorders, anxiety disorders, and complicated bereavements. She is trained in family systems, but uses a brief, solution-oriented approach to treating her clients. She is also trained in eye movement desensitization and reprocessing. Doctor Maidman has practiced in a variety of settings, including several local hospitals, crisis centers, and outpatient clinics. She has also consulted with major Twin Cities companies in the area of human resource selection and management.

Donna DiMenna, Psy.D., is a Licensed Psychologist, having obtained her Masters and Doctorate degrees from the University of St. Thomas in St. Paul, Minnesota. She has practiced clinically for the past 15 years in a variety of settings, including local hospitals, outpatient clinics, EAPs, and the Minneapolis School System. She currently maintains a private practice with an office in St. Paul. Her clinical work includes individual, couples, and family therapy with a specialization in personality and career assessment and organizational consulting. Doctor DiMenna is active in the Twin Cities counseling community, often facilitating groups and workshops.

To contact the authors, go to their Web site at www.readtwobooks.com and/or e-mail them at authors@readtwobooks.com.

Title Index

📖 Topic Index

A

C

D

I

M

P